USAF WARRIOR STUDIES

Richard H. Kohn and Joseph P. Harahan
General Editors

USAF WARRIOR STUDIES

Air Superiority in World War II and Korea, edited by Richard H. Kohn and Joseph P. Harahan, 1983
GPO Stock # 008-070-0489-5

The Command of the Air, by Guilio Douhet, New Imprint, 1983
GPO Stock # 008-070-0505-1

Condensed Analysis of the Ninth Air Force in the European Theater of Operations, 1984
GPO Stock # 008-070-0513-1

The Literature of Aeronautics, Astronautics, and Air Power, by Richard P. Hallion, 1984
GPO Stock # 008-070-0523-9

Over the Hump, by William H. Tunner, New Imprint, 1985
Available to Air Force agencies only from the Office of Air Force History

Air Interdiction in World War II, Korea, and Vietnam, edited by Richard H. Kohn and Joseph P. Harahan, 1986
GPO Stock # 008-070-00571-9

THE STRATEGIC AIR WAR AGAINST GERMANY AND JAPAN: A MEMOIR

Haywood S. Hansell, Jr.
Major General, USAF, Retired

OFFICE OF AIR FORCE HISTORY
UNITED STATES AIR FORCE
WASHINGTON, D.C., 1986

Library of Congress Cataloging-in-Publication Data

Hansell, Haywood S.
    The strategic air war against Germany and Japan.

    (USAF warrior studies)
    Bibliography: p. 295
    Includes index.
    1. Hansell, Haywood S. 2. World War, 1939–1945–
Aerial operations, American. 3. Japan–History–Bombardment, 1944–1945. 4. Germany–History–Bombardment, 1940–1945. 5. World War, 1939–1945–Personal
narratives, American. 6. Strategy. 7. Japan–Strategic
aspects. 8. Germany–Strategic aspects. I. Title. II.
Series.
D790.H264 1986 940.54'4973'0924 [B]   86–23749

Foreword

The Strategic Air War Against Germany and Japan is part of a continuing series of historical volumes produced by the Office of Air Force History in direct support of Project Warrior. Since its beginnings in 1982, Project Warrior has captured the imagination of Air Force people around the world and reawakened a keener appreciation of our fundamental purpose as a Service: to deter war, but to be prepared to fight and win should deterrence fail.

Military history helps provide a realistic perspective on warfare. Through the study of past events, we gain insight into the capabilities of armed forces and, most importantly, a sound knowledge of the policies, strategies, tactics, doctrine, leadership, and weapons that have produced success in battle. Each of us, in broadening our knowledge of air power's past, helps to maintain the most effective Air Force possible, now and in the future.

LARRY D. WELCII, General, USAF
Chief of Staff

United States Air Force
Historical Advisory Committee
(As of January 1, 1986)

Mr. DeWitt S. Copp
The Voice of America

Dr. Phillip A. Crowl
Annapolis, Maryland

Dr. Warren W. Hassler, Jr.
Pennsylvania State University

Brig. Gen. Harris B. Hull
USAF, Retired
National Aeronautics and
Space Administration

Dr. Alfred F. Hurley (Chairman)
Brig. Gen., USAF, Retired
North Texas State University

Dr. Haskell M. Monroe, Jr.
University of Texas at El Paso

Lt. Gen. Thomas C. Richards,
USAF
Commander, Air University

Gen. Thomas M. Ryan, Jr.
USAF, Retired

Lt. Gen. Winfield W. Scott, Jr.
USAF
Superintendent, USAF Academy

Mr. Eugene R. Sullivan
The General Counsel, USAF

Preface

The history of American air power is very short indeed. Military and naval histories span thousands of years. Military aviation history is encompassed in the lifetime of a single individual. The birth of powered flight is coincident with my own. In 1912 I got my first glimpse of an airplane. I was standing on the fairgrounds of the annual carnival in Manila, Philippine Islands, when a biplane beat its slow pace across the sky. An aged Filipino standing nearby said, in astonishment, "¡*Muy grande pollo!*" or "Very large chicken!" As a boy of nine I was in full agreement.

I mention this only to make a point. Military conflict on land and sea has been exhaustively reported and analyzed for centuries. The processes are well understood. The general principles have been distilled and tested. The experience and history of air war are in their infancy. They are measured in a few decades, actually in the span of my own lifetime. There has been only one major conflict involving application of air power on a grand scale. And yet that air experience has had a profound impact upon war, and upon nations in competition and conflict short of major war. The impact of space power has no history at all, but that impact may be even greater than the impact of atmospheric air power. There is dispute over the relative merits of historical experience and of abstract logic in the development of effective combat forces. Military aviation strategists must make the best of very limited historical experience and derive requirements based upon logic and forecast.

This book seeks to recount the air experience and development before World War II, to describe the objectives, plans and effects of strategic air warfare in Europe and in the Pacific, and to offer criticism, opinion, and lessons of that great conflict.

In retrospect I find that I have been singularly fortunate in my associations and assignments. I have been associated with many great men and have been in position to observe great events. In the decade before World War II, I had a priceless opportunity to work with Bob Olds, Harold Lee George, Ken Walker, Don Wilson, and Muir "Santy" Fairchild, under the guidance, inspiration, and benign protection of the Commandant of the Air Corps Tactical School at Maxwell Field, Col. John F. Curry. My associates also included Ira C. Eaker, who combined great ability as a staff executive with superlative leadership as Commanding General of the Eighth Air Force in England. I worked under that superb airman, Carl "Tooey" Spaatz, Commanding General, United States Strategic Air Forces in Europe. I was caught up in the dedication and driving spirit of Henry H. "Hap" Arnold, Commanding General, U.S. Army Air Forces, Air Member of the Joint Chiefs of Staff, and Commanding General, Twentieth Air Force. And I had the special privilege of working for the greatest soldier of our day, and perhaps of any day, a man of superb integrity and highest character: Army Chief of Staff Gen. George Catlett Marshall.

The observations contained in this book constitute a memoir, with all the shortcomings of faulty memory, bias, personal viewpoint, personal experience, and inadequate research that are implied in the term. They lead to speculation on probable results of alternative actions or conditions, and that speculation is likewise suspect because it reflects personal judgment. But the compendium may lead others to derive lessons and conclusions which fit into a broader mosaic.

This work does not, of course, aspire to the dignity of "history." Participants are notoriously poor historical observers. Participation induces bias. But there should be some limited value to the viewpoint of participants—if their opinions are properly screened to eliminate prejudice. After all, there is some virtue in the observation of the poet who wrote:

> The experts sit in serried rows
> And fill the Plaza Toros full.
> But only one there is who knows
> And he's the one who fights the bull.

These memoirs will not earn the "bull's ear," but the perspective is that of an aged matador.

Haywood S. Hansell, Jr.
Hilton Head, South Carolina

Acknowledgments

Since this is a personal memoir, I acknowledge my indebtedness on two scores: to those who shaped the perspective through which I viewed the events described in this book; and to those who helped in the preparation of the book itself.

My perspective and outlook were deeply influenced by my first commanding officer, Maj. Gen. Hugh J. Knerr, who prior to the war served with the 2d Bombardment Group at Langley Field. He impressed me as a dynamic and charismatic leader who imbued his outfit with his own integrity, devotion, and patriotic loyalty to the Air Corps. I owe a debt of admiration to Brig. Gen. Kenneth N. Walker for his enthusiasm and his faith in bombardment; to Lt. Gen. Harold L. George, whose perceptive prewar inquiry into the basic purpose and nature of strategic air warfare colored my outlook for the rest of my military career; to Maj. Gen. Donald Wilson for his method of logical research into fundamental target systems; to Gen. Muir S. Fairchild for his thoughtful approach to and appraisal of military philosophy, particularly as it pertains to strategic air warfare; to Gen. Ira C. Eaker for his dedication to performance as Executive to Gen. Henry H. Arnold, and as Commanding General, Eighth Air Force, for his courage and steadfastness of character in the harrowing first years of the great trial of the Eighth Air Force in combat. His dedication to the Air Force knows no equal. My outlook upon strategic planning and the conduct of air warfare was influenced by my service under Gen. Carl "Tooey" Spaatz and my admiration for his example of calm, courageous common sense and good judgment. And, I pay tribute to two great commanders for whom I worked and whose achievements—through signally different methods—I came to admire: General of the Army George C. Marshall, the epitome of integrity and cool dedication; and General of the Army Air Forces Henry H. Arnold, whose dynamism drove men to accomplish the impossible in the creation of the United States Air Force. All of these people influenced my military perspective and formed my military outlook.

The creation of the book itself benefited from many who helped, offered criticism, edited, and corrected the text. My gratitude to Maj. Gen. Cecil E. Combs knows no bounds. He offered intelligent and constructive criticism coupled with encouragement. His observations and contributions were well founded; he was an active participant in most of the events recorded in this memoir.

And I offer my thanks and acknowledgments to Lt. Gen. Raymond B. Furlong, USAF, Ret., former Air University Commander, and Col. Thomas A. Fabyanic, USAF, Ret., former Chief, Military Studies Division, Air War College, without whose enthusiastic support my previous books *The Air Plan That Defeated Hitler* and *Strategic Air War Against Japan*, on which this memoir is based, would probably not have been published. I especially appreciate the assistance of a very special scholar, Dr. Robert F. Futrell, a gifted professional historian who participated in the air war in the Pacific. His acknowledged scholarship and willingness to edit and review this manuscript have eliminated lingering fears of some gross error on my part.

The present form of the memoir is a compendium of the books mentioned above. This memoir has profited greatly from the talent and skill of Dr. Richard H. Kohn, Chief, Office of Air Force History; Col. John F. Shiner, Deputy Chief; and Dr. Joseph P. Harahan,

Historian, USAF, who consolidated, rearranged, and improved the sequential presentation of this book. Mr. Eugene P. Sagstetter, Office of Air Force History, edited the final manuscript; Mr. Ray Del Villar, USAF Directorate of Administration, Publishing Division, assisted with maps and charts; and Sgt. Glenn B. Reynolds, USAF, typed the final manuscript. Ms. Anne E. Johnson, Office of Air Force History, designed the volume and guided it through the publication process.

I also acknowledge my indebtedness to Mr. Robert T. Finney and Mrs. Irene P. Barnett of the Air University for editing an early edition of this manuscript. Mrs. Barnett gave of her talents so thoroughly that I feel she is better acquainted with this memoir than its author.

Finally, I express my gratitude to the editors of *Air University Review* for permission to use extracts from my articles which it has published, and to the editors of *Air Force Magazine* for permission to use my article "The Plan that Defeated Hitler," which appeared in the July 1980 issue.

H.S.H.

The Author

MAJOR GENERAL HAYWOOD S. HANSELL, JR., USAF (Retired), is a native of Atlanta, Georgia. A graduate of Georgia Institute of Technology (1924), he entered the U.S. Army Air Corps in 1928. Trained as a fighter pilot, he flew in the Air Corps Aerobatic and Demonstration Team (1932) led by Captain Claire Chennault. In the mid-1930s Hansell specialized in strategic bombardment, teaching tactics and doctrine at the Air Corps Tactical School from 1935 to 1938. Just prior to World War II, he went to Army Air Forces Headquarters where he helped draft the fundamental war requirements plan for the service. In 1942 he became Commanding General, Third Bombardment Wing (B–26s), Eighth Air Force, in the European Theater. Subsequently General Hansell commanded the First Bombardment Division (B–17s), Eighth Air Force, and in 1944–45 the XXI Bomber Command (B–29s), Twentieth Air Force, in the Pacific. The latter command was one of only two long-range B–29 commands conducting strategic air warfare against Japan. In 1946 he retired, suffering from a physical disability. During the Korean War (1950–53), the Chief of Staff, U.S. Air Force recalled him to active duty, assigning him as Chief, Military Assistance Program Headquarters, USAF, and subsequently as Air Member Review Board, Weapons Systems Evaluation Group, reporting to the Assistant Secretary of Defense, Research and Development and to the Joint Chiefs of Staff. After four years as a senior program manager and advisor, General Hansell retired again. He is the author of *The Air Plan That Defeated Hitler* (1972) and *Strategic Air War Against Japan* (1980).

Contents

Photographs

Maps and Charts

MAJ. GEN. HAYWOOD S. HANSELL, JR.

Chapter I

Integrating Strategy,
Air Doctrines, and War Plans

World War II witnessed the first full application of strategic air power in war. At this writing, in fact, World War II has provided the only such full-scale application. Because that great effort was unique, it should be worth analytical examination, not only in terms of actions and effects, but more particularly in terms of objectives, strategic plans, and results of operations designed to achieve these ends. A brief review of the development of U.S. strategic air doctrines and their nature at the outbreak of American participation in World War II should serve as a useful prelude to discussion of the strategic air war itself.*

Air Pioneers

Airplanes were used, of course, in World War I, although on a very limited scale. But even with the limited use and, for the most part, inconclusive results of air operations, proponents of air power began to appear. One of the most notable of these early proponents of the virtually untried air weapon was Lt. Gen. Jan C. Smuts, who headed a

---

*For a more detailed account of the origin and development of U.S. strategic air doctrine, see my *The Air Plan That Defeated Hitler* (Atlanta, Ga., 1972).

commission established by the British Cabinet to investigate the dual problems of air organization and home defense. The commission came into being largely as a result of popular dissatisfaction with the ability of the air defenses to deal with German Zeppelin and Gotha bombing attacks against London. The report, submitted to the British Prime Minister on August 17, 1917, stated:

> It is important for the winning of the war that we should not only secure air predominance, but secure it on a very large scale; and having secured it in this war, we should make every effort and sacrifice to maintain it for the future. Air supremacy may in the long run become as important a factor in the defense of the Empire as sea supremacy.

Smuts himself said in submitting the report of his commission:

> The day may not be far off when aerial operations, with their devastation of enemy lands and destruction of industrial and populous centers on a vast scale, may become the principal operations of war, to which the older forms of military and naval operations may become secondary and subordinate.

These were strong words regarding the potential of the new air weapon, coming as early as 1917. Smuts was a ground soldier speaking, not as one wedded to an historic art, but as a farsighted statesman. He was characterized by Air Marshal Sir John C. Slessor, Royal Air Force (RAF), in his memoir, *The Central Blue,* as "one of the greatest men of our time—of all times." Significantly, the report of Smuts's committee led to the establishment of the Air Ministry in December 1917 and the Royal Air Force in April 1918. Then, of course, there was Maj. Gen. Hugh M. Trenchard (later Marshal of the Royal Air Force Viscount Trenchard), who fended off attacks on the fledgling RAF by the other services and postulated advanced notions concerning the possibilities of the air arm.

Support for what we call today "strategic bombardment" came from other directions as well. For example, as early as 1916 the Italian aircraft manufacturer Count Giovanni B. Caproni proposed to destroy German and Austrian naval vessels by bomber attack against fleet bases. In January 1917, he argued that his large triplane bombers, if built in sufficient numbers, could destroy Austria's factories, thus ending the war with Italy's main opponent. In October 1917, Caproni, in collaboration with his friend Lt. Col. Giulio Douhet of the Italian Army, prepared a "Memorandum on the 'Air War' for the U.S. Air Service," in which he suggested that mass attacks made at night by long-range Allied bombers against industrial targets deep within Germany and Austria could definitely overwhelm the enemy by substantially reducing his war production at the same time that Allied production was increasing.

More must be said about Douhet. Actually, he had begun to write about military aviation as early as 1909. During World War I, he was imprisoned for a year (1916–1917) for criticizing Italy's wartime military policy. But Douhet, like Brig. Gen. William "Billy" Mitchell of the U.S. Army Air Service, whose career was parallel, became more influential in the post-World War I period. Douhet's wartime court-martial was expunged in 1920, and he was promoted to general officer rank in 1921. He completed his first serious treatise on military aviation—*Il Dominio dell' Aria*, or *The Command of the Air*—in October 1921. In this essay, he proved to be a strong proponent of strategic air warfare. In essence, he advocated creation of an independent air force made up of a fleet of bombers, to be accompanied by "battle planes"—bombers equipped with many guns to fight off hostile pursuit planes en route to strategic targets. This bomber force would win command of the air by attacking enemy aircraft factories and flying facilities and would destroy the enemy's will to resist by bombing his population centers. |

Soon after the end of World War I, airpower concepts were deeply influenced by two other military strategists. One was the great British military historian Capt. B. H. Liddell Hart. In his book *Paris*, Liddell Hart pointed out that Germany had surrendered when her armies were still powerful and her borders were still intact. The military power to wage war was still there but the civilian "will to resist"—to continue the struggle—had collapsed. Liddell Hart contended that prosecution of war is a product of two fundamental factors: *military capability* and *political will to resist* or persist. Either or both can be undermined, with resultant national defeat.

The other military strategist was Billy Mitchell. In the post-World War I period he was the most outspoken proponent of air power in our own country. The story of his advocacy of an independent air force and his insight into the potential of the air weapon has been told and retold and does not need repeating here. During the war, Mitchell had been exposed to ideas of other air pioneers, notably Trenchard, Douhet, and Caproni. He came out of the war convinced that an air force had a mission independent from the other services and, to be effective, air power should be concentrated in the hands of airmen. The extent to which Smuts, Trenchard, Caproni, and Douhet influenced Mitchell is speculative, but in the post-World War I period his espousal of a principal role—a war-winning role—for air power is indisputable.

Mitchell's ideas concerning air power came cascading in a stream of publications and public statements. So wide-ranging were his views, it is difficult to pin them down in one brief quotation. Perhaps, however, the principal thrust of his arguments was summed up in his statement before the House Committee on Military Affairs in 1926, when he declared:

> There has never been anything that . . . has changed war the way the advent of air power has. The method of prosecuting a war in the old days was to get at the vital centers of the country in order to paralyze the resistance. This meant the centers of production, the centers of population, the agricultural districts, the animal industry, communications—anything that tended to keep up war. Now in order to keep the enemy out of that, armies were spread in front of those places and protected them by their flesh and blood. You had men killing there, sometimes for years before these vital centers were reached. It led to the theory that the hostile army in the field was the main objective, which it was. Once having been conquered, the vital centers could be gotten at . . . In the future, we will strike, in case of armed conflict, when all other means of settling disputes have failed, to go straight to the vital centers, the industrial centers, through the use of an air force and hit them. That is the modern theory of making war.

War Department Doctrine

While Mitchell advanced ideas on the potential of air power far in excess of the capabilities of the air weapon of his day, the Army General Staff continued to be nourished on the time-honored concepts of warfare, which proclaimed the infantry was the "Queen of Battle." Within the War Department, the two decades after World War I were a period of conflict between the traditionally minded Army members of the General Staff and a new breed within the Army, the upstart airmen of the Army Air Corps. The conflict concerned both the place within the Army for the new air arm and, more specifically, the role of air power. Gen. John J. Pershing, recently returned from Europe as head of the victorious American Expeditionary Force and Chief of Staff of the Army in the early 1920s, threw the weight of his considerable personal prestige against air power. In fact, airmen might have been squelched into oblivion if the American public had not shown an interest in aviation. Public clamor was at least partially responsible for forcing the government to convene a series of military and presidential boards and commissions to inquire into the role and organization of aviation. The reports of these various investigative agencies played no small role in keeping the question of military aviation alive.

With one exception, the report of the Lampert Committee, which in many respects endorsed Mitchell's ideas, the reports reflected a general consensus that the air arm could serve a useful purpose as an adjunct to the Army and Navy. However, there was no place for a separate air force in the military establishment, and certainly there was no separate air mission. The prevailing view was summed up in the July 1934 report of the Baker Board, perhaps the best known of the various boards. It contended: "Our national defense policy contemplates aggression against no nation; it is based entirely upon the defense of our homeland and our overseas possessions, including protection of our sea and airborne commerce." The purpose of the Army was "to hold an invader while the citizen forces are being mobilized. . . . The idea that aviation can replace any of the other elements of our armed forces is found, on analysis, to be erroneous.

5

Since ground forces alone are capable of occupying territory, the Army with its own air forces remains the ultimate decisive factor in war."

Jimmy Doolittle, a member of the Baker Board and an experienced Army aviator, filed a minority dissent. He said, "I believe that the future security of our Nation is dependent upon an adequate air force. This is true at the present time and will become increasingly important as the science of aviation advances and the airplane lends itself more and more to the art of warfare." He maintained that a separate air arm was needed for the proper development and employment of military aviation.

The issues between the advocates of air power and older services were clearly drawn. The Army and Navy would only acknowledge the airplane as a useful auxiliary to the surface forces in the battle to defeat the enemy. Smuts, Caproni, Douhet, and Mitchell advanced ideas and concepts that embraced a war-winning potential for air power and advocated air attacks against "the vital centers, the industrial centers, the centers of population of the enemy nation," in order to destroy the capability and the will of the enemy to continue the war.

But these visionary concepts of the air pioneers lacked specifics. How does one go about destroying or paralyzing these vital centers? Are cities really the best targets? Are there other targets? How should air power be controlled and employed? What effect is intended and expected? In short, what strategic and tactical doctrines were needed to accomplish the ends?

To my knowledge, the Army Air Corps had no official body of doctrine in the early 1930s. It was a part of the Army. What little guidance the Air Corps received for the conduct of its operations was contained in training regulations issued by the War Department. But these instructions could scarcely be called doctrines for the employment of air power. While other branches of the Army had boards—the Infantry Board, the Cavalry Board, the Artillery Board—the Air Corps had none at the time. In the absence of similar Air Corps agencies, the Chief of the Air Corps relied upon the Air Corps Tactical School as a center for producing concepts of airpower employment. So in reality, the teachings of Air Corps Tactical School, as far as airmen were concerned, were the accepted doctrines of the Air Corps and served as guidance for forming strategic air plans. These American air doctrines and concepts of air strategy were evolved at the Tactical School in the 1930s.

Air Doctrine and Strategic Principles

The Air Corps Tactical School was established at Langley Field, Virginia, in 1920. Beginning as a Field Officers' School, it did not expand its scope of instruction and stress airpower employment until the end of the decade. Then, the school was blessed with a group of gifted leaders and independent thinkers—Robert Olds, Kenneth Walker, Harold Lee George, Donald Wilson, Muir "Santy" Fairchild—names honored by the Air War College, Air Command and Staff College, Air Force Academy, and throughout the modern Air Force. But there was another stalwart leader who has received less recognition, though he should be listed among the best. This was John F. Curry, Commandant of the Air Corps Tactical School from 1931 to 1935, a period when the principal texts were prepared for Air Warfare and Principles of Air Force Employment. Much of the basic strategy of American air power was developed under his regime. At a time when the War Department was threatening dire punishment from above, Curry protected the freedom of his faculty. He made possible the development of doctrines of air power which formed the basis for the creation of the Army Air Forces (AAF) and its employment in World War II. Under his leadership the school bridged the transition from broad generalities of pioneering air prophets to more pragmatic application of air power in attainment of specific objectives.

The early visionaries and proponents had made great claims for air power. Their strategic concepts all depended upon one basic *tactical* concept accepted by the Tactical School as a fundamental doctrine: bombers could *reach* their targets and *destroy* them. The *strategic* airpower doctrine fashioned at the school rested on five fundamental aphorisms:

1. Modern great powers rely on major industrial and economic

MEMBERS OF THE TACTICAL SCHOOL FACULTY

ROBERT OLDS, instructor
1928-1931

DONALD WILSON,
instructor 1931-1934;
department director 1936-1940

MUIR FAIRCHILD,
instructor 1938-1940;
department director, 1940

HAROLD L. GEORGE,
instructor 1932-1934;
department director 1934-1936

COL. JOHN F. CURRY, ACTS Commandant
1931-1935

BRIG. GEN. WILLIAM "BILLY" MITCHELL

9

systems for production of weapons and supplies for their armed forces, and for manufacture of products and provision of services to sustain life in a highly industrialized society. Disruption or paralysis of these systems undermines both the enemy's *capability* and *will* to fight.

2. Such major systems contain critical points whose destruction will break down these systems, and bombs can be delivered with adequate accuracy to do this.

3. Massed air strike forces can penetrate air defenses without unacceptable losses and destroy selected targets.

4. Proper selection of vital targets in the industrial/economic/social structure of a modern industrialized nation, and their subsequent destruction by air attack, can lead to fatal weakening of an industrialized enemy nation and to victory through air power.

5. If enemy resistance still persists after successful paralysis of selected target systems, it may be necessary as a last resort to apply direct force upon the sources of enemy national will by attacking cities. In this event, it is preferable to render the cities untenable rather than indiscriminately to destroy structures and people.

Since this philosophy had not been demonstrated in war, it was not universally accepted even in the Air Corps. There was little argument that nations needed industrial systems or that bombs could paralyze such systems. But the third premise ("the bombers will always get through") was vigorously protested by the pursuit people. However in 1932, when these concepts were first advanced, bombers rode the crest of technological achievement. They were just about as fast as the current fighters. Having the enormous advantage of the initiative, they could pick the time, place, altitude, and route of attack. Moreover, they could capitalize on the principle of mass, concentrating at the critical point. Defending pursuit planes possessed no such advantage. This was before the day of radar or even an observer corps. This still left one variable: Could the bombs be properly placed and, if so, how large a force was necessary to reasonably assure getting the requisite number of hits on the target? We worked up tables of probability based on peacetime, daylight, visual bombing practice. These served as a guide in selecting the size force that would assure the desired bomb hits and destruction.

Accepting these basic tactical precepts and doctrine, the Air Corps Tactical School turned to the problem of formulating strategic doctrines for the support of national policy with air power. National policy could vary within wide limits, and it was not feasible to cover all purposes and situations. The school concentrated its efforts on describing principles and doctrines involved in war with one or more modern, major powers. It accepted as the national strategic purpose the crushing of enemy opposition to the extent necessary for support or attainment of the nation's goals and aims. The school claimed that air power could break down the enemy's "will to resist" and "capability to fight" by:

1. Destroying organic industrial systems in the enemy interior that provided for the enemy's armed forces in the field.

2. Paralyzing the organic industrial, economic, and civic systems that maintained the life of the enemy nation itself. (Some of these systems supported both the capability to fight and to sustain a modern social and political structure.)

3. Attacking the people themselves, especially those concentrated in the cities. (The school considered this method an undesirable stratagem, one to be adopted only as a last resort.) The school recognized a fourth obligation of air power: the defense of one's own sources of power.

This was not, of course, the sole employment of air power. The flexibility of the air force enabled it to operate in parallel with or in support of the surface forces, and there would be occasions when this was the best employment. Still, the school believed the methods listed above constituted the unique contribution of strategic air power to the winning of wars. This line of reasoning ran directly counter to official War Department doctrine, which asserted the Air Corps had no mission beyond that of the army. The army alone could conquer and hold territory, the only way to win wars. To do this, the army would first have to defeat the enemy army, and the function of the Army Air Corps should be to support the army in this endeavor. The Tactical School did not deny the need of the army for air support. But it insisted there was another and vital function of air power—the waging of strategic air warfare beyond the scope of the battlefield.

Development of principles of strategic air warfare simply had to embrace offense and to consider basing of offensive air forces within range of foreign nations. But the War Department, reflecting national policy, strictly forbade any teaching other than defense of our borders. The school sought to overcome these limitations in two ways. If we were embroiled in a war involving major European nations, we could anticipate having allies who could furnish bases for our air forces. And official policy notwithstanding, strict adherence to defense would not win wars. The school therefore undertook to formulate doctrine for the air offensive against modern industrialized nations. In this regard, it introduced a subtle but very significant variation from the doctrines of Douhet and Mitchell. The latter advocated destruction of factories and industrial centers and population centers. The school favored destruction or paralysis of national *organic systems* on which many factories and numerous people depended, but also accepted the need for destroying a few highly important factories.

What were those critical organic systems whose destruction would paralyze a modern state? Being strictly forbidden to examine foreign countries, the Tactical School proposed to analyze the industrial might of America. An analysis of our own industrial, economic, and social complex and its vulnerability to air attack would serve for the development of doctrines and principles of air employment anywhere. Furthermore, the analysis would accord with national military policy, inasmuch as air defense was first priority and we needed to know what was most vulnerable to enemy air attack in order to plan defenses.

It soon became apparent that the very heart of our industrial system was the *electric power system*. Practically all our industrial and economic functions were totally dependent upon it. Then in order of importance were these systems: *transportation*, chiefly our *railroads*; *fuel*, including fuel-refining and distribution; *food* distribution and preservation; and *steel* manufacturing, the manufacturing process being vital to both the war-making capacity of the state, and to the operation of the economic and industrial functions of the state itself. In addition, there were a number of highly concentrated manufacturing factories whose destruction would add a crippling blow. Among these plants were electric generator, transformer, switch gear, and motor manufacturing; locomotive manufacturing; shipbuilding; aluminum and magnesium.

Viewing this concept, as applied to our own nation, the Tactical School concluded:

> Loss of any of these systems would be a crippling blow. Loss of several or all of them would bring national paralysis. As to repair of this devastation, it would seem obvious that any air force worthy of the name should be able to destroy faster than replacement could be effected. . . . The airplane gives us a weapon which can immediately reach the internal organization of an enemy nation, within range, and therefore bring about the defeat of that nation. The fundamental innovation lies in the fact that whole nations *now lie within the combat zone.*

As to strategic air intelligence, the school deemed it vital to planning and operations of strategic air warfare. It should be collected in time of peace and cover the economic, industrial, and social structure of potential enemies. On the question of counter-air force operations the school was moot. It was agreed that the "bombers could get through," but penetration of strong enemy defenses might prove intolerably costly. Defeat of the enemy air defense force might be necessary to assure the air offensive's success against the interior targets, and in any case would greatly increase the air attack's effectiveness. If so, the best method would entail air attack of enemy bases, enemy aircraft and engine factories, enemy sources of aviation fuel, and attrition through air combat attendant upon these missions.

The Tactical School took a look at one of our most troublesome problems—direct attack against enemy centers of population (the cities). Others, including Douhet, had advocated direct attack on cities. The school opposed the concept which was generally described as an attack on enemy morale. The idea of killing thousands of men, women, and children was basically repugnant to American mores. And from a more pragmatic point of view, people did not make good targets for the high-explosive bomb, the principal weapon of the air offensive. People can scatter, be evacuated, or be protected in shelters. On the other hand, the cities were control points in the complex fabric of the industrial structure—the management centers and focal points of management communications. If their evacuation could be forced, the industrial structure would suffer a serious blow. Dropping high-explosive bombs on selected focal points might destroy vital civic systems, render the cities untenable, and force their evacuation. A study of New York revealed that a very small number of hits on a few sensitive spots could cause collapse of the life-sustaining vital systems. These points included such sensitive elements as water supply conduits and pumping stations; railroads that literally carried the daily requirements of food; highway bridges and tunnels; and terminal facilities of the river and harbor barge system that served as a vast distribution switchyard for distribution of goods and food. This seemed a far better application of air power than scattering bombs in urban areas.

The school sought to sponsor another doctrine, one dealing with the tactical need for and provision of escort fighters to protect the bombers. Here it was unsuccessful, running into the adamant opposition of the Pursuit Section and the Pursuit Board. With plausible reasoning, the fighter experts asserted that a fighter with the range to accompany bombers would be so large and heavy that short-range interceptors could easily outfly and outfight them. Progress toward developing a long-range fighter was the two-place PB–2 produced by the Consolidated Aircraft Company. But the rear gunner was merely an unnecessary burden with little firepower. Very fast and maneuverable for its day and with relatively long range, the aircraft might have been developed into an effective escort fighter. However, the idea for its tactical employment was fuzzy, and there was no charismatic leader to support its doctrine. It is tragic that this was so, for the lack of long-range fighters nearly halted the air offensive in 1943. Seeking the only avenue open to them, the bombers increased armament and massed defensive firepower from tight formations.

In putting forth the preceding arguments, airmen at the school contended that, in seeking the ends of strategic air warfare in pursuit of national goals, offensive air forces could be used in several ways. They could be used as the primary war-winning force, supported or followed by land and sea forces, as suggested by Air Marshal Smuts.

Or they could function as a collateral force, coequal with land or sea forces, operating against separate but related objectives. In either event, the strategic air forces would have to have strategic intelligence peculiar to their own needs. To be effective in the pursuit of these two air strategies, air power demanded concentration of effort and unified command and control by an airman at the highest echelon of command. The very flexibility of air forces made possible diversion of the strategic element to a third role—support of land or sea force objectives. This could occur when there was a dearth of vital enemy industrial targets, the existence of an immediate national emergency, or the overriding authority of superior command. Hence strategic forces could be shifted to a support role. Still, if air forces were designed and structured solely for the role of supporting land or sea forces, they would be incapable of fighting effectively in a strategic war.

Besides the specific doctrines of air employment, the Air Corps Tactical School accepted and adapted the War Department Principles of War to air power. The most important were:

The Objective	Determine clearly what you want to accomplish and stick to it.
The Offensive	Only offensive action against the enemy will produce victory.
Mass	Concentrate the maximum possible effort toward attainment of the main objective. Do not permit the effort to be diverted from the principal purpose.
Economy of Force	The converse of the principle of mass. In all other operations use as little force as possible in order to concentrate mass on the principal effort.
Security	Unless the base of power is defended and secure, it will be very difficult to sustain the strategic offensive and to continue to prosecute the war.

The Tactical School devised a form, the Air Estimate of the

Situation for Strategic Air Warfare, to assist in determining the optimum application of offensive strategic air power. The form's rationale was fairly simple, the most significant considerations being: define clearly the purpose, the goal—what you want to accomplish; consider the obstacles and opportunities in the broad situation; list the actions (tasks) which, if successfully accomplished, would attain the purpose, *in order of desired priority*; consider the force needed to carry out each task; consider the capability of your own forces and determine which of the tasks come within your capability; consider the risks and possible losses of each task; select the tasks that will achieve your purpose most effectively without unacceptable risk and loss, and which come within your capability; prepare a plan to fulfill the selected tasks. We used this form in preparing all the strategic war plans. "Purpose" was the keynote: select targets that contribute most to the purpose. The rationale also underscored the principle of "Capacity of the Force." That is, do not attempt tasks beyond your capability. Keep your operations within the capability of the forces available. It is far better to destroy a few vital targets completely than to attack many targets inconclusively.

Though airmen at the Tactical School were slowly evolving a concrete body of doctrine for the employment of strategic air forces, the Army Air Corps had neither the organization nor the forces required to implement it. The closest the Air Corps came to achieve either in the 1930s was the establishment of General Headquarters Air Force (GHQ Air Force) and the appearance of the B–17 bomber.

The GHQ Air Force

In 1934 the Baker Board, while rejecting the concept of independent strategic air warfare, did recommend the creation of a consolidated, centrally controlled air strike force, the GHQ Air Force. GHQ would be the General Headquarters of the Army command in the field, and during wartime the Commander of the GHQ Air Force would be directly subject to the GHQ Commander. When the United States was not engaged in war, the GHQ Air Force Commander was responsible to the U.S. Army Chief of Staff. In keeping with the Baker

Board recommendations, the GHQ Air Force was activated in March 1935.

There were three views as to the purpose of the GHQ Air Force. One view saw it as GHQ Aviation Reserve. This was a role advocated for Army aviation after World War I. Parts of the GHQ Air Force would be apportioned out and attached to field armies and corps as the situation demanded. A second view saw the GHQ Air Force as a cohesive air-striking force to be employed as a unit in furtherance of the Army mission. Still a third view—one held by airmen—was that it was a unified striking force available for use beyond the sphere of activity of the Army as well as in support of the Army. In other words, airmen viewed the GHQ Air Force as an air force with missions of its own. The first Commanding General of the GHQ Air Force, Maj. Gen. Frank M. Andrews, felt no doubt about the issue and left no doubt in the minds of his associates. To General Andrews, the GHQ Air Force was an instrument of air power.

Actually, however, as the War Department underwent a series of reorganizations after 1939 in the face of the growing possibilities of U.S. involvement in World War II, the concept of a GHQ went out the window and with it the GHQ Air Force. The GHQ Air Force was too short lived to leave any outstanding legacy of air doctrine. But it had demonstrated in several dramatic flights that the bomber had superb flexibility and could quickly be deployed to remote bases. Significantly, despite the fight of airmen for acceptance of airpower theories, as late as 1939 the War Department was still saying: "The mission of the air component of the Army is to perform effectively the air operations devolving upon the Army in its assigned functions in the national defense. . . . Air operations beyond the sphere of action of the surface forces are undertaken in furtherance of the strategic plan of the commander of the field force."

American Strategic Air Doctrine

The Army Air Corps had no official basis on which to promulgate air doctrine. It was a part of the U.S. Army and doctrine was issued by the War Department for all branches of the Army. Nevertheless, by the 1930s the teachings and texts of the Air Corps Tactical School were accepted as doctrine within the Air Corps. The Army Air Corps considered that strategic air warfare embraced five optional categories:

1. a. Direct attack on enemy armed forces, including air forces on the ground and in the air; on concentration of troops; on naval and maritime elements; and on logistics in the combat zone.

b. Local air defense of friendly military forces and bases.

2. a. Indirect air attack of enemy armed forces by destroying the industrial elements which supplied and supported the enemy armed forces. Target objectives included industrial systems that made war production possible, such as:

(1) Electric power systems (generating stations, transformer and switching stations, dams and penstocks).

(2) Natural fuel, refining, and transfer systems; synthetic fuel production systems; transportation systems (rail, highway, canal, sea).

(3) Special factories and arsenals (aircraft and aircraft engine, tank, weapons, and ammunition factories; major interior depots; rubber production facilities).

(4) Basic war-supporting materials (steel plants, aluminum and magnesium plants).

b. Local interior air defense of friendly forces and installations vital to munitions manufacture.

3. Direct air attack on the economic and social systems and structure of the enemy state, including destruction or neutralization of major supporting systems (electric power, communication, basic economic industrial production, water supply, industrial and economic transportation, food-handling, food-production, food preservation and distribution, and management control).

a. Many of the national industrial systems and economic systems supported the enemy *capability* to sustain the armed forces and the ability to continue to fight. These were also vital to the continued operation of the state itself as a modern industrialized society—systems bolstering the political *will to resist* of the enemy nation.

b. Industrial and economic systems of the national state body were likened to the vital organic systems that give life and activity to the human body. Electric power was the heart, without whose continued function all directed activity is paralyzed. Transportation was the system of arteries carrying energy to the vital organs. Fuel systems were the metabolic functions that translate sources of energy to muscular action. Communications were the nervous system. All served the brain, the source of political decision. All were vital to the civil as well as to the military capabilities of the enemy state. Their paralysis undermine both the military *capability* of the enemy state and the social and political "*will to resist.*" They were pertinent to both 2 and 3 above.

4.   Direct air attack on enemy social centers, including cities and factory worker dwelling areas.

5.   Strategic air defense of one's own urban, industrial, economic, and base areas.

Within the constraints imposed on them, the airmen were thinking more and more about sustained, high-altitude bombing of selected industrial targets and supporting systems in order to attain national goals in war. Yet that was just the beginning, the expression of an abstract concept. To think and plan in practical terms, it was necessary to consider: What were our national goals and purposes, and what were the threats to those goals? Who were our potential enemies, and where in their industrial and social structure lay the weak links? How vulnerable were these targets? What measures would the enemy probably take to protect them? How far were they from our air bases? What new air bases would have to be acquired?

The problem was vastly complicated for it presumed knowledge about a nation which that nation naturally tried to hide. Much of the value of the bombing offensive, should there be one, would of necessity rest on intelligence data and the conclusions planners gleaned from it. In truth these specific questions were beyond the competence of the Tactical School. Strategic air intelligence on major world powers would demand an intelligence organization and analytical competence of considerable scope and complexity.

19

Strategic Air Intelligence

In 1940 the Office of the Chief of the Air Corps had an Information Division dealing chiefly with public relations, but the Air Corps had no Strategic Intelligence Division. Military intelligence was the province of G–2 of the U.S. Army General Staff and its prerogatives were jealously guarded.

A simple example is illustrative. As a new member of the Information Division in 1940, I undertook to promote inquiries I thought might be useful. Japan was not yet at war with the West but she was aligned with Germany and Italy, and Nazi Germany was actively engaged in war on her Western Front. It seemed likely the war would spread and Japan would extend her operations in China and the China Sea. If we should be drawn in, we might find the coast of China blockaded by Japanese naval power and inaccessible to us. In that case, if we wanted to support China and establish air bases there for attack of Japan, we would have to approach from India and Burma. I prepared a draft paper proposing that U.S. Army engineers be sent to survey the Burma Road and report upon the possibilities of maintaining military logistic communications.

I took the draft paper to my friend and classmate Capt. Andral Bratton, Far East desk, G–2. He enthusiastically endorsed the proposal and asked to keep the draft memorandum for discussion with his associates. In due course it came back to me through portentous channels. Brig. Gen. Sherman Miles, G–2 of the War Department, had sent it to the Deputy Chief of Staff, Maj. Gen. William Bryden, with a complaint that the Office of the Chief of the Air Corps had no business intruding in such matters. The Deputy Chief had passed the complaint to the Chief of the Air Corps with the comment that if the officers of the Information Division had no more useful occupation for their energies than this, he was prepared to disband the Information Division and transfer its personnel to G–2 where their talents could be directed to some useful purpose. Even General Arnold was miffed— and when he was miffed people soon found out about it. Doubtless he was embarrassed to be called down about an incident of which he had no knowledge. In sending the correspondence down to the Information Division, he penned the comment, "I am inclined to agree with General Bryden." The incident passed, but it served to slam shut the door connecting the Air Corps Information Division and G–2.

Not long thereafter the relationship—or lack of it—surfaced again. General Arnold had an informal conversation with Lt. Col. Truman Smith, recently returned from Berlin as the Assistant Military Attaché. Smith furnished General Arnold many details of the Luftwaffe and German aircraft production of which Arnold was ignorant. The general demanded to know why such information had not been passed to him previously. Obviously it was of vital importance to the Air Corps. He was informed that these and numerous other facts were reported to G–2. General Arnold went to General Miles, G–2, and posed the same question. He was advised that intelligence of this nature was restricted to members of the War Department General Staff (WDGS), and Arnold as Chief of the Air Corps was not a member of the General Staff and hence was not on the distribution list.

Arnold went directly to Chief of Staff Gen. George C. Marshall and requested authority to set up an air intelligence system with Assistant Military Attachés for Air at U.S. embassies abroad. General Marshall approved the request. Next, Col. Ira Eaker, Arnold's Executive Officer, sent for Maj. Thomas D. White and me. He described General Marshall's authorization, and said General Arnold directed us to get on with it. Tommy White was a gifted intellectual and a highly qualified Air Corps officer. Having extensive experience abroad, he was fluent in Chinese and French. He was also a recent graduate of the Air Corps Tactical School and the Army Command and Staff School at Fort Leavenworth.

After discussing the scope of the problem facing us, we divided the program into two broad parts: foreign collection, and strategic analyses. As Chief of the Air Intelligence Section, Tommy organized a system of Assistant Military Attachés for Air and the collection of information through them. He selected the attachés, brought them to Washington for orientation and instruction, and sent them abroad. He also arranged the channels for communication, which provided that

G–2 of the War Department General Staff should have copies of all pertinent reports.

I undertook the area of strategic air intelligence and analysis. I set up three subsections, or branches: one devoted to foreign air forces, including size, composition, equipment, disposition, tactical doctrine, and proficiency; another dealing with airports and air bases throughout the world, together with maps and weather data; and a third engaging in economic-industrial-social analysis of major foreign powers, culminating in analysis and description of vital and vulnerable systems and, finally, target selection and preparation of target folders.

This latter activity involved a completely new venture. The Army's G–2 gave us no help whatsoever. On the contrary, we ran into vigorous opposition to the collection and analysis of such information on the grounds that it did not relate to the proper role of military intelligence. We had to proceed on our own, pioneering in one of the most difficult, critical, and challenging areas in the field of intelligence. We knew correct collection and analysis was vital to the success of the strategic air effort. Moreover, miscalculations of any significant magnitude could completely discredit the concept. I believed foreign industrial analysis and targeting was the sine qua non of strategic air warfare. Without such intelligence and analysis there could be no rational planning for the application of air power. Douhet's statement to the effect that the selection of objectives and targets was the essence of air strategy was patently true.

Our approach to industrial analysis as a basis for targeting was not started from scratch. At the Tactical School we had laid out the methodology and, since we had no foreign intelligence, we used the industrial structure of the United States as a working model. It was an abstract exercise lacking in practical results, but it did help to focus attention on the importance of certain systems and factories: electric power; rail transportation; fuel; basic materials such as steel; food supplies and processing; water supplies; and armaments and aircraft factories.

In view of the world situation, the Strategic Air Intelligence Section naturally concentrated on the Axis powers. It was slow and tedious work, but ultimately we made a lot of headway with Germany and Italy. Japan, however, was a different story. The Japanese had established and maintained a curtain of secrecy that we found absolutely impenetrable. There were not even any recent maps available.

The rising concern in the United States about Hitler's Germany was of great value to us in our work. It led a number of gifted men to enter the service and contribute their special talents. Also, it made available modest sums of money for hiring civilian experts. We were fortunate to hire Dr. James T. Lowe, a specialist in diplomatic history and international relations. Another civilian-turned-military was Maj. Malcolm Moss, a man of broad experience in international business who had traveled extensively. We were also fortunate in enlisting the services of a man with a doctorate in industrial economics and one who was an expert in oil.

Our initial inquiries into the industrial-economic structure of Hitler's Germany focused attention on: electric power, as well as electric switching, transmission, and distribution systems, and sources of fuel; steel production, including sources and movement of raw material; petroleum production, distribution, and products, and synthetic processes; the aircraft industry, taking in engine and aircraft manufacturing plants and aluminum production; and transportation, the most prominent components being the railway, canal, and highway networks. Our analyses also encompassed Germany's nonferrous metal supply, machine tool production, and food processing and distribution.

Malcolm Moss made a particularly valuable suggestion with regard to the electric power system in Germany. He knew the electric power generating and distribution system of Germany was relatively new and had been built with capital borrowed largely from the United States. He also knew American banks did not lend large sums of money for capital equipment without carefully investigating the proposed structures. He suggested we inquire of the great international banks, particularly in New York, if they had drawings and specifications of German electric plants and systems. The results were fruitful and rewarding. Using these sources, together with scientific journals and trade magazines, we put together a comprehensive target study on the German electric power system and electric distribution system. It was even possible to prepare target folders, aiming points, and bomb sizes.

We also made substantial progress on information about petroleum and synthetic oil plants, partially through the same sources, in part from the oil industries, and to a degree through individuals. Fortunately, our civilian oil expert had worked in Germany, in the Rumanian fields at Ploesti, and in the Middle East. It was through his knowledge and analysis that we recognized the extreme importance and vulnerability of the German synthetic oil plants, and the related importance of the Ploesti refineries. Thus we were able to prepare target folders, aiming points, and bomb sizes for these target systems. In addition, we made an analysis of the German steel industry and its sources of raw materials. We were less successful in our analysis of German transportation, partly because of the extent of the rail and canal systems. But enough was discovered to place the transportation system high on the priority list of desirable targets.

Later in 1941, I had a chance to go to England as an observer. The express purpose of my visit was to explore British intelligence, in response to a generous invitation by the Royal Air Force, and bring home what I could. At the same time, I took a hard look at possible air base construction sites in England, since by this time British and American military leaders had met in Washington in what became known as the ABC Conferences. We knew if we should become involved in the war, we would probably be allied with Britain against Germany and that the bomber offensive, if we ever launched one, would probably be from bases in Britain.

My relations with the RAF and the Air Ministry were extremely gratifying. I spent much of my time with Gp. Capt. A. C. H. "Bobby" Sharp, and I was literally welcomed into the inner chamber of RAF intelligence. I had brought along digests of our own intelligence and was made more comfortable by the discovery that we had much to offer. On balance, we were better informed than the British on German electric power, petroleum, and synthetic products. The RAF was better informed on Germany aircraft and engine production, the German Air Force, and German transportation.

At the end of my visit I found myself happily loaded down with priceless gifts of intelligence. The burden was formidable. There was nearly a ton of it. Most of this was in the form of "target folders" rather than analysis of target systems, but it was very valuable and most gratefully received. I wondered how to get it back to the United States, since it was, for the most part, classified secret. In the end I was able to have it shipped back by air in an American bomber.

Planning for War

Immediately after my return to Washington in July 1941 I was transferred from the Strategic Air Intelligence Section, A–2, to the new Air War Plans Division. Thus I again came under Lt. Col Harold L. George and Lt. Col. Kenneth N. Walker. Until the division was enlarged, the task of organizing our efforts to meet the broad assignment of developing "overall plans for the control of the activities of the Army Air Forces" fell upon the three of us. In this crucial state of affairs, it was a formidable assignment embracing such questions as size, composition, equipment, disposition, and organization of the air forces. And these in turn invoked the need to adopt the optimum concept for the wartime employment of these forces. Moreover, it was axiomatic that employment must make its maximum contribution in support of overall national policy.

At the time, national policy was very difficult to define. Nowhere was it clearly and neatly described. It was apparent that President Franklin D. Roosevelt viewed the possibility of a Nazi victory with deep concern. For six months after the fall of France, Britain had stood alone. With the German attack on Russia in June 1941, Britain gained a breathing spell, but it seemed likely the Soviets would be defeated. If so, the whole might of the victorious German Wehrmacht would then be turned against Britain. Furthermore, the vast industrial complex of Europe would be available for the production of munitions, including the creation of massive German air forces. The prospect was ominous to say the least. President Roosevelt seemed to favor American intervention before the collapse of Britain should make it a lost venture.

The United States as a whole was nowhere near such a mood. Most Americans seemed to cling to the hope that we could save the remnants of freedom and democracy in Europe by providing material aid to Britain. They were even willing to extend such aid to Soviet Russia in the belief a surviving Communist regime was a much lesser threat than a triumphant Nazi Germany. They were willing to extend our naval screen far out into the Atlantic and to prepare for active defense of the entire Western Hemisphere. But they were not ready to take the step of active participation in the war in Europe. Roosevelt had to retreat from his semi-belligerent policies on several occasions when it was clear that most of the American people were not willing to go so far. His Far Eastern policies caused little public concern. The American people simply could not believe Japan would challenge the United States in open warfare.

Until American policy firmed considerably, the best we could do for guidance was to determine in broad terms the general characteristics of the force requirements America seemed most likely to need. For those characteristics, we naturally turned back to lengthy discussions we had had on the subject back at the Air Corps Tactical School. We had reasoned that armed forces, as instruments for the furtherance of national policy, might be called upon to perform in three ways. One was the active acquisition of foreign territory. This would place primary reliance on land armies, and this objective seemed remote. However, taking temporary military action abroad in support of our national interest seemed increasingly probable. If so, chief dependence might be on the air force, or it might rest upon land armies, with naval and air forces operating in support roles. The possibility that aggressive action by forces unfriendly to the United States might compel us to take some action to protect our national interests and to force a halt upon the aggressor seemed a distinct possibility and received careful consideration. Air power might play the dominant role here. The third possibility, national and hemispheric defense, would require primary reliance upon air power for air defense and might call upon air power to repel any invasion.

Three dictators hostile to the United States were driving toward domination of important parts of the world. They threatened completely to upset the balance of power and with it world peace. Adolph Hitler and Benito Mussolini had completed the conquest of much of Europe and the Balkans and were verging on the conquest of western Russia and North Africa. England might either fall or be forced into a humiliating accommodation. On the other side of the world the Japanese warlords were tearing China and Southeast Asia apart. Meanwhile a fourth dictator, Joseph Stalin, though hardly a friend of America, was a most valuable asset in resisting Hitler. And it seemed likely he too would be overwhelmed.

Strategic Guidelines

If in mid-1941 there were no firm national policies on which to structure our national defense, there were at least certain strategic guidelines. In September 1940 the Tripartite Pact had brought Japan openly into the Axis camp. At about the same time, the unexpected collapse of France, followed by the epic Battle of Britain, had opened the eyes of many American political and military leaders to the possibility of a world dominated by Hitler in the West and by Japan in the East. As a result, the President decided to offer material aid from the "arsenal of democracy" to those fighting the Axis. Also, after consultation with the Secretaries of War, Navy, and State, the President concluded that some formal military staff conversations with the British were in order. There followed a series of secret joint meetings in Washington at the end of January 1941, conferences known to history as ABC-1.*

The British personnel attending were Rear Adm. Roger M. Bellairs and Rear Adm. Victor H. Danckwerts, representing the Royal Navy; Maj. Gen. Edwin L. Morris, representing the British Army; and Air Vice Marshal John C. Slessor, representing the Royal Air Force. The United States personnel attending were Rear Adm. Robert L. Ghormley, Rear Adm. Richmond K. Turner, Capt. Alan G. Kirk, and

---

*ABC-1 is the short title for the report of these British-American joint meetings. Starting on January 29 and ending on March 29, 1941, representatives of the two staffs held fourteen sessions and discussed military and naval strategy, joint operations, geographical responsibilities, force structure, command arrangements, and limited operational plans.

Capt. DeWitt C. Ramsey, all of the U.S. Navy, and Col. Omar T. Pfeiffer, U.S. Marine Corps. Lt. Gen. Stanley D. Embick, Brig. Gen. Sherman Miles, and Brig. Gen. Leonard T. Gerow represented the U.S. Army, and Col. Joseph T. McNarney, from the War Plans Division of the General Staff, represented the Army Air Corps. Although there were "rated" air officers of the United States present, there was no official representative of United States air power in a position corresponding to that of the RAF representative.

On an informal basis the Plans Division and Intelligence Division of the Office of Chief of the Air Corps cooperated very closely with Air Vice Marshal John Slessor and members of his staff and with Colonel McNarney. One of the most vital and fruitful developments of this informal relationship was a detailed exploration of the potential air base capacity of the United Kingdom, a capacity found to be several times greater than air planners in the United States had anticipated.

Our informal plans for possible deployment of the U.S. Army Air Forces to England had been predicated upon and limited by an analysis of existing airports. After making allowance for RAF requirements for air bases, it appeared the remainder would drastically restrict American air force deployment. Group Captain Sharp, who was in Washington on logistic matters at this time, produced a survey of suitable sites in England on which air bases could be built. It completely revolutionized our ideas of the potential capacity for accommodating U.S. air units. This discovery had an immense effect upon the dimensions of the air offensive that might be sustained from Britain and the potential scope of American air participation. The results that might be obtained from such an air offensive became a major aspect of combined offensive strategy.

The agreements and conclusions reached by the ABC–1 conferees were furnished to Roosevelt and Churchill in March 1941. The results of these conversations on the subsequent strategic developments of the war were profound. As a consequence, the U.S. Air Force owes an immense debt to Sir John Slessor and Colonel McNarney. The salient features of these conversations, predicated on the contingency the United States might be compelled to participate in the war, included these points: Since the Atlantic-European area was deemed to be the decisive theater, the primary effort would be exerted there. Offensive measures in the European area would embrace a sustained air offensive against military power, supplemented by air offensives on other enemy regions contributing to that power. Italy would be eliminated early on. Raids and minor offensives would be conducted initially against the Continent. Support would be given to all neutrals and belligerents who opposed the Axis. Forces would be built up for an eventual offensive on Germany, and positions from which the offensive could be launched would be captured.

This agreement was incorporated with the war plans being prepared by the War and Navy Departments, and on May 14, 1941, the Joint Army and Navy Board approved the war plan known as Rainbow No. 5.* It was subsequently approved by the Secretaries of War and the Navy. When the Air War Plans Division of the Air Staff came into being in July 1941, it found itself in solid accord with the ABC conversations and with Rainbow No. 5, the overall war plan envisioning Great Britain and the United States standing against Germany, Italy, and Japan.

War in Europe

As Hitler's armies cut their paths of victory through Europe, a mounting wave of apprehension engulfed the Roosevelt administration in Washington. Programs for expansion of the armed forces were presented to a reluctant Congress. One such program called for expansion of the Army Air Corps to fifty-four groups. It was presented to Gen. George C. Marshall, Chief of Staff, early in 1940. On conclusion of the presentation by Capt. Laurence S. Kuter, General Marshall asked a penetrating question: "Why is this a fifty-four group program? Why not fifty-six, or sixty-four?" As usual,

---

*In 1939 American war planners adopted the term "Rainbow" to describe a series of plans outlining the broad national strategic goals of the United States. They called the plans Rainbow because earlier war plans, written in the 1920s and 1930s, had been labeled with colors "orange," "red," etc. The single-color plans had anticipated wars against a single nation. By 1941 the conquests by Germany, Japan, and Italy had altered the assumptions of all previous American war planning.

General Marshall had gone directly to the root of the problem. What purpose was to be sought? What was the objective? Did it require fifty-four groups to attain that objective? Why? What was the strategic plan?

When the next opportunity arose for presentation of a major program, General Marshall's lesson was remembered. The planners asked themselves what was expected to be achieved with the force? What was the purpose?

Concern over Hitler's aggressive acquisitions in Europe produced other reactions in America. In June 1941 Secretary of War Henry L. Stimson, acting on General Marshall's recommendation, established the Army Air Forces. General Arnold, Chief of the Army Air Force, was permitted to set up a staff for the AAF resembling the War Department General Staff but at a lower level. It included Personnel, Intelligence, Operations and Training, Materiel, and Air War Plans Divisions. Lt. Col. Harold George at the time commanded the 2d Bombardment Group containing all the B–17s of the AAF (all thirteen of them). He was reassigned to Washington to organize and operate the Air War Plans Division of the Air Staff, arriving on July 14.

The next major force-structuring effort grew out of a new presidential inquiry. On July 9, 1941—some two weeks after Hitler had mounted his massive attack on Russia—Roosevelt asked the Secretaries of War and Navy to prepare an estimate of "the overall production requirements required to defeat our potential enemies." There was as usual a short deadline for a reply. Because the Joint Army and Navy Board could not agree upon an operational strategy, the War and Navy Departments each put together its needs separately. The burden of writing the War Department's response fell upon the War Plans Division of the WDGS. That division proposed to estimate air requirements, coordinate them with ground requirements, and append the air details to its report as Annex 2, Air Requirements. Colonel George, Chief of the fledgling Air War Plans Division, asked that his division be allowed to prepare the Air Annex. General Arnold made the necessary arrangements.

The War Plans Group of the infant Air War Plans Division

consisted of two people: Lt. Col. Kenneth N. Walker as Chief of the Group, and myself, Chief of the European Branch—two chiefs and no Indians at all. Harold George devoted his full time to the project, and that made three. He succeeded in having Larry Kuter, on duty with G–3 of the General Staff, temporarily assigned to the division. The four of us were faced with the task of preparing a strategic air plan for conducting war on a worldwide scale, and determining the forces to carry out such a plan. We would be constrained only by the physical capability of the United States to produce the recommended forces.

In this latter regard, we had the benefit of advice and counsel from the supply people at Dayton, with Maj. Max F. Schneider serving as a priceless liaison. By the time we got authority to proceed, there were just seven days left for submission of the plan and report. We had one definite asset going for us: We had spent years together as instructors in Bombardment and Air Force at the Air Corps Tactical School. We embraced a common concept of air warfare and we spoke a common language. Then, too, I had spent the past year as head of the Strategic Air Intelligence Section of the Office of the Chief of the Air Corps, amassing and analyzing economic and industrial intelligence on the Axis powers. That intelligence now proved invaluable.

Harking back to General Marshall's comments as well as to our own teachings, we realized the first requirement for our plan was a statement of purpose—a strategic objective. What should the air force try to achieve? What was the overall purpose? That was the fundamental keystone to plans, requirements, and operations. But that purpose was not only missing from our instructions; it was exceedingly hard to define.

The President's letter had called for defeat of our potential enemies. This was important guidance. Although he did not specify who our potential enemies were, there could be little doubt they were the Axis powers. His call for defeat cleared the air of any compromise objective, such as containment or deterrence. And we had two other significant guidelines. In passing the air requirement responsibility to the Air Staff, Brig. Gen. Leonard T. Gerow, Chief of the War Plans Division, had stipulated that the provisions of joint British-American conversations (ABC–1) and the U.S. current war plan (Rainbow No. 5) should be followed. The ABC–1 report called for strategic offensive operations against the European Axis powers as a maximum effort and strategic defensive operations in the Far East, with minimum diversion of forces from the main effort. It said: Offensive measures in the European area will include a sustained air offensive against German military power, supplemented by air offensives against other regions under enemy control which contribute to that power.

But what should be the relationship of air power to the achievement of the national purpose and to land and naval forces? Air forces were flexible, but special types of aircraft were best suited to specific roles, and the selection and provision of aircraft would depend upon the major role to be assumed by air power. Even in defeating the European Axis powers there was a wide range of strategic air purposes to be weighed:

a. Should the "sustained air offensive against German military power" seek to crush the war-making capability of the Third Reich by air warfare alone? If so, it would be necessary to destroy not only the industrial structure supporting the German armed forces, but the industrial and economic structure upholding the state itself.

b. Or should the "sustained air offensive" seek to undermine the war-making capability of Germany and pave the way for invasion of the Continent, with subsequent strategic air operations weakening Germany's willingness and capability to fight, in a continuing strategic air effort coordinated with the land campaign?

c. Or should the sustained air offensive seek only to guarantee the success of the invasion, and devote its entire strength to the support and success of the land operations, which would become the sole reliance for final victory?

d. And what were the requirements for home defense?

The targets, the types and number of aircraft, and the organization of the air forces would vary with each of these options. Selection of a basic overall strategy was the sine qua non of air planning. And the problem was further compounded by the knowledge that the plan would have to pass through the gauntlet of the War Department General Staff, culminating in a presentation to General Marshall. If he did not approve, the whole scheme would simply be discarded.

Marshall was himself a farsighted, broad-minded leader who had shown strong support for air power. But many Army officers still adhered to the official statement of Army doctrine: the sole mission of the Army Air Forces was the furtherance of the mission of the mobile army.

We knew a strategy oriented solely to invasion and air support of ground warfare in Europe involved troublesome prospects, including long and perhaps disastrous delays. We knew the War Plans Division had concluded it would take two years to build a merchant marine capable of transporting and supplying the necessary ground forces. And it would take another six months to prepare them for invasion. An air offensive could be launched in half the time. Furthermore, the War Plans Division was frank in admitting that Hitler's seasoned war machine would have to be seriously weakened before we could hope to defeat the German Wehrmacht on the ground. In any event, the German air forces would have to be defeated before an invasion could be undertaken. There was general agreement that a successful air offensive, which would include defeat of the Luftwaffe, must precede any invasion. There was less unanimity as to what other purposes the air offensive should try to accomplish.

We wrestled as a group with this fundamental problem. The final solution was a statement of objective and a plan leaning heavily toward victory through air power. But it provided for air support of an invasion, and afterwards combined operations on the Continent if the air offensive should prove inconclusive. If the air offensive succeeded in destroying the German ability to support the war or in bringing about capitulation, so much the better. The closer the air offensive came to finality, the greater the ease and less the cost of invasion.

In the Air Plan we described the overall objective of the air mission in essentially these terms:

a. To wage a sustained air offensive against German military power, supplemented by air offensives against other regions under enemy control which contribute toward that power (ABC–1).

b. To support a final offensive, if it becomes necessary to invade the Continent.

c. In addition, to conduct effective air operations in connection with hemisphere defense and a strategic defensive in the Far East.

d. The basic concept on which this plan is based lies in the application of air power for the breakdown of the industrial and economic structure of Germany. This conception involves the selection of a system of objectives vital to the continued German war effort and to the means of livelihood of the German people, and *tenaciously concentrating all bombing* toward the destruction of those objectives. The most effective manner of conducting such a decisive offensive is by the destruction of precise objectives, at least initially. As German morale begins to crack, area bombing of civil concentrations may be effective.

e. It is improbable that a land invasion can be carried out against Germany proper within the next three years. If the air offensive is successful, a land offensive may not be necessary.

In the plan we acknowledged that the German Air Force, especially the German fighter force, would have to be defeated before an invasion could be contemplated. And such a defeat might also be necessary to the prosecution of the air offensive itself. Hence defeat of the German Air Force was accorded first priority among air objectives ('an intermediate objective of overriding importance"), to take precedence over the primary air objectives themselves.

As for primary objectives, the plan called for destruction and disruption of:

a. Electric power. Disruption of a major portion of the German electric power system.

(1) Nearly all industry—civil as well as military—finds its roots in electric power. The German electric power system, the second largest in the world, was greatly expanded for this war. Even so, it is operating at a fifty-percent greater rate than that of Great Britain. It is vital to the German war effort and is highly important to civil life.

(2) The electric power system might be likened to the neuro-muscular system of the human body. Disruption would vitiate controlled action. It is estimated that destruction of fifty targets would bring about collapse.

b. Transportation. The German transportation system is carrying an extremely heavy load, divided about as follows: seventy-two percent of German transportation is carried out by the railroads, twenty-five percent by canals and waterways, and three percent by long-haul truckage. The transportation system bears the same relationship to the German corporate body as the bloodstream to the human body. Without a free flow of transportation, raw materials could not reach processing plants, manufactured parts and supplies could not reach factories and assembly plants, and finished products could not reach consumers, whether they be armed forces or civilian institutions. Forty-one targets, consisting of marshaling yards, bridges, canal locks, and inland harbors are set up for the accomplishment of this objective.

    c. Petroleum and synthetic oil.

    (1) German military vehicles and transportation, the German Air Force, the German Navy, and (a large block of) German industry are dependent upon petroleum products.

    (2) The blockade has cut off external sources, other than Rumania, leaving the Reich heavily dependent upon a group of synthetic oil plants. Twenty-seven synthetic plants plus the refineries at Ploesti in Rumania are set up to accomplish this objective.

    In summary, the plan called for destruction of these target systems and targets:

German Air Force	18 airplane assembly plants
	6 aluminum plants
	6 magnesium plants
Electric power	50 generating plants and switching systems
Transportation	47 marshaling yards, bridges, and locks
Synthetic petroleum	27 synthetic plants
Total	154 targets

How many planes?—How many people?

Bombing requirements for the destruction of each target, including repeat attacks to prevent restoration, were computed, using target dimensions and characteristics and tables of bombing probability. Force requirements were based on providing ninety-percent probability of obtaining the number of hits to destroy each target. Accuracy was degraded by a factor of two and one-fourth to take care of bombing accuracy under combat conditions. Allowances were made for aborts and losses. Based on weather records, the monthly rate of operations from British bases was taken at five. Finally, the total of bomber sorties was computed, and the number of bombers needed to accomplish the entire task in six months at the rate of five missions a month was determined. The key element in the entire plan was the proviso that the full bomber force should devote its entire strength to these targets for six months after it had reached maturity. Invasion would follow if necessary. Requirements for hemispheric defense were also estimated. The allowances for the defensive measures needed in the Far East were skimpy, to say the least. It was presumed the U.S. Navy would be the primary agency for this requirement.

The air plan specified that the offensive be conducted chiefly from bases in England, using B–17s and B–24s, and from bases in Northern Ireland and the vicinity of Cairo, Egypt, using future long-range bombers (B–29s). But the plan covered a contingency that bordered on disaster. Hitler's armies were slashing into Russia and would soon approach the gates of Moscow. If Russia should be defeated, Hitler could rebuild his air forces using all the resources of Europe. He could then mass his forces for a final assault on Britain, and Britain might also succumb. If so, the British air bases would no longer be available. To meet this contingency, the plan envisioned the development and production of 44 groups of 4,000–mile bombers (B–36s)—to press the war from bases in the Western Hemisphere. Still the strategic plan presumed British bases would in fact continue to be available. If these air operations against industrial targets were not conclusive, the plan suggested direct attack on cities as a last resort. But we never accepted attack on civilian populations as the main method of air warfare. We provided for air support of an invasion of France if the air offensive should not be conclusive after 6 months of undiluted effort. The air plan afforded massive additional tactical air forces for air support of an invasion and for subsequent combined operations on the Continent. Actually the Tactical and Air Defense Air Forces and Strategic Air

PLANNED AIR OFFENSIVE AGAINST GERMANY (AWPD-1)

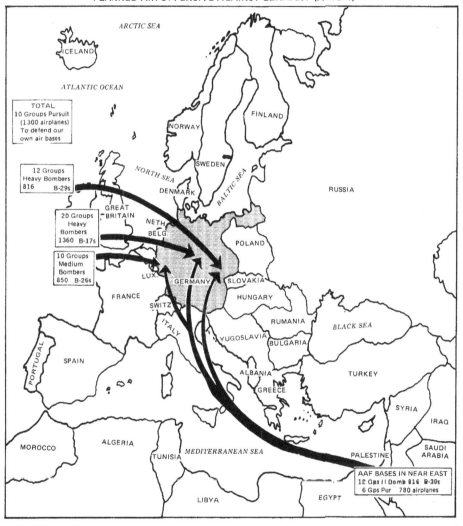

Forces were approximately equal in numbers: 12,000 first-line and unit reserve aircraft in each.

To pursue this strategy, the plan (Air War Plans Division I, or AWPD–1) called for some 61,800 aircraft (including 37,000 trainers), as well as 180,000 officers and 1,985,000 enlisted personnel—a total of 2,165,000 men and women. The scope of the air proposal was simply staggering. The personnel strength of the Army Air Forces in 1940 stood at about 51,000. The plan proposed an expansion to 2,165,000 in 3 years, a 42–fold increase. The aircraft inventory in 1940 was about 6,000, about half of these were obsolescent combat aircraft and the rest trainers. The plan proposed a 10–fold increase in 3 years. Furthermore, it called for production capacity to replace the combat elements of the force (about 26,000 combat aircraft) every 5 months. The heavy bomber component called for nearly 11,000 4–engine bombers. Combat replacements would require 770 4–engine bombers per month for the air offensive against Germany alone, and 416 fighters. The Army Air Forces had received 61 4–engine bombers in 1940. Shortly before that, the War Department had told the Congress that the Army needed no 4–engine bombers at all.

Although strategic air operations could begin on a limited scale about twelve months after the outbreak of war, it was not expected that the air offensive would be in place at full strength in England until about eighteen months after M–day. Thus, the full six months of strategic air warfare would end about twenty-four months after the outbreak of war. The invasion force should be positioned by that time. There would ensue a period of two or three months during which the strategic air forces could be applied in direct assault preparatory for invasion, and the ground forces could make final preparations for amphibious invasion, if by that time it were still necessary to storm the coast of France. (See charts on page 117.) Even if effective German resistance were broken by the air offensive, an occupying force would be needed. It would keep order, support an interim government, and ensure adherence to peace terms. The opposition to such an occupying force might be considerable, but the enemy capacity for massive, organized resistance should be broken by that time.

RELATIONSHIP OF STRATEGIC AIR OFFENSE
IN
PLANNING GRAND STRATEGY—WAR IN EUROPE
(VICTORY PROGRAM — AWPD–I)

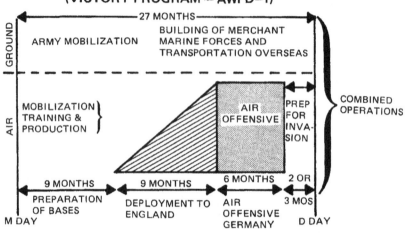

The plan was completed and submitted to the War Plans Division, WDGS, before General Arnold returned from Argentia, Newfoundland, where he had gone with President Roosevelt and General Marshall to meet with Prime Minister Churchill and his staff. The plan had been checked with Robert A. Lovett, Assistant Secretary of War for Air, at literally the eleventh hour. As a document it was not impressive-looking—pages typed and mimeographed; pen-and-ink corrections; charts black and white, hastily prepared and crudely pasted together. Finally, the entire War Plans document (including AWPD–1) was bundled off to the Government Printing Office.

The Air War Plans Division Plan No. 1 (AWPD–1) stipulated these total force requirements:

TOTAL AIR FORCE GROUPS REQUIRED

Heavy bombers (B—17, B—24)	47
Very heavy bombers (B—29, B—32)	24
Very long—range bombers (B—36)*	44
Fighters	54
Others (Primarily for support of ground forces)	82
TOTAL	251

TOTAL MILITARY AIRCRAFT PRODUCTION REQUIRED
(Including unit equipment and initial reserves)

Strategic Forces

Bombers, Heavy		9,775	
Heavy (B—17/24)	3,995		
Very heavy (B—29/32)	2,040		
Very long—range (B—36)	3,740		
Fighters (escort)		2,000	
		TOTAL	11,775

Tactical and Air Defense Forces

Bombers Medium, Light, and Dive	3,244		
Fighters	6,748		
Reconnaissance Aircraft	1,917		
		TOTAL	11,909

Transports	1,064		
		TOTAL	1,064
	TOTAL COMBAT AND OPERATIONAL AIRCRAFT		24,748

Trainers	37,051		
		TOTAL	37,051
		TOTAL MILITARY AIRCRAFT	61,799

TOTAL MILITARY PERSONNEL REQUIRED   2,118,625

Once war had begun, it would be necessary to replace the combat units (Total Combat and Operational Aircraft 24,748) every 5 months to account for combat attrition. This would require production of approximately 59,400 combat aircraft per year.

---

*The B—36s were required in case Britain would collapse.

39

The plan became Annex 2, Air Requirements, of the War Department report, which became "The Victory Program." But the Joint Army and Navy Board, in forwarding the full report, took scant notice of the air plan. The board said: "Naval and air forces may prevent wars from being lost, and by weakening enemy strength may contribute greatly to victory. . . . It should be recognized as an almost invariable rule that only land armies can finally win wars."

Finally on August 30 we faced the crucial test. General Marshall; W. Averell Harriman, the President's representative to Russia; General Arnold; Lt. Col. Muir S. Fairchild; several members of the General Staff; William S. Knudsen of General Motors, Inc., and other officials from war production listened to the presentation. There were questions and some expressions of dissent. Reserving his comment until all others had been heard, General Marshall said: "I think the plan has merit. I should like the Secretary and Assistant Secretaries to hear it." That statement by General Marshall to General Arnold marked a crucial turning point in the evolution of American air power. This was the moment of conception of the United States Air Force. General Marshall was its godfather. He could so easily have said: "The proposal is totally out of keeping with the program for the rest of the Army. Cut it in half!" Instead he said: "I think the plan has merit." It was a magnificent decision and a typical example of his towering character.

Briefed on September 1 with General Marshall present, Secretary of War Stimson showed a gratifying appreciation of the strategic concept. General Marshall offered encouraging comments. At last Stimson turned to Colonel George and said: "General Marshall and I like the plan. I want you gentlemen to be prepared to present it to the President." A tentative date for the meeting and intensive preparations for the presentation were under way, when Pearl Harbor threw all arrangements into disarray. Loss of the opportunity to brief the President on the detailed plans for strategic air warfare was a cruel disappointment. It is quite likely Roosevelt's quick intelligence would have prompted him to make detailed inquiries, and perhaps he would have embraced the scheme with the same comprehension that characterized the reactions of Marshall and Stimson. Missing that presentation, the President never fully grasped the war-winning potential of air power.

Nonetheless, AWPD-1 became the basic blueprint for the creation of the Army Air Forces and the conduct of the air war. As part of The Victory Program it was approved for production. Since the production quantities were derived expressly from the plan of operations, approval for production clearly implied approval of the scheme of operations. In the absence of other guidance, AWPD-1 became the accepted and authoritative statement of air strategy until issuance of AWPD-42 a year later. Still, AWPD-1 was never formally endorsed by the Joint Chiefs of Staff. After the Pearl Harbor attack, the Air War Plans Division hastened to amend AWPD-1. One principal change was more air forces for the Pacific to help compensate for the loss of U.S. capital ships. Another was to add a large number of air transports, since it was apparent a heavy burden of overseas communications would have to be met by air. The new estimate was called AWPD-4, but it was not much different from AWPD-1.

BOMB DAMAGE TO THE BALL BEARING FACTORIES at
Schweinfurt, Germany. In attacking this vital industry, the AAF
attempted to slow down the wheels of the German war machine.

Chapter II

Planning the Strategic
Air War for Europe

The Japanese aircraft that destroyed the U.S. Navy's battleline at Pearl Harbor on the morning of December 7, 1941, produced reverberations that extended far beyond the Pacific. The attack roused an apathetic America into a fury of resentment, resulting in a tidal wave of emotion that swept over the carefully reasoned plans which had been prepared to meet a war emergency. This wave of emotion affected civilians and military alike. America had watched the progress of the war in Europe and Far East with bemused and pacific apprehension. Suddenly, after Pearl Harbor, there was a call for action, and the call riveted attention on the Pacific and Far East—upon the Japanese—not upon Hitler and his Nazis.

U.S. military planners had not been idle after the outbreak of war in Europe. Despite the pacifists prevailing in the country, the possibility of the United States being drawn into the conflict was very real. The plans devised in a calmer and more logical atmosphere specified that the initial effort be launched against Axis Europe. The war against Japan would be restricted to the strategic defensive pending the defeat of Hitler. Then, and only then, would America transfer her might to the Pacific and defeat the Japanese. During the defensive phase in the Pacific, the U.S. fleet would seek out and defeat the Japanese fleet if the opportunity occurred. However, the primary effort and the priority of resources would be concentrated on crushing Hitler.

With the loss of the battleships on December 7, meeting the Japanese fleet on the high seas would have to be postponed. Even so, emotions were running high and reversal of the "Europe first" strategy and early assumption of the offensive against Japan appeared probable. The order of priority in building and deploying our forces was likely to veer in that direction.

Following the sneak attack, the Germans damaged their cause by promptly declaring war against the United States. Still, this act did not stem the tide of opinion that demanded instant retaliation against Japan in the Pacific. It was not the Germans who had attacked us—it was the Japanese. The U.S. Navy understandingly welcomed this public surge toward reprisal. For over a generation the Navy had looked toward the day when it could sweep the Pacific Ocean of the Japanese. Now it had been seriously depleted of capital ships and patriotic men who manned them. Add to this the affront to the pride of an organization that had built the world's greatest fighting machine at sea. The logic of a "Europe first" strategy seemed surely to be overcome by the surging waves of emotion.

Almost immediately after Pearl Harbor, Prime Minister Churchill announced his intention to come to America to join President Roosevelt for consultations between the new Allies on combined grand strategy. He may have sensed the American impulse to turn west against Japan rather than east against Axis Europe in the new situation. He announced he would bring his military staff, the Chiefs of Staff Committee. It consisted of the Chief of the Imperial General Staff, Sir Alan F. Brooke; the First Sea Lord, Sir Dudley Pound; and the Chief of the Air Staff of the Royal Air Force, Air Chief Marshal Sir Charles F. A. Portal. They would be supported by the members of the British Joint Plans Committee and Joint Intelligence Committee.

We viewed this approaching visit with alarm and some misgiving. The British interservice staff organization was competent and experienced. As yet, we had no similar committee organizations prepared to confer with the British. Moreover, our plans and desires were in complete disarray as a result of Pearl Harbor.

The President met this situation by appointing the U.S. Joint Chiefs of Staff Committee. Initially, it was to consist of the Chief of Staff of the Army and the Chief of Naval Operations. On the initiative of General Marshall, the President accepted General Arnold, AAF Chief, on the committee. This would satisfy Churchill's suggestion that there be an American "opposite member" to the Chief of the Air Staff of the Royal Air Force. But Roosevelt issued no formal directive defining General Arnold's position. At the meetings, held between December 22, 1941, and January 14, 1942, Arnold remained in the background, speaking only on technical air matters.

Adm. William D. Leahy, U.S. Ambassador to France, had recently returned to become the President's personal Chief of Staff. Initially he attended the meetings of the Joint Chiefs of Staff Committee to keep Roosevelt informed of the committee's proceedings and discussions. Thus, he had much the same role as that of Lt. Gen. Sir Hastings L. Ismay, Churchill's military assistant, who attended the meetings of the British Chiefs of Staff Committee.

The new "Joint Chiefs of Staff" set up supporting committees. Chief among them were Joint Plans, Joint Strategic, Joint Intelligence, and Joint Logistics.

Joint Strategic Planning

The Joint Strategic Committee and the Joint Intelligence Committee supported the Joint Chiefs of Staff through the Joint Plans Committee, which initially consisted of Rear Adm. Richmond K. Turner, USN (Chairman); Col. Thomas T. Handy, USA; and Col. Harold L. George, USAAF. Colonel George assumed command of the Air Corps Ferrying Command in April 1942 (redesignated Air Transport Command in June 1942). Maj. Gen. Carl Spaatz then became the Air member, with Col. Howard A. Craig serving as his deputy.

The functions of the Joint Strategic Committee were described in these terms:

To prepare such strategical estimates, studies, and plans as may be directed by the Joint Staff planners, and to initiate such studies as the committee may deem appropriate.

The estimates and studies produced by the Joint US Intelligence Committee and the Joint US Strategic Committee should represent the considered, composite convictions of each committee. In their studies and deliberations preliminary to committee conclusions, it is intended that the members of these committees should present their individual views regarding the matter under consideration. When higher authority has reached a decision or had issued a directive, the committee concerned will be guided accordingly.

The original membership of the Joint Strategic Committee included:

Capt. Oliver M. Read, USN
Col. Ray T. Maddocks, USA
Capt. Bertram J. Rodgers, USN
Lt. Col. Jesmond D. Balmer, USA
Capt. Forrest P. Sherman, USN
Lt. Col. Albert C. Wedemeyer, USA
Maj. Homer L. Litzenberg, Jr., USMC
Maj. Haywood S. Hansell, Jr., USAAF

On a Friday morning, I received orders reassigning me immediately from the Army Air Forces, where I was Chief of the European Branch of the Air War Plans Division, to the War Department General Staff Corps. I was ordered to report to the Joint Strategic Committee at its new offices on Monday morning. As a member of this committee, I found myself in the midst of the massive machinery which was trying to deal with problems of worldwide proportions. I was told that my loyalties in my new job were to be devoted to the Joint Chiefs of Staffs and that I must divest myself of service allegiances and all prejudices relating to one branch of the military service.

There were only four offices for the eight members of the committee. Each office had a large double desk at which two officers, of different services, sat. Each desk had one "in" basket, one "out" basket, and one "hold" basket. Every effort was made to force us into concerted action and to divorce us from service loyalties. We were a group of strangers, four from the War Department and four from the Navy Department. The senior officer was Navy Captain Read. He acted as chairman initially, but alternated with Colonel Maddocks at the Army's insistence.

The military beliefs of the various members of the Joint Strategic Committee were as different as the members themselves, reflecting the divergent backgrounds of the individuals and their training. Of the eight committee members, I was unfortunately the only graduate of the Air Corps Tactical School, though the school had graduated many Army, Navy, and Marine Corps officers. I, for one, was familiar with Air Corps doctrine which taught that wars, once entered upon, should be won in the sense that victory should make possible the attainment of national war aims and that victory involved overcoming the enemy's "will to resist" and capability to continue the fight, while preserving one's own. That end could be sought by:

1. Providing security for one's own sources of power.

2. Defeating the enemy's forces in battle.

3. Destroying (or cutting off) the war-supporting industrial structure supplying the instruments with which the enemy fought.

4. Destroying or debilitating the industrial systems supporting both the war-supporting and the civil-social, life-supporting vitality of the enemy State.

5. As a last resort, destroying great numbers of the enemy people or depriving them of the means to support themselves, particularly the masses dwelling in the cities.

Of these options, air power might be employed to achieve 1, 3, 4, and 5, or to assist the Army and Navy in achieving 2 or 3. This Air Corps concept obviously was not unanimously adopted by the committee. In fact, there was no unanimity—no common ground—on which the members of the Joint Strategic Committee might move in unison toward recommending a joint overall strategy for the conduct of the war.

With the exception of Colonel Wedemeyer, the members of the Joint Strategic Committee were unaware of the Air Corps' views on air power and certainly were not ready to accept them. The Army members considered that victory could come only through invasion of the enemy's territory and defeat of the enemy's army. The Navy was prepared to go along with this view, with the clear understanding that invasion could not possibly be considered until the Navy had defeated the enemy navy and secured the lines of communication. Thereafter, the Navy was ready to support the amphibious assault and protect the lines of communication—leaving the rest to the Army, supported by the air forces. As the Air Corps member, I contended the enemy could best be defeated by strategic air power. The Joint Strategic Committee was treading in troubled waters. The potential of strategic air power to be the decisive element in achieving victory continued to be disputed until the end of the war.

We were just getting acquainted when we received our first directive from the Joint Chiefs of Staff. As the meeting was called to order, a burly Marine captain entered, bearing a locked and sealed briefcase. He wore side arms and an armed guard accompanied him. With much ceremony, he removed a message from his briefcase and received a signed receipt. The message was from the Joint Chiefs of Staff by way of the Joint Plans Committee. It was a masterpiece of directness and simplicity asking in effect: "What should be the strategic concept of the conduct of the war?" Making no reference to previous plans or policies and making no effort to influence our views, the message left the field wide open. This was typical of the open-mindedness of General Marshall. Unfortunately, however, the directive furnished no statement of national purpose or national objective of the war to serve as guidance for our formidable task. Nor did we, as the Joint Strategic Committee, seek to interpret national attitudes and statements of policy to serve as guidance. At our first meeting, however, we did agree upon a sensible first step: we called upon the Joint Intelligence Committee for a presentation of the world intelligence situation.

The Joint Intelligence Committee presentation was gloomy indeed. All of Western Europe had become a German citadel, and Hitler's armies were at the gates of Moscow. The Germans had suffered a rebuff, but this was attributed as much to the winter weather as to Russian counterattack. The Joint Intelligence Committee estimated that Russian resistance would collapse within three months after fighting resumed in the spring. That would be in about six months. The Japanese were pressing relentlessly onward with no sign of weakening. Corregidor in the Philippines might hold out for a while, but it would simply be bypassed. The Joint Intelligence Committee estimated that the Germans and Japanese might join hands in the vicinity of Karachi, India, within the year. Taking note of these facts, opinions, and predictions, we sought to evaluate them. In our deliberations, the great question marks were the Russian Army and the capability of Britain to hold out.

The Russian Army gave no reason for optimism. Little was known of it, but that knowledge was hardly encouraging. Stalin had killed off great numbers of the professional military in the purges of the 1930s. Thereafter, the Russians had instituted the commissar system, whereby every military commander had a Party member at his elbow. This new Russian Army had not fared well against the very small adversary of Finland in 1939 and 1940. Rumor indicated the Communists had then abandoned the commissar system. Later, however, we learned this was not true. The Soviets were extremely secretive and treated their Allies as potential enemies.

The great Russian Army had permitted itself to suffer the disastrous effects of surprise the previous summer when Hitler had unleashed 163 divisions against them on June 22, 1941. How the Germans could amass 163 divisions on the Russian border without alerting the Russians to their danger remains a mystery. Actually Stalin had been warned, both by the British and by his own agents. The summer campaign of 1941 by the Germans had produced one of the wonders of military history. Using bold tactics of wide envelopment and deep penetration by Gen. Heinz Guderian's armored forces, closely supported by the Luftwaffe, the Germans cut out huge chunks of Russia. By following up with foot soldiers moving forward at an amazing pace, the Germans simply ingested over a million Russian prisoners at a rate which surely taxed the prisoner-of-war facilities to the utmost.

In the winter of 1941–1942, the hope of continued Russian resistance on any major scale seemed dim indeed. If Russian resistance faded away, what then? Numerous Germans would be released for redeployment against the British. The British had preserved their security through the Battle of Britain. But it was problematical that Britain could succeed a second time. With the European industry available for producing new armaments, the deficiencies leading to the defeat of the Luftwaffe in the Battle of Britain could be corrected. Heavier bombers and longer-range escort fighters might accomplish what the He–111 bombers and the Me–109 fighters failed to do. The submarine campaign might be extended until it did indeed starve Britain into submission or accommodation. Then all would be lost, and America would face either the extension of German power into South America, or the prospect of an uneasy peace subjecting the vast resources and markets of Europe to German exploitation. But what could be done about it? More specifically, what could the United States do about it?

The Victory Program* had shown it would take two years to raise the armies and build ships to transport them to Europe for massive combined invasion of Fortress Europe, even if the British were able to survive and persist. Two years seemed quite hopeless.

We had been spared the agony of deciding whether to go to war. The Japanese had made that decision for us. But the Joint Strategic Committee would have been well advised to preface its deliberations with a determination of national purpose and national military objectives. The first was, unfortunately, ignored. The latter was commonly agreed to be "victory over our enemies." The victory must be so convincing as to permit our statesmen and political leaders to set whatever course was best for the postwar world.

The committee faced two options in terms of national grand strategy: (1) strategic offensive against Axis Europe and strategic defensive against Japan; (2) strategic defensive of the Western Hemisphere and strategic offensive against Japan. The committee

---

*The response by the Secretaries of War and Navy to the President's letter of July 9, asking for "estimates of production required to defeat our potential enemies" was called *The Victory Program*, of which AWPD–1 was Annex II. After Pearl Harbor only the Air Plan, AWPD–1, remained feasible to accomplish in the new situation.

further faced several options in terms of military force application, whether there should be primary emphasis on invasion, or sea blockade, or strategic air attack, or a combination of the three. Earlier, Roosevelt and Churchill had clearly favored a joint offensive in Europe as a first priority. But this was before the catastrophe of Pearl Harbor and the proximate defeat of Soviet Russia. At this point, the Joint Strategic Committee felt free to make a new military appraisal. In fact, the committee looked upon this as a requirement in view of the directive from the Joint Chiefs.

The direction most of the members of the committee would favor soon became evident. If the salvation of Europe was hopeless, then it would be stupid to waste resources on a doomed venture and leave the Japanese undisturbed while they consolidated their expanding areas of conquest. In short, insofar as grand strategy was concerned, the majority of the committee tended toward option (2)—strategic defensive of the Western Hemisphere and strategic offensive against Japan, abandoning Europe as hopelessly lost. As to military force application, the Navy wanted primary emphasis on defense of the Western Hemisphere by the Navy and gaining naval domination of the Pacific. Ultimately, this meant gaining sea superiority in the critical areas vital to Japan and finally supporting an invasion. Army members stoutly contended that invasion, whether in Europe or Japan, was the decisive maneuver for victory.

I was the proponent of air power as the chief instrument of victory. Although my interests included air defense and air support of surface operations, they centered on strategic air warfare. And I was not prepared to write off Europe as already lost. There were many principal ways to apply air power. (We do not need to go into them here as they pertained to the air war against Germany. They are described elsewhere.) The significant point was that a Nazi victory in Europe would create a condition wherein we could not sustain a prosperous life in peace. Acknowledging this, authorities at the very highest levels had already approved the offensive against Germany as our main effort. To this end, our first military effort was an air offensive, as described in AWPD–1. Regardless of how black the picture looked, we simply had to do our utmost to save Europe to save ourselves. In defense of my position, therefore, I briefed the committee in detail on the air plan, which proposed first priority on a sustained and unremitting air bombardment of Germany from English bases.

The purpose of the air offensive was (1) to debilitate the German war machine through destruction of war industries and undermine the "will to resist" of the German state by selective bombing, (2) topple the German state if possible, and (3) prepare for support of an invasion, if that should be necessary. More specifically, AWPD–1 called for the operation of 1,060 medium bombers (B–25s and B–26s), 3,740 heavy and very heavy bombers (B–17s, B–24s, and B–29s), and 2,000 fighters against Germany from bases in England, Northern Ireland, and Egypt. In addition, 3,740 very-long-range bombers (B–36s) would operate from bases in the Western Hemisphere. There would be 6 months of intensive and undiluted bombardment of 154 selected industrial targets:

German Air Force	30
German electric power system	50
German petroleum system	27
German transportation system	47
	154

The primary air objectives were described in some detail with regard to Axis Europe; they were less definitive as to Japan.

Days and nights of bitter but earnest arguments ensued within the committee. The weight of committee sentiment and conviction gravitated steadily to the Pacific. Committee members had spent their professional lives studying military history, and most were inclined to accept a strict interpretation of the Joint Army and Navy Board's precept expressed in September 1941, in The Victory Program: "Naval and air power may prevent wars from being lost and, by weakening enemy strength, may greatly contribute to victory. By themselves, however, naval and air forces seldom, if ever, win important wars. It should be recognized as an almost invariable rule that only land armies can finally win wars." Invasion of Europe by land armies before the collapse of Russia appeared a very remote possibility.

Growing impatient, the Joint Chiefs of Staff sent a message demanding an answer to their question. Colonel Wedemeyer and I favored a grand strategy of Axis Europe first, even though the prospects of victory in Europe looked very grim indeed. A head count showed that nearly all our committee members, three-fourths in fact, were for abandoning Europe as beyond salvation and for constructing a defense of the Western Hemisphere and an offense against Japan as soon as forces, especially naval ones, could be provided. They were ready to acknowledge the loss of Europe and Britain as a hopeless cause and assume the offensive against Japan at the earliest possible time, culminating in the invasion and conquest of the Japanese home islands.

I was motivated by a number of convictions to turn our maximum effort to the defeat of Hitler. A year's study as head of the Strategic Air Intelligence Section of A–2 led me to a firm belief that Germany was susceptible to defeat from the air. I had estimated and evaluated the force requirements to achieve this aim. I knew the air offensive would not have to be delayed two years; it could begin in the near future and reach massive proportions in a little over a year and a half if it were accorded top priority. I knew base areas could be furnished in Britain. And a tour in England as an observer of the war convinced me Britain would fight and go on fighting so long as there was one ray of hope. We could supply that ray.

I also felt that victory over Hitler was essential to America's future well-being. Failure to preserve Europe could produce a situation in which a Nazi-dominated Europe could become too strong for our economic competition or our military security. This was not so for the Far East. Failure to thwart Emperor Hirohito of Japan would lead to discomfort but not disaster. Colonel Wedemeyer also believed that we should do everything in our power to defeat Hitler and save Europe. He, too, felt that a Europe dominated and exploited by Hitler could prove to be a disaster for the future of America.

Together we persuaded our associates. The recommended grand strategy sent to the Joint Chiefs through the Joint Plans Committee envisioned a strategic offensive against Axis Europe as the maximum national effort until Nazi Germany was decisively defeated. Concurrently, there would be strategic defensive operations in the Pacific with the least diversion of available forces from the main thrust against Hitler. An all-out strategic offensive would be launched against Japan immediately after Hitler's defeat. The initial mode of offensive operations against Axis Europe would be through a combined strategic air offensive by the Royal Air Force and the U.S. Army Air Forces from bases in England. It would be directed against the German Air Force and the war-making and civic-sustaining resources of the German state. Preparations for an invasion of the Continent and sustained and combined air and surface warfare would be provided. Massive tactical air forces to support ground operations would be made ready in time. The proponents of strategic air warfare hoped an invasion would not be needed, but Allied grand strategy could not be pinned to that hope alone.

This grand strategy was accepted by the U.S. Joint Chiefs of Staff and was formally accepted by the Combined Chiefs of Staff on December 31, 1941. The agreement contained the following paragraph:

The essential features of the American-British Strategy as adopted by the Combined Chiefs of Staff on December 31, 1941, based on the principle that only the minimum of force necessary for the safeguarding of vital interests in other theaters should be diverted from operation against Germany, were:

(a) The realization of the victory programs of armaments, which first and foremost requires the security of the main areas of war industry.

(b) The maintenance of essential communications.

(c) Closing and tightening the ring around Germany.

(d) Wearing down and undermining German resistance by air bombardment, blockade, subversive activities, and propaganda.

(e) The continuous development of offensive action against Germany.

(f) Maintaining only such positions in the Eastern theater as will safeguard vital interests and deny to Japan access to raw materials vital to her continuous war effort while we are concentrating on defeat of Germany.

It is interesting to note that the Combined Chiefs of Staff recognized that *defensive security of the sources of power, the main areas of population, and war industry, must be ensured before any offensive operations could be sustained.*

One would expect this would settle the dichotomy over early offensive against Japan, but this was not so. The U.S. Navy was not content with a defensive role and demanded the acceptance of a "limited active defense" against Japan, with forces assigned for this purpose. Specifically, Navy officials wanted a U.S. Army strategic air force assigned to support naval forces in the South Pacific. The crux of the disagreement focused on communications between Hawaii and Australia. I demurred against furnishing a strategic air force to the Pacific which would compete with requirements for Europe. Nonetheless, the other committee members agreed with the Navy's contention that the line of communication to Australia through New Zealand was vital to the war effort, and there must be provided a mobile air force of long-range aircraft to operate with the mobile naval surface forces. The idea was appealing and had merit—if we had forces to support it.

I agreed that the area was important but could not agree that a long-range air force should be provided for operations in that area. Actually, we had no long-range air forces at all. The Eighth Air Force was to be organized for deployment to England at the earliest possible moment. But it was not even in existence. We were short of long-range bombers and trained crews, and we were straining to form such an air force for the air offensive against Axis Europe. To set up another long-range air force for operations in the South Pacific would dilute our sparse resources beyond recognition. This was the first of many efforts—some of them all too successful—to divert long-range bombers from their agreed first priority job: the attack on Germany.

The request by the Navy for creation of an Army Air Forces strategic air force to be deployed to the South Pacific to operate under naval command was approved by the majority of the members of the Joint Strategic Committee. This was, I suspect, the first "split-paper" submitted to the Joint Chiefs, and they were not pleased. Delivering an official admonition to our committee to be recorded on the personal record of each member, they directed us to reconvene and come up

55

with an agreed recommendation. General Arnold called me in and gave me a "personal admonition" to go on my record.

We reconvened in continuous session. Colonel Wedemeyer, who had always inclined to a "Europe first" strategy, recognized the danger in setting up a competing demand for a strategic air force in the South Pacific. He joined me and we worked as a team. Little by little the others came around—the Navy members most reluctantly. Finally, we came to agreement on the need for concentrating forces for the chief effort against Axis Europe with a minimum of diversion elsewhere. We submitted our unanimous findings, which were accepted. I rather thougnt General Arnold would remove the record of my personal admonition, since I had won my point, and I am sure he would have if he had thought of it. But apparently it did not occur to him.

I do not think it wise to make too much of these incidents. I doubt if the Joint Chiefs would have endorsed the recommendation first favored by the majority of our committee—abandoning Europe as irrevocably lost and turning our energies to defeat of Japan. But it is possible they might have. President Roosevelt and Prime Minister Churchill would certainly have overridden any recommendation to that effect. Yet, if Germany had not declared war on the United States so promptly, the President would have had to face alone the wave of anger against Japan. I think it quite possible that, under those circumstances, our main effort might have been in the Pacific. The incidents have, I think, two points of significance.

First, if Germany's declaration of war against the United States had been omitted entirely or had been delayed, Churchill would have found it difficult to arrange for immediate conversations on British-American grand strategy on a worldwide basis. And it would have been difficult for him to bring the Chiefs of Staff Committee and their supporting committees with him. Since there would have been no immediate need for a U.S. air member to balance the Chief of Staff of the Royal Air Force, it is quite likely the initial composition of the U.S. Joint Chiefs of Staff (if such a committee were appointed at all) would have embraced only the Chief of Staff of the Army and the Chief of Naval Operations, together with the President's personal

Chief of Staff. Without air membership, the U.S. Joint Chiefs in their deliberations on grand strategy would have embraced the argument that Britain could not be saved by surface warfare, and they would probably have endorsed the decision to abandon support of Britain as infeasible and to make defeat of Japan the primary American military objective.

Second, the Navy never really abandoned its adherence to the concept that equal priority should go to the war in the Pacific—to the defeat of Japan. By the time the final plans for invasion of the Japanese home islands were approved in 1945, the Navy had completed an enormous armada in the Pacific, including 10 new battleships and 13 rebuilt old ones and 109 aircraft carriers of assorted sizes. Nearly all of these ships had been committed or laid down in 1942 and 1943. They had enjoyed equal priority with the needs and demands of the Army and the Army Air Forces for new armaments, even though these resources were destined for the secondary, defensive effort in the Pacific, not to the principal offensive against Axis Europe. The enormous carrier force was equipped with multiple aircraft complements and combat crews for each carrier. These, too, shared equally in resources with the Army Air Forces, which were committed to the top priority strategic effort against Axis Europe. No one will deny the magnificent performance of these forces in the Pacific. But their production schedule was not in accord with the agreed joint strategy, and it competed with and jeopardized the buildup of forces for the chief effort.

My tenure with the Joint Strategic Committee was not long. In May, Maj. Gen. Dwight D. Eisenhower asked me to head an air plans office in the European Theater of Operations, and in June I went to England where he promoted me to brigadier general. My replacement on the Joint Strategic Committee was Col. Earle E. "Pat" Partridge. I went from that job to command a wing and an air division in Eighth Air Force.

AWPD-42

In August 1942 the President again asked for an estimate

involving aircraft. He wanted to know the number of military airplanes that should be produced in 1943 to attain air supremacy. I was temporarily called back from England to direct preparation of a new air plan (AWPD–42). Air War Plans Division–1 (AWPD–1), written in September 1941, had been a "contingency plan," in case we should go to war. But AWPD–42 was essentially a "requirements" plan specifying munitions, bases, and air needs to carry out an agreed strategy. This time the requirements would include aircraft for our allies as well as ourselves, since we continued to want the wherewithal to conduct significant air operations. AWPD–42 retained the basic structure of AWPD–1. The defeat of Germany remained the first priority and the air offensive against Japan was still deferred. Unchanged was the primary strategic purpose of undermining and destroying the capability and will of Germany to wage war. This would be done by destroying the war-supporting industries and economic systems upon which the war-sustaining and political economy depended.

The air operations contemplated for 1943 and 1944 were:

1. An air offensive against Axis Europe to:
    a. Defeat the German Air Force.
    b. Destroy the sources of German submarine construction.
    c. Undermine the German war-making capacity.

2. Air support of an Allied land offensive in Northwest Africa.

3. Air support of Allied nations' land operations to retain the Middle East.

4. Air support of surface operations in the Japanese Theater to regain base areas for a final offensive against Japan proper, including:
    a. Land operations from India through China, reopening the Burma Road.
    b. Amphibious operations from the South and Southwest Pacific toward the Philippine Islands.

5. Hemispheric defense, including antisubmarine patrol.

The air objectives were described as primary and intermediate, with overriding priority given to the intermediate ones:

58

(German) Fighter aircraft assembly plants
Bomber aircraft assembly plants
Aero engine assembly plants

The primary ones were:

(German) Submarine yards
Transportation targets (rail and canal in Germany)
Electric power system
Synthetic oil plants
Aluminum plants
Synthetic rubber plants

When inaugurated, the strategic offensive against Japan would resemble that for Germany. It would seek to undermine and destroy the capability and will of the Japanese people to wage war by destroying the industries and systems upon which the war industries and the civilian economy relied.

In comparison with operations and priorities called for in AWPD–1, worldwide operations revealed by 1942 some weakening of resolve to keep the maximum possible air strength directed toward the primary strategic air offensive, the destruction of the vital elements of Germany. Northwest Africa was drawing off air forces to support land operations. Land operations in the Middle East were likewise diverting air elements. And surface operations to regain base areas in the Far East, as distinct from operations for a strictly defensive purpose, were also absorbing air power. By necessity, all these absorbed air forces could have been employed in the primary strategic effort, the air offensive against Germany. Yet the latter had not even started in any meaningful sense, and the delay would be further extended if these diversions continued to grow.

As for the air offensive against Japan, it was too early to give anything more than general guidance in terms of objectives and targets. Nevertheless, AWPD–42 recognized that the strategic air offensive against Japan would follow the defeat of Germany, and proposed the following targets:

Aircraft engine plants
Submarine yards
Naval and commercial bases
Alumina and aluminum plants
Iron and steel
Oil
Chemical plants
Rubber factories

There were two striking omissions from this list: the Japanese electric power system and the transportation system (including shipping, harbor and repair facilities, inland seas transportation routes and waterways, and railroads). The omission of the electric power system stemmed from the cursory analysis by A–2. This fostered the general belief that electric power was produced in a multiplicity of small hydroelectric generating plants which would render the system as a whole practically invulnerable to attack. The analysis had not been made in depth and did not include the distribution system. However, there was ample time for a further detailed examination, and failure to conduct it was a costly error.

The total approved aircraft production requirements for the Army Air Forces, the U.S. Navy, and our allies came to 127,000, of which 85,300 would go to the Army Air Forces.

Distressing Diversions

The first threat to the air offensive against Germany came distressingly soon. Prime Minister Churchill vigorously advocated an invasion of North Africa. It would have to be supported with heavy bombers at the expense of the air offensive against Germany. The American Joint Chiefs took the position that an invasion of North Africa was militarily unwise. As General Marshall pointed out, it was a tangential thrust, at right angles to the proper axis of attack—the assault of Germany itself. The North African invasion would swallow up vast military resources at the expense of the principal effort, while doing very little toward defeating the Reich in Europe. General Arnold vigorously supported this position with special stress on the cost to the strategic air offensive against interior Germany. Adm.

Ernest J. King, Chief of Naval Operations, believed the margin of priority of Germany over Japan was very small and any diversion of resources away from Germany should go to the Pacific, not to the Mediterranean.

President Roosevelt weighed both the military arguments against diversion to North Africa and the political arguments calling for some visible evidence of military success. The air offensive against Germany was not well enough understood to meet political demands, nor were its true dimensions really grasped by the President. Invasion of France was out of the question in 1942 and probably in 1943. At this point (mid–1942), both the British and the Americans had only a string of stinging defeats—except for the defensive Battle of Britain—to show for their war efforts. Churchill was coming under increasing political attack at home, and his possible political defeat would be a dreadful disaster. The Prime Minister's arguments for operations in North Africa and the Mediterranean had two longer range objectives: freeing the sea lanes through the Mediterranean to India and Australia, and adoption of a main thrust toward Germany by way of the Balkans and the "soft underbelly." Such a push would run interference against the Russian drive that might engulf all of Western Europe. The President agreed to the North African venture.

The Air War against Axis Europe

The problems of grand strategy plagued Brig. Gen. Ira C. Eaker from the day in February 1942, when he and his small advanced staff of six people landed in England and set up the VIII Bomber Command, Eighth Air Force. Eaker lacked a clear, authoritative, written statement of purpose. What was the VIII Bomber Command expected to accomplish? What was the grand objective? Where did that grand objective fit into the scheme of international purposes? Did American air power have an independent but coordinate task to accomplish, or was it a supporting element, paving the way for and assisting the decisive campaigns of the ground forces? What was to be the relationship between VIII Bomber Command and RAF Bomber

Command, and between VIII Bomber Command and the U.S. Theater Commander?

Eaker himself understood well enough the objective General Arnold had in mind, from the latter's verbal instructions. But he had no written directive or letter of instructions describing his purpose and giving him the authority to pursue it. The VIII Bomber Command Commander had been a supporter and disciple of Billy Mitchell. He had attended the Air Corps Tactical School, where Mitchell's broad concepts had been translated into specific concepts and principles. He had also been thoroughly briefed on AWPD-1, the plan for the development of the Army Air Forces and their operations in the European Theater. As mentioned earlier, that plan expressed the objective of U.S. Army Air Forces in a war against the European Axis Powers in these terms: "To conduct a sustained and unremitting air offensive against Germany and Italy to destroy their will and capability to continue the war and to make an invasion either unnecessary or feasible without excessive cost." The primary targets were listed as the disruption of Germany's electric power system, transportation system, and petroleum system. The German Air Force, especially the German fighter force, might make it excessively expensive to make deep penetration to reach these primary targets. Hence, the German fighter force was described as an *intermediate objective* and given an "overriding priority," even higher than the primary targets whose destruction was expected to cripple the German state and its ability to continue the war. Neutralization of the German fighter force would have the added value of being absolutely essential to any consideration of invasion. To accomplish this aim, AWPD-1 specified building Eighth Air Force to 10 groups of medium bombers (850 B-25s and B-26s), 20 groups of heavy bombers (1,360 B-17/B-24s) based in England, 12 groups of very heavy bombers (816 B-29s) based in Northern Ireland, and 10 groups of fighters (1,300 P-47s and P-38s) based in England—a total of 4,328 aircraft, including unit reserves.* Clearly this was a concept of air power coordinate with any other forces, land or sea, and designed to have a war-winning role in Allied grand strategy. Obviously the Eighth Air Force would have to establish and maintain its individual identity and integrity if it was to perform such a role.

Eaker subscribed to this concept wholeheartedly and he never swerved from it. But AWPD-1 had been prepared before Pearl Harbor and had been approved by the President solely as part of the Victory Program, as a guide for production. When the Joint Chiefs of Staff organization was created in late December 1941, the Chiefs refused to approve AWPD-1 as a basis for strategic operations. The Navy particularly objected, saying the plan dealt with matters important to the Navy, but that Navy officers had not participated in its development. Furthermore, Pearl Harbor had radically changed the situation.

On January 13, 1942, the Joint Chiefs did approve dispatching a bomber force to England to join with RAF Bomber Command in attacks on the European Axis. On January 27 the Combined Chiefs agreed that the first two U.S. heavy bomber groups available were to be assigned to an American bomber command in the British Isles, to "operate independently in cooperation with the British Bomber Command."

Arnold probably had no authority to issue Eaker a "Letter of Instructions" to prepare to implement AWPD-1. Had Arnold made an issue of it at the time he most likely would have lost. What he may have told Eaker in private has not been disclosed, but there was no

---

*The number of groups and aircraft were later described in AWPD-42 (August 1942) as: heavy bombers, 42 (2,016); medium bombers, 15 (960); fighters, 25 (2,500). Unit reserves would boost these totals an estimated additional 50 percent: 3,024 heavy bombers, 1,440 medium bombers, and 3,750 fighters in the theater. These changes reflected the decision to rely upon the continued security of bases in England. (AWPD-1 provided for the substitution of B-17s and B-24s for the B-36s in order to meet the contingency of the loss of England as a base area.) In AWPD-42 the B-29s were also replaced with B-17s and B-24s, since these bombers had adequate range to reach the targets in Germany, and the long-range B-29s, when they became available, would be needed in the Pacific. It also reflected the transfer of fighters from the air defenses of the Western Hemisphere. (Most of these fighters were transferred to the Tactical Air Forces, where they became excellent fighter-bombers). The total number of aircraft to be based in England became 8,214, including unit reserves.

need to explain intentions. Arnold, Spaatz, and Eaker had worked together for twenty years to develop air power. They understood each other. Probably Arnold was wise in waiting until he had deployed this massive force to England before raising the issue of grand strategy. As it was, officially he told Eaker to go to England to study RAF Bomber Command operations and to prepare the way for reception of U.S. bomber units.

When Eaker arrived in England in early February 1942, he reported to the Commanding General, U.S. Army Forces in British Isles, Maj. Gen. James E. Chaney, an Air Corps officer. Chaney had received no special instructions regarding Eaker and proposed to quarter Eaker in his theater headquarters, staffed chiefly by ground officers, and to exercise command over him like all other U.S. Army elements in England. Eaker needed all his tact and ingenuity to avoid being absorbed. He succeeded in evading this fate by seeking headquarters near RAF Bomber Command, thirty miles outside London, in order to carry out his instructions from Arnold.

But there Eaker encountered his second major problem. Air Marshal Sir Arthur Harris, Commander in Chief, RAF Bomber Command, was the soul of hospitality, but he was bent upon having the American bombers join Bomber Command in night operations against German cities. This threatened the absorption of VIII Bomber Command into RAF Bomber Command and the abandonment of the American strategic air concept of selective target destruction, which required daylight operations so as to distinguish and attack specific targets. It was here Eaker displayed his remarkable talent for "amicable disagreement." He and Harris became and remained fast friends. But Eaker steadfastly refused to accept Harris' urgent recommendations and appeals.

When Generals Eisenhower and Spaatz arrived in England on June 24, 1942, to be the U.S. European Theater Commander and the Commanding General, Eighth Air Force, respectively, each carried a "Letter of Instructions." Spaatz had received verbal instructions from Arnold and the letter, signed by Arnold, was brief, dealing exclusively with channels of communication. Eisenhower's letter, more detailed, constituted the real directive under which all U.S. Army units in

England, including the AAF, were to operate in the United Kingdom. All air units initially based there were to be integrated into the Eighth Air Force. General Spaatz, as commander, was to have his own headquarters and staff, and provision was to be made for bomber, fighter, ground-air support, and air service commands. Eisenhower's letter talked about strategic control of AAF operations vested in the British government and expressed through Air Chief Marshal Portal, RAF, as agreed by the Combined Chiefs of Staff. It was assumed the instructions to Eisenhower meant general strategic directives on purposes and broad objectives. His instructions did not include designation of targets or tactical control of operations. The broad objective for the AAF in the European Theater of Operations was described in the letter. It was to gain air supremacy over western continental Europe in preparation for and support of a combined land, sea, and air movement across the channel into continental Europe.

The letter made no mention of a place for air power in grand strategy and gave no strategic objective or list of strategic targets save for gaining air superiority to prepare for and support an invasion of the Continent. Nor were there any instructions to Eisenhower to offer support for a strategic air offensive. No authority for strategic air decisions was specially vested in General Spaatz as Commander of the Eighth Air Force. As executive agent of the Combined Chiefs of Staff, Air Chief Marshal Portal exercised broad strategic direction. Final authority rested with General Eisenhower as theater commander, commanding all U.S. Army forces in the European Theater of Operations.

Spaatz and Eaker had no overriding authority or responsibility for directing the strategic air offensive of the Eighth Air Force, except as they were able to assume such authority by persuasion. Fortunately they were both able, persuasive commanders, but their freedom of action was limited and could be withdrawn at the discretion of the theater commander. Thus the prospects for an effective American strategic air offensive seemed dim, even if the forces promised for England should arrive on schedule and should not be diverted. When Eisenhower departed the European Theater to become commander in

MAJ. GEN. HENRY H. ARNOLD. Chief of the AAF, (center) meets with his staff to plan war strategy, ca. fall 1941. Staff members include: (left to right) Col. Edgar P. Sorenson; Lt. Col. Harold L. George; Brig. Gen. Carl Spaatz, Chief of Staff; Maj. Haywood S. Hansell, Jr.; Brig. Gen. Martin F. Scanlon; and Lt. Col. Arthur W. Vanaman.

AAF COL. STANLEY T. WRAY, Commander, 91st Bomb Group; Maj. Gen. George E. Stratemeyer, Chief of Air Staff, Headquarters, AAF; and Brig. Gen. Hansell, Commander, 1st Bomb Wing, attend a dedication ceremony at Bassingbourn, England, in April 1943.

BRIG. GEN. HANSELL listens to Maj. Gen. Follett Bradley, AAF Air Inspector, during a visit to 305th Bomb Group, Chelveston, England, on May 21, 1943.

BRITISH AIR CHIEF MARSHAL SIR ARTHUR HARRIS (left) meets with Lt. Gen. Frank M. Andrews, Commanding General of U.S. Forces in the European Theater, and Maj. Gen. Ira C. Eaker, Commanding General, Eighth Air Force, on March 25, 1943.

chief of the forces invading North Africa, he took Spaatz with him—and more than half of Eaker's bombers as well.

Late in 1942, Maj. Gen. Muir S. Fairchild was a member of the prestigious Strategic Survey Committee of the Joint Chiefs of Staff that supplanted the Joint Strategic Committee. The committee was charged with examining the progress of and recommending changes in the grand strategy that had been formulated by the Joint Strategic Committee. General Fairchild was disturbed by attacks being made on the air strategy proposed in AWPD–42. He discovered that the Joint Intelligence Committee, containing no air member, was challenging the validity of the basic strategic airpower contention. Specifically, the committee questioned the effect on the outcome of the war of the destruction of industrial targets. Fairchild therefore proposed that a group of top U.S. industrial leaders be assembled to assess the impact of destruction of selected targets upon industrial production. His idea was to look at the primary targets listed in AWPD–42 and assess the impact of their destruction. He also proposed to list industrial targets, in priority, whose destruction would contribute most to the collapse of the German capability and willingness to continue the war.

During the first week of December 1942, General Arnold (without reference to the Air War Plans Division) sent Fairchild's draft proposal to Col. Byron E. Gates, head of the Office of Management Control. Arnold's memorandum read:

> Have the group of operations analysts under your control prepare and submit to me a report analyzing the rate of progressive deterioration that could be anticipated in the German war effort as a result of the increasing air operations we are prepared to employ against its sustaining sources. This study should result in as accurate an estimate as can be arrived at as to the *date* [emphasis added] when the deterioration will have progressed to a point to permit successful invasion of Western Europe.

The emphasis upon invasion is significant, and was a source of some confusion to the Committee of Operations Analysts.

Meantime, the issue of incorporating U.S. bombers into RAF night operations continued to boil. The issue was not confined to RAF Bomber Command. Although Air Marshal Harris did not personally refer the matter to the British Air Ministry, the latter took strong opposition to General Eaker's daylight operational concept. Eaker was caught between two millstones. Over his bitter protest he had lost his most experienced and effective bomber groups to the North African campaign. Then the very people who had robbed him were castigating him unmercifully for failing to undertake effective air operations against Germany. Unfortunately, the criticism was just as caustic from the United States as from the Air Ministry. Whereupon that most powerful and persuasive personality, Winston Churchill, Prime Minister of England, entered the fray.

In early 1943, at the Casablanca Conference of the Allied heads of State and the Combined Chiefs of Staff, Churchill protested the Eighth Air Force daylight bombing at a luncheon with the President. He secured Roosevelt's tentative agreement that the Eighth should be directed to abandon the American air strategy of selective target attacks and join RAF Bomber Command in night operations against German cities. When General Arnold learned of it, he sent for Ira Eaker, now a major general and Eighth Air Force Commander since Spaatz departed to join General Eisenhower in the Mediterranean Theater. Arnold explained the situation. Eaker for once lost his customary aplomb. He told General Arnold that if he, Arnold, was prepared to abandon his objective and adopt an air strategy that could neither paralyze Germany's war-making industry nor make feasible an invasion, he, Eaker, wanted no part of it, and Arnold could find another air commander. Arnold grinned and said he had anticipated such a response and had arranged a meeting between Eaker and Churchill two days hence, to see if the Eighth Air Force Commander could dissuade the Prime Minister.

Eaker sequestered himself with his aide, Captain James Parton, and prepared his argument. He knew that Churchill preferred brevity; like most high officials he had neither time nor patience to wade through lengthy documents. The first draft of the digested arguments prepared by the two totaled some twenty-three pages. Eaker then called upon his skill of exposition, a natural talent sharpened by a year of law at Columbia University. The final draft consisted of eight simple, declarative assertions, filling half a page.

On the occasion of his momentous meeting with Prime Minister Churchill, General Eaker said he understood that the Prime Minister was always willing to weigh both sides of an issue, and he had prepared a brief paper. Churchill read the statements slowly and with evident relish at their pithy clarity. Eaker then had the opportunity to explain and expand his arguments. He raised no criticism of night bombing by the RAF, but argued that it would fit in with the daylight bombing by the Eighth Air Force to provide continuous pressure. "We'll bomb the devils day and night and give them no rest." At the conclusion of the meeting Churchill said:

> Young man, you have not yet convinced me you are right, but you have persuaded me that you should have further opportunity to prove your contention. How fortuitous it would be if we could, as you say, "bomb the devils around the clock." When I see your President at lunch today, I shall tell him that I withdraw my suggestion that U.S. bombers join the RAF in night bombing, and that I now recommend that our joint day and night bombing be continued for a time.

It was, I believe, one of the most critical decisions of the war. If Prime Minister Churchill's recommendation had stood, if Eaker's argument had not been persuasive, the results would have entailed:

a. Standing down the Eighth Air Force for modifying equipment and retraining. The B–17s and B–24s would need to be shielded against exposing exhaust and supercharger turbine light for night operations. That would have been quite difficult because they used exhaust gas turbines to drive their superchargers and the light would have been quite prominent at night. Most of the guns and gunners would require removal, since they would be relatively useless at night.

b. The navigators would need training for higher expertise in celestial navigation.

c. The bombardiers would require retraining for night bombing.

d. The bombardment aircraft would need British navigation and position equipment (Gee and Oboe) pending refinement and provision of American H2X radar bombing equipment.

e. Provision would have to be made for night landing of large forces and for prevention of collision in congested air space being used by both forces.

But most important of all, it would have entailed abandonment of American grand strategy and a radical change in air strategy. Americans were convinced that solely by destruction of selected vital target systems could German war-making and war-sustaining capability be wrecked. Certainly the German Air Force could not be eliminated by night bombing; hence there could be no invasion. And the night attack of German cities might prove insufficient to cause German capitulation, as seemed probable in the view of American air strategists. If so, victory in Europe might elude the Allies, and the objectives of grand strategy would probably be lost entirely if this change in air strategy were adopted. It is even likely American strategic air priority would have shifted to the Pacific.

It was, in my opinion, the crucial turning point in the conduct of the war in Europe. Its outcome hung upon the convictions and the persuasiveness of Ira Eaker. He gambled his career that this was one of "the things that can be changed and should be changed," and ultimate success proved his wisdom. It was a testimonial to Eaker's forthright and courageous support of strategic purpose and objective. He succeeded in persuading the Prime Minister to reverse himself on a position that Churchill had emphatically endorsed and had committed himself to the President. Eaker's gift for "amicable disagreement and persuasion" never stood him in greater service. And in the process he earned the admiration and respect of the Prime Minister. It was a magnificent achievement.

The Casablanca Directive

The Casablanca Conference of January 1943 brought forth another signal accomplishment: the Casablanca Directive for the prosecution of the Combined Bomber Offensive (CBO). It ranks, I think, with AWPD–1 and AWPD–42 as one of the finest air documents of the entire war. While Eaker's hand was discernible in its formulation, the document itself appears to have been fathered by a greatly gifted British airman, Air Vice Marshal Sir John Slessor, Assistant Chief of Air Staff for Policy. Eaker and Jack Slessor were close friends, and they shared a common view of air power. It was Slessor who had provided for "a sustained air offensive against Germany" as a key element in the joint strategy of the American-British Conference (ABC–1) agreed upon in February of 1941. Eaker had kept Slessor abreast of American strategic thinking. Slessor was thoroughly familiar with AWPD–1 and AWPD–42 and the objectives expressed in both American plans. He was thoroughly familiar with the target systems of each, the tactics proposed, and results expected. Eaker and Slessor were eye to eye in terms of airpower's contribution to victory and the place of strategic air power in grand strategy. Slessor said American plans and objectives had great merit, though they may have been somewhat optimistic in some respects.

Slessor's document, "The Casablanca Directive," specified vigorous prosecution by both British and American air forces toward a common grand strategic objective, optimizing the special strength and capabilities of each air force toward that common goal. As described in the directive, the ultimate objective of British and American strategic air forces was: "The progressive destruction and dislocation of the German military, industrial and economic system, and the undermining of the morale of the German people to a point where their capacity for armed resistance is fatally weakened." Pending preparation and approval of a plan for the Combined Bomber Offensive, the Casablanca Directive called for destruction or neutralization of:

    a. German submarine construction yards.
    b. The German aircraft industry.

    c. German transportation.
    d. German oil plants.
    e. Other targets of war industry.

These targets were taken directly out of AWPD–1 and AWPD–42, with one important omission: German electric power. That target, however, could be included in "other targets of war industry."

The directive endorsed both American and British grand strategy for air power, and recognized both RAF doctrine and experience and American tactical doctrine. The Eighth Air Force and RAF Bomber Command could operate as coordinate members of a team progressing toward a common destination, without being literally tied together. RAF Bomber Command was free to continue its chosen air strategy using the bombers designed for that method; the Eighth Air Force was free to pursue its doctrine of destruction of selective targets by daylight bombing, using day bombers and fighters. Together they would contribute toward an agreed grand objective, the "fatal weakening" of Nazi Germany. The Combined Chiefs and the President and the Prime Minister approved the directive. At one stroke air grand strategy had been accepted and approved. Air power would take its place with land power and sea power.

No agreement was reached concerning an invasion of northern France, which the British opposed; but neither was there agreement against it; and the Casablanca Directive made no mention of it. The objective of the air forces was not directed to attainment of air superiority over European beaches and support of an invasion. It focused upon dislocation and disruption of the German state, and its capability and willingness to continue the war. If the German state was "fatally weakened," it was going to fall. It might or might not take a push in the form of an invasion to cause it to topple, *provided the strategic air forces were built up on schedule and were fully employed without dilution or diversion from the intermediate objective and the primary targets for six months at full strength.* Final decision on invasion of northern France was postponed. In the meantime, tactical air forces would be built up to support such an invasion. Eaker's cup was surely running over.

From Policy to Operational Plans

At General Arnold's suggestion, and with Air Chief Marshal Portal's endorsement, a joint U.S. Army Air Forces-RAF team was set up in Eaker's headquarters in 1943 to prepare a plan for carrying out the Casablanca Directive. The team consisted of members of Eaker's staff, the two B–17 wing commanders of the Eighth Air Force (Brig. Gen. Frederick L. Anderson and myself), representatives of the Air Ministry and RAF Bomber Command, and a representative from the British Ministry of Economic Warfare. I was chairman of the planning team.

Col. Charles P. Cabell, who had been one of Arnold's special advisors, arrived at General Eaker's headquarters on March 23, 1943, carrying the list of potential target systems prepared by the Committee of Operations Analysts. General Eaker then turned to the planning team to prepare the strategic plan of operations and select the target systems which would come within the capability of Eighth Air Force while contributing most to the accomplishment of the objective, after considering the scheduled growth of the force and the potential combat losses. The operational plan would also set up a proposed time schedule.

To direct this planning team, I had been called in from my 1st Bombardment Wing Headquarters. General Frederick Anderson was brought in from the 4th Bombardment Wing and, at General Eaker's request, Air Chief Marshal Sir Charles Portal furnished the very able Air Commodore Sidney O. Bufton, RAF, Director of Bomber Operations at the Air Ministry. Sidney Bufton was a most valuable addition to the planning team. He had been, and continued to be, an important contributor to the bomber offensive. Gp. Capt. Arthur Morley, RAF, was also a member, as were Maj. Richard Hughes (one of the original members of the Strategic Air Intelligence Section), Lt. Col. John S. Hardy, and Lt. Col. Arthur C. "Sailor" Agan, Jr., all from General Eaker's staff. Colonel Cabell also participated. Even though the team set up by General Eaker bore no official designation, it might be called the CBO Planning Team, seeing that it produced the plan for the Combined Bomber Offensive from the United Kingdom and the Mediterranean.

The plan would differ from AWPD-1 and AWPD-42 in one important respect. The former were "Requirement Plans," designed to prescribe what should be accomplished and what was needed. The plan for the CBO was a "Capability Plan." Its purpose was to prescribe what should be done to achieve an objective with forces already committed to production.

The salient features of the plan were as follows:

I.   Objective: The Casablanca Directive.

II.   Primary Target Systems: The report of the Committee of Operations Analysts has concluded that the destruction and continued neutralization of some sixty targets, among nineteen target systems, listed in priority, will gravely impair and might paralyze the western Axis war effort. The priority list of the nineteen target systems is: German aircraft industry, with first priority on fighter aircraft, including assembly plants and engine factories; ball bearings; petroleum; grinding wheels; nonferrous metals; synthetic rubber and tires; submarine construction yards and bases; military motor transport; general transportation systems; coking plants; steel; machine tools; electric power; electric equipment; optical precision instruments; chemicals; food production; nitrogen and the chemical industry; antitank machinery and antiaircraft machinery. There are several combinations among the industries studied that might achieve this result. From the systems suggested by the Committee of Operations Analysts, six systems comprising seventy-six precision targets have been selected: German aircraft industry; submarine construction yards and bases; ball bearings; oil; synthetic rubber and tires; military transport vehicles.

III.   Intermediate Objective—German Air Force: The German fighter strength in Western Europe is being augmented. If the growth of the German fighter strength is not arrested quickly, it could become literally impossible to carry out the destruction planned for the strategic air offensive, and thus to create the conditions necessary for ultimate decisive action by our combined forces on the continent. Hence, the successful prosecution of the air offensive against the principal objective is dependent upon a prior (or simultaneous) offensive against the German fighter strength.

IV.   Integrated RAF-United States Army Air Force Offensive: The combined efforts of the entire United States and British bomber forces could produce the results required to achieve the mission prescribed for this theater. Fortunately, the capabilities of the two forces are entirely complementary.

The tremendous and ever-increasing striking power of the RAF bombing is designed to so destroy German material living conditions and economic facilities as to undermine the willingness and ability of the German worker to continue the war.

It is considered that the most effective results from strategic bombing will be obtained by directing the combined day-and-night effort of the United States and British bomber forces to all-out attacks against targets which are mutually complementary in undermining a limited number of selected objective systems.

V.   General Plan of Operations: The plan of operations is divided into four phases. The depth of penetration, the number of targets available, and the capacity of the bombing forces increases successively with each phase.

VI.   Forces Required:*

First Phase—800 U.S. heavy bombers on hand by July. Depth of penetration—generally limited to range of escort fighters. (There is one notable exception—the ball-bearing factory at Schweinfurt.)

Second Phase—1,192 U.S. heavy bombers on hand by October. Depth of penetration—400 miles from bases in England.

Third Phase—1,746 U.S. heavy bombers on hand by January 1944. Depth of penetration—500 miles.

Fourth Phase—2,702 U.S. heavy bombers on hand by June 1944. Depth of penetration limited only by operating radius of action of bomber aircraft.

If the forces required as set forth above are made available on the dates indicated, it will be possible to carry out the mission prescribed in the Casablanca Conference. If those forces are not made available, then that mission is not attainable in mid–1944.

In view of the ability of adequate and properly used air power to impair the industrial source of the enemy's military strength, only the most vital considerations should be permitted to delay or divert the application of an adequate air striking force to this task.

Upon completion, the CBO plan was presented to General Eaker and, after considerable discussion, he approved it. It was later given to the new European Theater Commander, Lt. Gen. Frank M. Andrews, and he also concurred. Meanwhile, the RAF members of the

---

*Actually, this was a reflection of the total number of aircraft scheduled for delivery.

committee made similar presentations to Air Chief Marshal Sir Charles F. A. Portal, Chief of the Air Staff of the Royal Air Force.

General Eaker took the plan to Washington and personally turned it over to the Joint Chiefs of Staff on April 20, 1943. In a masterful briefing made without reference to written matter, he won their approval and personal commendation for his performance.

Change in the Casablanca Directive

After the plan for the Combined Bomber Offensive was referred to General Andrews, and apparently after General Eaker left for Washington, a sentence was added to the Casablanca Directive. The source of the change is not clear, but it seems likely to have been added by Air Chief Marshal Portal. This new sentence read: "This is constructed as meaning so weakened as to permit combined operations on the Continent." The original Casablanca Directive, approved by the Combined Chiefs of Staff, President Roosevelt, and Prime Minister Churchill, did not include this sentence. It is hard to believe that the approved directive could have been altered without their knowledge. But there is no proof that their concurrence was either sought or received.

Unaware of the change, the planning team that developed the CBO plan used the original Casablanca Directive as the air objective. Quoting from the plan circulated to the Combined Chiefs of Staff on May 15, 1943:

> 1. *Problem*: To provide a plan to accomplish, by a combined U.S.-British air offensive, the "progressive destruction and dislocation of the German Military, industrial, and economic system, and the undermining of the morale of the German people to a point where their capacity for armed resistance is fatally weakened;" as directed by the Combined Chiefs of Staff at Casablanca.

No reference is made to any amendment or appendix to the directive. However, the plan transmitted on April 15, 1943, by Air Chief Marshal Portal to General Arnold, Commanding General, AAF, has this quotation:

1. *The Mission*: The mission of the U.S. and British bomber forces, as prescribed by the Combined Chiefs of Staff at Casablanca, is as follows:

To conduct a joint U.S.-British air offensive to accomplish the progressive destruction and dislocation of the German military, industrial, and economic system and the undermining of the morale of the German people to a point where their capacity for armed resistance is fatally weakened. *This is constructed as meaning so weakened as to permit initiation of final combined operations on the Continent* [emphasis added].

Air Chief Marshal Portal may have added the sentence after discussions with his associates on the Chiefs of Staff Committee. The addition may have been meant to win support for the strategic air offensive from the Army and Navy members, whose principal interest was in surface warfare. Or it may have reflected General Arnold's known concern for support of a cross-channel strategy, which General Marshall strongly endorsed. The invasion, tentatively scheduled for mid-summer 1944, was on the agenda for the upcoming Trident meeting in Washington.

Whatever the cause, the added sentence cast doubt upon the real intention of the Casablanca Directive. If the sentence had said: "This is constructed as *including* so weakened as to permit initiation of final combined operations on the Continent," it would have been more palatable to the airmen. As it was, three basic interpretations of the Casablanca Directive were now in evidence.

For instance, RAF Bomber Command considered the "undermining of the morale of the German people" as the significant clause leading to the "point where their capacity for armed resistance is fatally weakened." This did not necessarily entail killing large numbers of people. It did entail depriving them of homes, heat, light, water, urban transportation, and perhaps food. Homeless, hungry workers and civilian employees, they reasoned, do not produce munitions and, like soldiers who are wounded, are a greater impediment to the state at war than dead ones. Also, factories deprived of workers and utilities as a byproduct of urban bombing are useless as sources of combat munitions. Finally, there was the added hope that civilians might become so discouraged as to lose their willingness to support the war.

In contrast, the U.S. Strategic Air Forces looked upon "the progressive destruction and dislocation of the German military, industrial, and economic system" as the path to the "fatal weakening," and believed it could best be done by destroying selected targets in Germany. "Fatal weakening" meant the impending collapse of the entire German state, not simply a breach in the coastal defenses of France. A structure that has been "fatally weakened" is doomed to collapse.

The differences between British and American airmen were not so deep as might appear on the surface. The responsible air commanders generally agreed on the suitability of the strategic objective to be attained. The debate was over method and was related more to operational equipment and capability and survivability than to the need for "fatal weakening" per se. It will be recalled that at first the RAF was committed to the doctrine of daylight, precision attacks, but the bombers available to carry out the mission could not withstand the Luftwaffe's determined attacks. Hence the heavy British Stirlings and Lancasters, which sacrificed armament for bomb-carrying capacity, switched to night area type bombing. Indeed, the British were so sure bombers could not survive German fighter attacks by day that they repeatedly tried to convince the Americans that the basic doctrine of high altitude, precision bombing in daylight would fail.

On their part, the American planners felt they had fully measured the compelling desirability of precision bombing against the dangers inherent in daylight attack. As indicated earlier, they believed survival was possible through heavy defensive firepower and proper concentration of bomber formation flying. They knew it was risky, but destruction of selected vital targets through precision bombing was so important that the risk, as well as the reduced bombload caused by heavy armament, was regarded as acceptable. Effectiveness of the bomber offensive should be measured against the impact upon the German national war machine, not simply in terms of bomber losses.

Top-level soldiers and sailors of both nations—and to a large degree the President and Prime Minister as well—considered the chief purpose of the Combined Bomber Offensive to be something quite different from that envisioned by the airmen. To them the real goal of the bombing offensive was making possible an invasion of the Continent. In their view, the "fatal weakening" meant the destruction and dislocation of the German military system which would ordinarily oppose the invasion. "This is construed as meaning so weakened as to permit initiation of final combined operations on the Continent."

From the standpoint of the airmen, the added sentence to the Casablanca Directive would have been more acceptable had it read: "This is construed as *including* so weakened as to permit initiation of final combined operations on the Continent." They believed the primary objective was "the progressive destruction and dislocation of the German military, industrial, and economic system, and the undermining of the morale of the German people to the point where their capacity for armed resistance is fatally weakened." That purpose encompassed destruction of targets in Germany, not softening up beach defenses and restricting military movements in France.

After the Joint Chiefs of Staff accepted General Eaker's plan and the Combined Chiefs of Staff approved it at the Trident Conference on May 18, 1943, Sir Charles Portal, acting as executive agent for the Combined Chiefs, issued a directive to proceed with the Combined Bomber Offensive. The Eighth Air Force by day and the RAF Bomber Command by night were thus launched upon their parallel and coordinate efforts, to cause the fatal weakening of the willingness and capability of the German people to pursue the war. The Combined Bomber Offensive (code name Pointblank) was under way.

The two strands of strategic thought—decisive weakening of interior Germany by air power, and air preparation for decisive air-ground operations on the Continent—clashed with each other due to the restriction in timing. Originally, the plans had specified six months of air offensive *before* direct preparation for invasion. However, the campaign in North Africa and the Mediterranean (opposed by the Joint Chiefs on military grounds) delayed by about four months the crucial assault on the German air forces from bases in England. This telescoped by a like time interval the period between the completion of the offensive against the *intermediate objective* (defeat of the German

Air Force) and the readiness of the ground forces for invasion. The four months of air attack of the primary objectives (the industrial and economic targets in Germany) were postponed until after the invasion.

The dichotomy in strategic concepts for the prosecution of Pointblank came to a head about ten months after Trident, when General Eisenhower as Supreme Commander, Allied Expeditionary Forces, demanded concentration of the strategic air forces upon targets in France to prepare for the invasion. This was right after the crippling of the German air forces in the last week of February 1944, but before the main assault upon the targets in interior Germany could be carried out in force.

The Casablanca Conference had brought another blessing to General Eaker and the Eighth Air Force. General Marshall selected Lt. Gen. Frank M. Andrews, former Commanding General of the GHQ Air Force and an Air Corps officer, as European Theater Commander, replacing General Eisenhower who had moved to North Africa.

Andrews was the number one airpower leader and advocate of his day. Perhaps the most skillful pilot in the Air Corps, he was also the leading senior air strategist as well. His experience was broad. He had been the first GHQ Air Force Commander in 1935 and had organized and trained that pioneering element of American air power. In 1939 he had been selected by General Marshall to be G–3 of the War Department General Staff, the first airman to head a major WDGS division. Eaker hailed his arrival in England with joy. But joy turned to tragedy when Andrews was killed as his bomber crashed against a mountain in Iceland where he was making an inspection of American forces. At the same time, Eaker was flying back to London from Washington.

Andrew's replacement as European Theater Commander was Lt. Gen. Jacob L. Devers, an Army ground officer. It is doubtful if any other officer in any guise, with or without pilot's wings, could have equaled Devers' contribution to the Eighth Air Force. He quickly absorbed and embraced Eaker's strategic airpower concepts and backed them to the limit of his authority. Eaker and Devers became a unified command team whose binding elements were dedication to strategic purpose and friendship born of mutual admiration and respect.

Chapter III

Execution and Evaluation

During the early period, when bomber units of the Eighth were finding themselves and tempering their quality in the heat of combat, success or failure hung upon the human factor that had to sustain the greatest strain of all—the morale of the combat crews. The cutoff in the promised flow of additional units in the buildup of the bomber force and the absence of replacements for groups already at war, caused by the diversion of heavy bombers to the Mediterranean Theater, placed an almost intolerable strain on the morale of the crews. The morning after each mission saw the number at the breakfast table dwindle. By March 1943 the crews of the initial groups were at less than half strength. Each mission was costing between five and six percent in combat casualties, and missions were running at the rate of five per month. Because the force was so small, each mission was a "maximum effort."

At coffee tables and in mess halls and reading rooms, the crews developed a new and morbid game. Graphs were plotted, replotted, discussed, and examined. The graphs were of two kinds. The less sophisticated type of curve was plotted with the ordinate as percentage of strength remaining, and the abscissa as an expression of time in months. When the straight line crossed the abscissa, in about three months, everyone would be gone. It did little good for the mathematicians among the crews to spot the fallacy in this simple forecast and to

BOMB LOADING AT AN 8TH AIR FORCE BASE IN
ENGLAND—1943. (Courtesy USAF Art Collection)

show the line was really a curve, and there would actually be twenty percent left after three more months, instead of none. Like most mathematical approaches, this icy logic was of more interest to academicians than to aircraft combat crews, and at best it was of little comfort. The "combat tour" of twenty-five missions was held out as an element of hope, but the chances of completing a combat tour if the combat units still did not get replacements were about one in five (about twenty percent), and this was not encouraging.

The importance of promptly replacing combat losses is clearly illustrated in these survival expectations. If replacements had been promptly made, the chance of survival of each crew would have been forty-four percent at the end of four months instead of twenty-seven, and the chances of surviving a full twenty-five missions would have been nearly two in five. Fortunately, the forces did begin to increase and the replacements to flow about the middle of the year.

Schweinfurt-Regensberg Raids

Toward the end of June 1943, Brig. Gen. Frederick L. Anderson, who had been a member of the planning team for the Combined Bomber Offensive, moved up from 4th Bombardment Wing Commander to command the VIII Bomber Command. He and Eaker at once went to work preparing for the first assault upon the ball-bearing factories at Schweinfurt and the Me–109 assembly plant at Regensburg. The plan for the Combined Bomber Offensive had called for the deep penetration of Germany to reach Schweinfurt as soon as it would be possible to launch a force of 300 bombers. The ball-bearing factories were so vital to Germany's prosecution of the war and so concentrated as a target that it was resolved to attack them as early as possible, even before long-range fighters were available, lest the Germans sense their vulnerability and disperse the factories. The story of the two missions against Schweinfurt has been ably told. One of the best descriptions is that by Thomas M. Coffey in *Decision Over Schweinfurt*. The mission was daring and innovative. The objective was sound, as attested by Albert Speer, German Minister of Munitions, who said: "In those days, we anxiously asked ourselves how soon the enemy would realize that he could paralyze the production of thousands of armaments plants merely by destroying five or six relatively small (ball-bearing factories) targets." He was asked after the war what would have happened if there had been concerted and continuous attacks on the ball-bearing industry. He replied: "Armaments production would have been critically weakened after two months and after four months would have been brought completely to a standstill."

This strategic objective was obviously well chosen. The stakes were very high and the cost was heavy. Weather destroyed the coordination of the attacks, and German fighters took their toll. Two targets in close proximity were chosen: the 1st Bombardment Wing attacked the ball-bearing factories at Schweinfurt; the 3d Wing attacked the Me–109 factory at Regensburg and then flew on to bases in North Africa. Of the 230 bombers of the 1st Bombardment Wing that took off for Schweinfurt on August 17, 1943, led by Brig. Gen. Robert B. Williams, 34 did not return—a loss rate of 15 percent. The 3d Wing, led by Col. Curtis E. LeMay, suffered even more. Of the 146 bombers that had taken off for Regensburg, only 122 reached the landing bases in North Africa, a loss rate of 16½ percent. The bombing had been good but the bombs used against Schweinfurt had not been heavy enough. Though the buildings were destroyed, the heavy machinery survived. Restoration of these factories became the No. 1 priority of Albert Speer's ministry. In the next 2 months, just as the available supply of bearings was approaching exhaustion, the factories commenced to recover production. The attacks on Schweinfurt were repeated on October 14, with 291 Flying Fortresses dispatched on the mission. Sixty did not return, a loss rate of 20½ percent. While the bombing was good and the destruction extensive, no air force could continue attacks with such loss ratios. The ball-bearing factories were again rebuilt, but it was a close call for the Germans. To keep producing, single factories were sending individual motorcycle messengers to Schweinfurt to bring back dispatch cases of bearings.

These events are well known. Who can speculate on the anxiety and anguish of Eaker and Anderson which were pitted against their

SA.628
SCHWEINFURT BALL BEARING INDUSTRY
14.10.43.

APPROXIMATE BOMB PLOT

• Position of well defined bursts
  Areas of heavy concentration
+ Approximate location of fire
  Target areas
  Areas in which incendiary bombs fell

BOMBING RESULTS of the Third Bombardment Division's mission over Schweinfurt, Germany, October 14, 1943.

BRIG. GEN. HANSELL, Commanding General, 1st Bomb Wing, (left) greets Col. Curtis E. LeMay, Commander of the Wing's 305th Bomb Group, beside a Boeing B-17.

A SEVERED JU-88 AT BRUNSWICK, GERMANY, testifies to the AAF's determination to break the back of the German Air Force.

EIGHTH AIR FORCE BOMBERS strike a ball-bearing factory at Stuttgart.

THREE AMERICAN OBSERVERS examine the twisted ruins of the Kugelfischer ball-bearing works at Schweinfurt, bombed repeatedly by Allied forces.

B-17 FLYING FORTRESSES OVER SCHWEINFURT.

AT THE WAR'S
END, SCHWEIN-
FURT LAY RAV-
AGED BY CON-
TINUOUS AIR
ATTACKS.

determination to perform these vital missions? If the first mission called for courage, the second added iron will. Only the prospect of assuring victory, shortening the war, and saving thousands—perhaps hundreds of thousands—of lives bolstered the will of the commanders, at a cost which would have overwhelmed men of lesser caliber than Eaker and Anderson.

The Schweinfurt missions had indeed been costly, too costly to pursue at that rate of combat losses. The escort fighters, whose assistance had been predicted, were sorely needed. Penetration of German air space had to be limited until long-range fighters could be provided. The solution came in the form of droppable auxiliary tanks. Why no one had thought of this earlier defies explanation. The Germans had used this device to extend the range of the Me–109 in the Spanish civil war. But the technical solution was not as simple as would first appear. The tanks had to be pressurized to force the gasoline up to the engine carburetor. And the logistic problem of providing tanks in adequate quantity at the last minute was formidable also. A thousand fighters using two tanks each and operating five missions a month would expend ten thousand tanks monthly. It really was not possible to provide such quantities from English resources, and that many tanks took up a lot of transatlantic shipping space. But by the end of September 1943, P–47 fighters with drop tanks escorted bombers all the way from bases in Britain to a target in Germany— Emden. By October they were reaching Munster. By November the record of the Thunderbolts stood at 273 for a loss of 73. The toll of American bombers lost dropped correspondingly. The range of escort improved with the arrival of P–51s in October, and by March 1944 it extended to a radius of 850 miles from base. The bomber offensive was revitalized.

Reorganizing U.S. Strategic Air Force for the Combined Bomber Offensive

General Arnold, in a discussion with Air Chief Marshal Portal during the Quadrant Conference at Quebec in August 1943, questioned the feasibility of getting maximum operational use out of bombers stationed in England, in view of the winter weather. Air Marshal Portal agreed and pointed out the desirability of operating from Italy, especially in view of the proximity of two great German fighter factories near Vienna. Together these plants were estimated to be assembling about sixty percent of German fighter production and could be reached from Italian bases. Portal expressed again his deep concern over the mounting strength of the German fighter force. This decision to base major strategic air forces in Italy was made after the decision to invade Italy, and was not one of the reasons for making the invasion.

On October 9, 1943, General Arnold submitted to the Joint Chiefs of Staff a plan for splitting U.S. air power in the Mediterranean by creating two air forces. One, the Fifteenth, would be a strategic air force, to be employed in the Combined Bomber Offensive. The other, the Twelfth, would be a tactical air force and would keep on supporting surface operations in the Mediterranean. The six groups of heavy bombers currently assigned to the Twelfth would be transferred to the Fifteenth, and would be augmented by fifteen additional groups diverted from the buildup of the Eighth.

The Combined Chiefs of Staff approved this plan on October 22, after consultation with General Eisenhower. General Spaatz was named Commander of the U.S. Army Air Forces in the Mediterranean Theater, and Maj. Gen. James H. Doolittle was named Commander of the Fifteenth Air Force. General Doolittle continued to serve as Commander in Chief of the Northwest African Strategic Air Force. Initially, the Fifteenth included two groups of B–25 and three of B–26 medium bombers.

Headquartered at Foggia in Italy, the Fifteenth was programmed to consist of twenty-one heavy bombardment groups, seven fighter groups, and one reconnaissance group by March 31, 1944. It was to remain under the control of the Mediterranean commander but would operate in furtherance of the Combined Bomber Offensive. It would be available on an emergency basis to support the surface forces in the Mediterranean.

This arrangement left much to be desired as to coordinating the participation of the Fifteenth Air Force in the Combined Bomber

Offensive. The problem was resolved at the Sextant Conference in Cairo in December 1943. After some debate, coupled with polite dissent on the part of the British, General Arnold succeeded in creating the Europe-wide U.S. strategic air command for which he had striven so long. The Fifteenth and Eighth Air Forces were linked in the U.S. Strategic Air Forces in Europe under the command of General Spaatz. At the same time, General Eisenhower was chosen to command the Allied Expeditionary Forces for the invasion of France. He elected to take with him General Doolittle, whom he had come to trust and admire, to command the Eighth Air Force, which would support the invasion. Also, Mediterranean Allied Air Forces was formed, under the command of Lt. Gen. Ira C. Eaker.

General Spaatz set up Headquarters of the U.S. Strategic Air Forces on January 1, 1944, in London, exercising command jurisdiction over the Eighth and Fifteenth Air Forces. General Eaker assumed command of the Mediterranean Allied Air Forces, headquartered in Italy. Maj. Gen. Nathan F. Twining relieved General Doolittle as Fifteenth Air Force Commander. Maj. Gen. Frederick L. Anderson moved from Commanding General, VIII Bomber Command, to become Deputy Commander for Operations for General Spaatz; Maj. Gen. Hugh J. Knerr became Deputy Commander for Administration. General Eisenhower established Supreme Headquarters Allied Expeditionary Forces (SHAEF) in London.

The commander of the Allied tactical air forces for the invasion had already been designated at the Quadrant Conference in Quebec. He was Air Chief Marshal Sir Trafford L. Leigh-Mallory, who had commanded No. 12 Group of RAF Fighter Command in the Battle of Britain, and had succeeded Air Vice Marshal Keith R. Park as Commander of No. 11 Group after the battle. He had eventually become Air Officer Commanding in Chief, RAF Fighter Command. His previous experience had been related to Army cooperation. He was unfamiliar with broad strategic air warfare, and he had never had the benefit of service at high levels of the Air Ministry or on matters involving the various committees serving the British Chiefs of Staff Committee.

The Air Offensive against the German Air Force

With the arrival of General Spaatz, intensive preparations were undertaken for an all-out offensive against the German Air Force, including the aircraft and engine factories, in furtherance of Pointblank. Though weather continued to frustrate intentions, there were three successful radar bombing attacks against the I. G. Farbenindustrie chemical works at Ludwigshafen, which presented a good radarscope return. There was one fleeting opportunity for visual bombing on the German aircraft and engine factories, and the Eighth seized upon it.

On January 11, the forecast indicated a brief break in the clouds over central Germany. The Eighth sent a major force against high-priority targets of the German aircraft industry. Three divisions, comprising 663 B–17s and B–24s, were dispatched to the following targets: FW–190 fighter production at Oschersleben; JU–88 (multi-purpose aircraft) production at Halberstadt; and Me–109 fighter parts and assembly plants at Brunswick. The weather, bad at the bases, did not clear as expected en route, and two of the air divisions were given recall orders. Fighter escort was furnished but it was difficult to carry out. In the Eighth Air Force, there was just one group of P–51s that could cover at the target. Only the 1st Bombardment Division and one combat wing of the 3rd Bombardment Division went on to the targets. One hundred thirty-nine bombers attacked Oschersleben, 52 bombers attacked Halberstadt, and 47 bombers attacked the Brunswick targets.

The P–51 group put up a magnificent fight but was badly outnumbered by defending German fighters. The 1st Bombardment Division lost 34 bombers. Total losses were 60 bombers, no fighters. But the bombing had been good, considering the heavy fighting, and the results were creditable. The formations attacking Oschersleben put 51 percent of their bombs within 1,000 feet of the aiming point for an average radial error of about 1,000 feet and a circular error probable (CEP) of about 930 feet. The two groups bombing Brunswick did much better, placing 73 and 74 percent of their bombs within 1,000 feet of the aiming point, for an average CEP of 750 feet. Photo reconnaissance showed very extensive damage.

By a strange quirk of irony the Fifteenth Air Force was even more hampered by winter weather than the Eighth. It had been confidently expected that weather would be more favorable for the bomber offensive from Mediterranean bases than from English ones. In the winter of 1943–1944 the reverse was true. The Fifteenth did get off to an auspicious start. On November 2, the second day after its creation, the Fifteenth launched a successful attack against the very important Messerschmitt plants at Wiener Neustadt, near Vienna, that were turning out many Me–109 fighters. Production dropped from 218 in October to 80 in November and to 30 in December. Foul weather prevented any followup.

The opportunity to deal a crushing blow to the German Air Force required about a week of visual bombing weather. General Spaatz was especially anxious to find three days of clear weather over central Germany. But bad weather persisted, and the plan prepared for execution in January continued to be postponed. This produced an interesting aberration in logic.

The diversion of heavy bombers by the Joint Chiefs of Staff away from the Eighth Air Force had left the Eighth far short of its requirements in the CBO. The force was not large enough to strike telling blows during the periods of good weather. But those same Chiefs of Staff who had weakened the Eighth expressed dissatisfaction with its performance in the fall of 1943 on the ground that it had not achieved its "overriding intermediate objective'—the defeat of the German Air Force.

With the passage of time, the cross-channel invasion (Overlord) loomed closer and closer on the horizon. Overlord simply could not be undertaken if the German Air Force continued to be a strong and vigorous menace. American ground planners in particular grew increasingly insistent that the German Air Force be removed as a significant threat. Many wanted to drop all the primary target systems of Pointblank and leave only one—the intermediate objective. This would then call for the defeat of the German Air Force, not simply as a matter of overriding priority, but of sole priority.

Change in Pointblank Directive by the Combined Chiefs of Staff (February 1944)

There were more and more insistent demands for a change in the Pointblank directive. Eaker and Spaatz opposed this change, asserting that the German Air Force was already in top priority, but that the war would not end with a successful lodgment in Normandy. The contribution of the Combined Bomber Offensive went far beyond the defeat of the German fighter force; it included the disruption of the whole supporting structure of the German state.

The problem was temporarily resolved on February 13, 1944, when the Combined Chiefs of Staff issued a new directive for the Combined Bomber Offensive. The new objective was stated as:

The progressive destruction and dislocation of the German military, industrial, and economic systems, the disruption of vital elements of lines of communication and the material reduction of German air combat strength, by the successful prosecution of the combined bomber offensive from all convenient bases.

The priorities of primary target systems were revised. First priority was German single-engine and twin-engine airframe and component production, and Axis-controlled ball-bearing production. Second priority was installations supporting the German Air Force. Other target systems in their order of priority were:

a. Crossbow targets (V–1 German missile installations).

b. Berlin and other industrial areas, to be attacked by RAF Bomber Command and U.S. Strategic Air Forces in Europe (by radar), whenever weather or tactical conditions proved suitable for such activities but not for operations against the primary objectives.

c. Targets in southeast Europe (cities, transportation, and other suitable objectives in the Balkans and in satellite countries). These would be attacked by the Mediterranean Allied Air Forces supported by the Fifteenth Air Force, whenever weather or tactical conditions prevented operations against Pointblank objectives or in support of important land operations in Italy.

The guidance stipulated for the conduct of combined operations was: "Mutually supporting attacks by the Strategic Air Forces of both nations pursued with relentless determination against the same target areas or systems, so far as tactical conditions allow."

In this restatement of the objectives of the Combined Bomber Offensive, reference was made again to destruction and dislocation of the German military, industrial, and economic system. But the original primary targets were not listed. Undermining of morale and the fatal weakening of German willingness and ability to fight had been dropped. Defeat of the German Air Force had been emphasized. Although reference to specified industrial target systems as primary targets had been deleted, those primary targets had not been specifically canceled. An invitation had been offered to use Pointblank forces for attacks against cities and transportation and other suitable targets in the Balkans, or for the support of ground operations in the Mediterranean Theater. A new element of significance had been added: "disruption of vital lines of communication." Vital to what? The German industrial and economic system? Or to the movement of German forces and supplies? Was this concept introduced at the request of General Eisenhower who embraced the transportation plan with such single-minded determination?

What had happened to oil, synthetic rubber and tires, and motor transport vehicles? Presumably the submarine yards and bases had intentionally been dropped. The submarine building yards were no longer a principal concern. The submarines had been defeated or their menace reduced. Their omission was not surprising. The position may well be taken that the reference to "other targets" should be construed as new or additional targets and not an indication that the previously prescribed primary targets were not still in high priority. It seems inconceivable anyone would have suggested deletion of oil and rubber.

Actually, this was apparently the interpretation placed on the new directives by the operating heads, Spaatz and Harris. Both U.S. Strategic Air Forces and Bomber Command kept oil in high priority. Transportation (communications) appeared with increasing frequency in the operations that followed. Neither Spaatz nor Eaker nor Harris objected to putting German fighters at the top of the list. As a matter of fact, they had been there all along. This change in directive almost surely stemmed from the Joint Staff—coming up from the Joint War

Plans Team for Europe through the Joint Plans Committee and the Combined Plans Committee to the Joint and Combined Chiefs of Staff. It was certainly a departure in tone from the concepts put forward in the earlier plans stemming from the War Plans Division of the Air Staff.

Big Week

In the last week of February 1944 the long-awaited opportunity to strike a lethal blow at the German Air Force finally arrived. The forecast pointed to a week of visual bombing weather over Germany. On the 20th of February, the Fifteenth Air Force found itself committed to local operations in support of the ground forces in the Mediterranean, from which General Spaatz could not extricate it. So the Eighth, assisted by fighters of the Ninth, launched the attack.

The mounting of this mission, ushering in Big Week and culminating in a mortal blow to the German Air Force, involved one of the crucial command decisions of the war. The plans had been prepared and the orders issued earlier. Envisioned was an all-out assault of 3 successive days on the German fighter factories. The forces and their commanders anxiously awaited the predicted break in the weather. February weather, often bad, was at its notorious worst in 1944. The night before the proposed assault found the skies solid and the icing conditions severe. Throughout the night, weather aircraft ascended and returned, bearing reports of the cloud and icing conditions: ceiling 500 feet, tops of clouds 12,000 feet, heavy icing. It would be necessary to start takeoffs before dawn because the hours of daylight were so short at this time and latitude.

As the crucial hour approached, weather planes reported the tops of clouds at 8,000 feet with heavy icing conditions on the way up. It was still dark on the ground, with limited visibility. The heavily loaded bombers would have to take off, go on instruments for the climb through clouds with heavy icing conditions, and assemble into combat boxes, combat wings, and air divisions in the dark. The fighters would be especially taxed. They were heavily laden with fuel drop tanks, and they were not as well instrumented as the bombers. Furthermore, there was no assurance that the weather at the bases would clear for landing. It is one thing to take off over a thousand heavy bombers and nearly a thousand fighters on instruments. It is quite a different thing to try to land them in instrument weather with no instrument landing equipment. It was quite possible the entire Eighth Air Force and a large part of the Ninth might be lost on a single mission. Maj. Gen. Frederick L. Anderson, Deputy Commander for Operations for General Spaatz and one of the finest bomber commanders of the war, was deeply concerned but strongly favored the attack. For hours he had been urging Spaatz to make a firm decision to go. Finally, when the last moment for action had arrived, Spaatz told Anderson to issue the order to go. The risks were so great and the conditions so unfavorable that none of the subordinate commanders was willing to take responsibility for the launch without a direct order from General Spaatz personally. Spaatz quietly and firmly issued the order to go. It was a momentous, dangerous, and highly successful command decision.* It was another crucial decision in the course of the war. The back of the German fighter force was broken in bitter fighting in the last week in February. The opportunity did not occur again in the next two months. The weather did not make it possible. If General Spaatz had not taken that bold command decision, the air forces could not have guaranteed air superiority over the beaches of Normandy in June, and almost certainly there would have been no invasion at that time.

In the best tradition of cooperation, RAF Bomber Command the night before had struck Leipzig, in the area of the U.S. penetration. On February 20, 16 combat wings of the 3 air divisions of the Eighth Air force, numbering over 1,000 heavy bombers, took off in heavy weather, supported by 17 groups of escort fighters from the Eighth and Ninth Air Forces. In addition the RAF furnished 16 fighter squadrons. Twelve German aircraft factories were the targets, 2 being

---

*From a conversation with General Cabell who had been at "Park House," General Spaatz's headquarters on the outskirts of London at the time. Cabell, who had commanded a combat wing of the Eighth Air Force, recalled that he was asked his opinion. He said in his judgment the mission, though marginal, was feasible. General Spaatz turned to General Anderson, who had been urging approval of the operation, and quietly made the decision to "go."

as far away as Posen in Poland. Bombing was good and losses were slight. That night RAF Bomber Command struck with 600 bombers at Stuttgart, a city vital to the aircraft industry. The Fifteenth was grounded by weather on the 21st, but the Eighth again took off in force. Broken cloud cover at the targets reduced the accuracy of bombing.

On the 22d the Fifteenth participated by attacking the large aircraft plant at Regensburg, and the Eighth put forth another maximum effort. However, adverse weather again plagued the Eighth. Two divisions, though airborne, had to abandon their primary targets, and the other found its targets partially obscured. German fighter opposition was vigorous on the 22d, and the Eighth lost 41 bombers out of 430 sorties. The Fifteenth lost 14 bombers of the 183 dispatched. The escort fighters claimed 60 German fighters for a loss of 11.

On the 23d the English weather was so poor that no missions were scheduled by the Eighth. The Fifteenth, however, sent 102 bombers against a ball-bearing plant in Austria. On the 24th the weather over Germany opened up again and another maximum effort was launched. This time the target list included Schweinfurt again, the target that had cost 60 bombers out of 291 on October 14. The B–24s of the 2nd Air Division of the Eighth lost heavily to German fighter attacks: 33 planes out of 239. The Schweinfurt force lost 11 of the 238 B–17s dispatched. The Fifteenth attacked an aircraft component plant at Steyr, Austria. The Fifteenth lost 17 bombers on this strike. The intensity of the air battles is reflected in the claims. The bombers claimed 108 German fighters destroyed, the escort fighters 37.

In an unprecedented string of luck, the weather was again favorable on the 25th. Both the Fifteenth and Eighth attacked German aircraft factories in southern Germany. The Fifteenth launched 400 bombers, of which 176 attacked the main target at Regensburg. The rest, having insufficient range, were dispatched against other targets. Bearing the brunt of the German fighter assaults, the Fifteenth lost 33 bombers on the Regensburg mission. The Eighth lost 31 out of 738. All forces bombed their primary targets with generally good accuracy.

In this week of maximum effort to paralyze the German aircraft industry and defeat the German Air Force before the fast-approaching deadline for the Normandy invasion, the Eighth and Fifteenth Air Forces launched 3,800 bomber sorties against Combined Bomber Offensive targets (3,300 by the Eighth, 500 by the Fifteenth). Tonnage of bombs dropped roughly equaled the total tonnage dropped by the Eighth in the first year of its operations. The Eighth lost 137 heavy bombers, the Fifteenth 89, an overall average of about 6 percent per mission. Escort fighter sorties totaled 2,548 for the Eighth, 712 for the Ninth, and 413 for the Fifteenth. Total escort fighter losses were 28. Even with escorts, the bomber losses per sortie were nearly 5 times as great as those of the escorting fighters. The RAF in this combined effort made night attacks against 5 cities associated with the industries and areas of the daylight effort, using 2,351 sorties, with a loss rate of 6.6 percent.

The U.S. Strategic Bombing Survey (USSBS) reported after the war that those operations against the aircraft industrial system damaged seventy-five percent of the buildings producing ninety percent of German aircraft. While the German aircraft industry showed an amazing ability to recuperate, and German aircraft were soon coming off the production line, the effect upon German air power was catastrophic. Whether from the bombing of aircraft industries or from the vicious air battle, or both, the German Air Force never rose again to its past performance.

The back of the German Air Force was broken in February 1944. The Allied strategic air forces, assisted by fighters of the Ninth (Tactical) Air Force, had defeated the German Air Force and attained the neutralization of the Luftwaffe, the "intermediate" objective. They were now ready to turn in force to the primary target systems. But it was late in the day. The plans had called for six months of maximum-scale operations with the forces at full maturity to produce the "fatal weakening" preliminary to invasion. Only three months remained before D–day, and much of the power of the air offensive would be diverted from the primary objectives of the CBO and absorbed instead in operations intended to soften up the German ground forces and delay movements directly threatening the Normandy beaches. This diversion of strategic air forces to short-term, ground-operation goals was insisted upon by General Eisenhower over the vigorous protest of General Spaatz.

Big Week, for a variety of reasons, had achieved its basic purpose. The resistance of Luftwaffe Fighter Command was broken, but it was still capable of vicious spasms of fighting. Even so, the strategic air forces with their heavy bombers and long-range escorts could choose their targets almost anywhere in Germany and penetrate the defenses to reach them without incurring intolerable losses.

Controversy over Employment of the U.S. Strategic Air Forces

It was the supreme irony that the U.S. Strategic Air Forces, having won their crucial battle at such cost in blood and guts, having attained the "overriding intermediate objective" that had stood in the way of the primary strategic objectives, then faced an even more formidable obstacle to the prosecution of the strategic air war. This was the determination of high authorities and commanders to divert the power of the strategic air forces away from those primary objectives and apply it in a support role for the furtherance of the ground forces objective. The conflict was not simply between air and surface strategists. There were important air commanders who led the fight to use the strategic air forces for ground support. But the responsible strategic air commanders stood together in opposing such diversion.

At the end of March, the U.S. Strategic Air Forces arrayed against Axis Europe were:

	groups
U.S. Eighth Air Force, heavy bombers	39
U.S. Fifteenth Air Force, heavy bombers	21
Total	60

(About 2,800 aircraft in operational units)

U.S. Eighth and Ninth Air Forces, fighters	32
U.S. Fifteenth Air Force, fighters	12
Total	44

(About 3,600 fighters)

This force compares with AWPD–1 and AWPD–42 in the following manner:

	Groups
AWPD–1, heavy bombers	44
AWPD–42, heavy bombers (including North Africa and Middle East)	49
AWPD–1, pursuit	21
AWPD–42, pursuit (including North Africa and Middle East)	39

Until Big Week in the war on the German Air Force, the U.S. Strategic Air Forces had been in a period of growth and adolescence, perhaps "stunted growth" would be more accurate. The theories and doctrines of the Air Corps Tactical School had been pursued with an inspiring faith in spite of disappointments and the shocking effect of air battles of unprecedented dimensions. But the real test, in terms of results compared with plans and expectations, lay still ahead. The first year of combat had sorely tried the basic concept that the bombers could get through. When Kenneth N. Walker was a first lieutenant and the bombardment instructor at Maxwell Field, he had stoutly professed that "a properly planned and organized air attack, once launched, cannot be stopped." The realities of air combat had led to modifications in equipment and tactics, but the spirit behind that doctrine had not wilted in the heat of fire. But now, when the real opportunity to apply strategic air power was here, other influences rose to frustrate its achievement.

As the date for the invasion came closer, General Eisenhower was concerned only with results that would be felt in time to assist troops in establishing their beachhead. The factor which, second only to the German Air Force, had been the greatest source of worry to the ground commanders and planners responsible for the Normandy invasion was the rate of buildup of Allied and German divisions in the critical invasion area. Could the Allies transfer divisions and supplies over the channel and across the open beaches faster than the Germans could shift divisions by land to meet them? If the answer was "no," then the great adventure was doomed to failure, with international effects difficult to visualize. One solution was to delay enemy movements by air attacks, especially against the railroads.

Air Plans in Preparation for Overlord

When General Eisenhower arrived in England in January 1944, bringing his Mediterranean Team with him, he also brought strong convictions about the employment of strategic air forces which were not in step with the convictions of the U.S. Strategic Air Forces Commander. The SHAEF Team in the controversy consisted of RAF Air Chief Marshal Sir Arthur W. Tedder, RAF Air Chief Marshal Sir Trafford L. Leigh-Mallory, and Lt. Gen. Lewis H. Brereton, Commander of the U.S. Army Ninth Air Force. They advocated a concentrated air offensive against rail communications in France, involving some 75 to 110 rail bridges, marshaling yards, and maintenance facilities—to make northern France a 'railroad desert" and hamper German movements to the Normandy beaches. All Allied air forces, strategic as well as tactical, would be exclusively devoted to this purpose. In the process it was hoped the remaining fighters of the Luftwaffe would arise to the challenge, affording an opportunity to reduce German air fighter forces by combat attrition. The campaign was to begin as soon as possible after Big Week.

The strategic air war team in the controversy comprised General Spaatz, U.S. Strategic Air Forces Commander, supported by General Eaker and the Commanders of the Eighth and Fifteenth Air Forces and Air Chief Marshal Sir Arthur T. Harris, commanding RAF Bomber Command. They proposed an intensive air offensive against Germany until mid-May, then an interdiction campaign against railroads in northern France. General Spaatz wished to focus on German oil resources and production to dry up the gasoline resources of German air and motorized units. The German fighter forces had been crippled but not eliminated. Spaatz hoped by attacking oil to reduce German air fighter forces through combat attrition. Spaatz contended that the German fighter units were currently concentrated in central Germany and the German fighters would have to remain there and fight for their fuel sources if we continued the strategic air offensive. They were not consolidated in France, and they would not defend French railroads, even if we did assault them. In strategic air attacks against oil, they could be pinned down in central Germany and hence would not be used in Normandy. Spaatz asked for fifteen days of visual bombing by the Eighth Air Force and ten by the Fifteenth Air Force to pursue this strategy. About three weeks before D–day all air forces would then turn to interdiction of communications in France. Air Chief Marshal Harris decried the value of selective precision bombing against the synthetic plants themselves, and preferred area bombing against German cities. However, at first he supported Spaatz and suggested that RAF Bomber Command cooperate with U.S. Strategic Air Forces in attacking cities in central Germany.

Marshal of the Royal Air Force Sir Charles F. A. Portal ultimately swung to the exclusive transportation plan (in France only) proposed by Tedder and Leigh-Mallory, after the controversy had become a major issue and Eisenhower had taken such a strong stand for transportation. Spaatz appealed to General Arnold, but Arnold refused to be drawn into the controversy, saying it was Eisenhower's right to decide. General Eaker came up from the Mediterranean Theater and supported General Spaatz. On March 26, General Eisenhower decided in favor of Tedder and Leigh-Mallory, endorsing the transportation plan for air interdiction of France.

The German fighter forces were still formidable, and it was essential they be kept away from the invasion area. For the defense of the Normandy beaches the Germans had these aircraft:

On D–day	160 (80 operational)
Reinforcements in the ensuing month totaled	600
Luftflotte III—facing invasion—had by the end of June	287 single-engine, day
	89 single-engine, night

By the end of July	244 single-engine, day
	404 single-engine, night
By the end of August	324 single-engine, day
By the end of September	296 single-engine, night

Luftflotte Reich—in central Germany and charged with the air defense of vital installations of the interior—had:

	Single Engine	Twin Engine	Night
In June	287	103	322
In July	311	257	102
In August	273		418
In September	420		665

Obviously it was important to keep these forces pinned down in central Germany.

The control and direction of the strategic air forces passed to General Eisenhower at the end of March (although the formal transfer did not take place until midnight of April 13/14) and stayed there until September 14, 1944. The problem associated with command was as controversial as the plan for employment. Eisenhower was determined that his control of strategic air forces should be absolute and untrammeled. Because he had been fearful of opposition in this regard he was more adamant in his demands. Arnold had assured Eisenhower personally just after his appointment as Supreme Commander, Allied Expeditionary Forces, that he fully endorsed this demand.

General Spaatz was completely agreeable to this arrangement for Overlord, that is to say, for the time needed to ensure success of the invasion. Overlord was the campaign to establish a secure lodgment on the Continent; it was not the campaign for the subsequent defeat of Germany. Spaatz believed the maximum contribution of the strategic air forces toward victory would be to destroy the war-supporting structure of interior Germany. He wanted to resume the strategic air war as soon as the success of the invasion was assured.

The British were reluctant to place Bomber Command and Coastal Command under Eisenhower. They were willing for Fighter Command to go with its Commander, Leigh-Mallory, into the Allied Expeditionary Air Force for Overlord. This did not mean, however, that Leigh-Mallory would be at liberty to transfer large blocks of Fighter Command to the Continent. Fighter Command would return to Air Ministry control once the Allied expeditionary forces were on the Continent. Air Chief Marshal Leigh-Mallory considered that his title as Air Commander in Chief, Allied Expeditionary Air Force, should give him command of all air forces engaged in Overlord.

Air Chief Marshal Harris and General Spaatz were content to come under the direction and control of General Eisenhower. Nevertheless, the two were determined not to accept subordination to Leigh-Mallory, whose knowledge of and attitude toward the use of strategic air forces were held suspect by both. In this they were supported by Generals Arnold and Marshall and by Marshal of the Royal Air Force Sir Charles Portal. The issue was finally resolved by placing the strategic air forces directly under General Eisenhower, with Air Chief Marshal Tedder directing their operations in the transportation plan (France) for Eisenhower and coordinating their efforts with Leigh-Mallory.

There was lively dissent as to the most profitable way to disrupt rail traffic: by attacking marshaling yards and railroad shop facilities, or by destroying bridges. Both methods were tried, the latter proving better on later examination. The overall result was satisfactory. The U.S. and British strategic air forces and the medium bombers and fighter-bombers of the U.S. Ninth Air Force devoted almost all of May to assaulting rail transportation in France. The interdiction of German rail movement to the Normandy area was effective. In the

THE 91ST BOMB GROUP strikes enemy installations at Oscherleben, Germany, on February 20, 1944.

Left: LT. GEN. JO-SEPH T. MCNAR-NEY, Army Deputy Chief of Staff, (left) and Gen. Carl Spaatz visit the 381st Bomb Group, Ridgewell, England, on April 19, 1944.

Below: ETO COMMANDER LT. GEN. JACOB L. DEVERS, Secretary of War Henry L. Stimson, and Maj. Gen. Ira C. Eaker review bombing documents at Thurleigh, England, July 13, 1943.

words of General Spaatz, the attack on German transportation "opened the door for invasion."

To provide additional assurance against interference by the German Air Force, intensive strikes were made on its nearby airfields. By D–day the airfields in the area closest to Normandy had received 6,717 tons of bombs, 3,197 of which were delivered by the Ninth Air Force, 2,638 by the Eighth, and the remaining 882 by the RAF. Actually this was a normal and proper operation for the tactical air forces, rather than the strategic air forces.

On the first day of the invasion, June 6, 1944, the Allied air forces combined their strategic, tactical, and air defense components in direct support of the landings. They launched 13,000 sorties that day. The Luftwaffe was able to reply with about 300 sorties, producing literally no effect whatever. Not a single daylight attack was made by the Luftwaffe. One of the primary purposes prescribed in all the strategic air plans (AWPD–1, AWPD–42, and the Combined Bomber Offensive) had been accomplished. The Luftwaffe had been rendered powerless to effectively oppose either the land invasion or the continued air offensive.

After the lodgment in Normandy had been secured and the breakthrough achieved at Saint-Lo, the Ninth U.S. Army Air Force and the RAF Second Tactical Air Force, under general supervision of Air Chief Marshal Leigh-Mallory, should have taken over the tactical support function, leaving the strategic air forces free to resume their mission of air warfare. After all, Eisenhower had in the Ninth Air Force alone more combat aircraft than the Germans could muster in the entire Luftwaffe. And in addition he had the Second Tactical Air Force, RAF. Furthermore, the Luftwaffe had been defeated and contained by the strategic air forces. However, shortly after D–day the problem was complicated by the initiation of the German V–1 missile attacks. Air defense of England fell upon RAF Fighter Command, and naturally this responsibility was picked up by Leigh-Mallory. As the assaults intensified, an alarmed British Government insisted that all available means should be employed to alleviate them. Leigh-Mallory concluded that the strategic bomber forces were best suited for this purpose.

General Arnold had long since discovered that heavy bombers were not the optimum weapon for destroying the very heavy structures from which some of the missiles were launched. He had been at some pains to find out the best method of attacking these structures. Intensive photographic reconnaissance coupled with a commando raid that had seized a set of construction drawings made it possible for Arnold to construct a typical V-weapon site in Florida. Many attacks were made upon the structures, using various size bombs and different types of delivery. It was concluded that very-low-altitude assaults by single fighter-bombers with 2,000–pound bombs were the most destructive. Brig. Gen. Grandison Gardner—who had done so much for the bombing probability methods at the Tactical School—supervised the tests. He was sent to England to convey his results.

For some reason Leigh-Mallory was not impressed with these experiments, asserting that the heavy bombers were the only salvation. General Arnold's restrained prodding did not move him. It was weeks before he tried the low-altitude, fighter-bomber method, and then he chose to use smaller bombs. Nonetheless the demonstration was persuasive.

As a result of these controversies the Combined Bomber Offensive suffered another serious setback. The primary targets of the CBO slipped to third priority. It was a long time before most of the strategic air forces were rescued from these diversions and redirected toward their principal goals. As is always the case—the ground commander was reluctant to release control after he had obtained it. And even after direction of the strategic air forces had been returned to the Combined Chiefs of Staff, General Eisenhower constantly demanded their use.

Fortunately, General Eisenhower did respond in part to the persistent arguments of General Spaatz and permitted the occasional return of the strategic air forces to their primary objectives when he felt that the immediate needs of the ground forces were not paramount. But the chief strategic targets in Germany were left relatively free of the major power of the strategic air forces for slightly over three months after the invasion—a total of about six and a half months after Big Week. The strategic air forces were called upon frequently to render close support in specific ground operations. This function they performed with a promptness that confirmed both the virtue and the weakness of flexibility in air forces.

At last on September 14, 1944, the U.S. Strategic Air Forces and the RAF Bomber Command were permitted to resume the air offensive described in the Combined Bomber Offensive, which the Combined Chiefs of Staff had approved. But even after that, the strategic air forces continued to be diverted to the support of the ground campaigns, and just three-fifths of their might was directed against the strategic targets in the interior of Germany.

With the beginning of the Combined Bomber Offensive, the basic planning phase—that seemingly unexciting, largely unrecognized but absolutely essential prelude to effective combat—was over. What remained to be seen was whether the strategy so ardently and carefully propounded would really be followed with unrelenting perseverance, whether the forces called for would be provided or dissipated and dispersed to other demands, and whether the effects of the bombing offensive would bear out the contentions and expectations described in AWPD–1.

It is far beyond my ability to adequately describe the frustrations, disappointments, fragile hopes, determination, and soaring zeal that were mixed in the cauldron to make AWPD–1 and the plans modifying it. The frantic efforts to meet deadlines, the disagreements, the uphill fight against entrenched and hostile opinion, the dedicated crusade for the new role of air power, the slumbering dread that we might be wrong—that we might persuade our leaders to take a path that would lead to disaster—put a heavy burden on all of us, and initially upon Lt. Col. Harold L. George (Air War Plans Division Chief) in particular. We were, in truth, probing the future, seeking to apply a doctrine conceived in theory and wanting the years of experience that could point the path to follow. It was similar to our attempts today to begin a space doctrine, before the risks are known, before the technology needed if space became a battle area is a reality, and before likely offensive measures and countermeasures can really be described.

Back at the Air Corps Tactical School before the day of radar, the theory of overflying an enemy's armed force and striking the vital element of his homeland seemed as simple as it was attractive. But how to accomplish this feat against a great power, riding the crest of victory and equipped with the latest creations of munitions technology, was a practical problem of immense dimensions. Even if we penetrated to the selected targets without unacceptable losses and destroyed those targets, how could we predict with assurance the effect upon the viability of the German nation? We could but use the best intelligence available, and make the most careful estimates. This we did with AWPD–1 and the follow-on plans. That the plans turned out as well as they did was, in part, due to good fortune. But it was also due in large measure to the years of debate at the Air Corps Tactical School and, in no less degree, to men like Harold George who had the vision to see the potential of air power and the courage to risk their careers for what they felt was right. Such vision is rare. Moral courage is rarer still, and the combination is truly priceless.

After the war, Harold George remarked to General Arnold that AWPD–1, which had forecast the number of U.S. combat groups within two percent and missed the final total of officers and men by only five and a half percent, showed some pretty accurate forecasting. "Quit slapping yourself on the back," General Arnold said wryly. "You're not such a smart forecaster. We just followed your plan in building the Army Air Forces. No wonder the results look the same."

The force structure prescribed in AWPD–1 was mostly within the power and control of General Arnold, once AWPD–1 had been approved as a guide for production. But the strategic deployment and employment of those forces as laid down in AWPD–1 were chiefly outside his control. They were influenced by joint and combined commands and alliances and subject to the vicissitudes and surprises of the climate of war. These aspects of the plan fared well, but still they bore the imprint of AWPD–1. Combat experience dictated changes in tactics, but the basic strategic concepts and doctrines stood up astonishingly well. Examination and analysis of the effects of the strategic air offensive against Nazi Germany proved to be the "proof of the pudding."

Change of Command

In December 1943 Maj. Gen. Ira C. Eaker suffered a traumatic disappointment that would have broken a man of lesser fiber. When General Eisenhower was selected to lead the invasion across the English Channel and was designated Supreme Commander, Allied Expeditionary Forces, at the Sextant Conference in Cairo in December 1943, he demanded the right to bring with him his principal team members from the Mediterranean Theater. Among them were Lt. Gen. Carl Spaatz and Maj. Gen. James H. Doolittle. This meant that Eaker would be displaced as Commanding General, Eighth Air Force.

It was a staggering blow to Eaker, who had literally created the Eighth Air Force, nursed it through an adolescence fraught with ills of every sort, and brought it to full stature as a proud and effective fighting machine. Now he was to leave it just as it was set to wage decisive strategic air warfare. He protested in vain. On January 8, 1944, after a testimonial dinner by the RAF, he departed for the Mediterranean Theater to become Commander in Chief, Mediterranean Allied Air Forces. It was a position of responsibility and prestige, but nothing could really compensate for the loss of the Eighth.

If the Eighth Air Force had to lose a gallant commander, it could not have hoped for a better replacement. General Doolittle was a charismatic leader and a superb tactician. One of his first and most successful decisions came after Big Week. His forces, together with the Fifteenth Air Force and the fighters of the Ninth Air Force in England, broke the back of the German fighter force. He issued orders for the release of the escort fighters to seek out and destroy the enemy in the air wherever they were found. Under Doolittle's command, the Eighth showed what can be done with a fine instrument of air power. The reports of the U.S. Strategic Bombing Survey bear eloquent testimony. In early 1944 General Doolittle ordered fighter commanders to pursue until the German fighters were destroyed. Commanders could exercise judgment in leaving the bombers to search for the enemy, under the doctrine that such action accelerated destruction of the German Air Force.

Fighters grew more numerous, and while going to and returning from rendezvous they engaged and destroyed any enemy they could find. Thus a virtual stream of fighters moved along the path of the bombers from base to rendezvous to target and back to base. Increased range made this possible. By March 1944, P–38s had a potential radius of 585 miles; P–51Bs 650 miles with two 75–gallon tanks. This was extended to 850 miles with 108–gallon tanks for P–51s. On May 29, 1944, P–51s furnished target support at Posen, Poland (over 700 miles from base) and returned accompanying the bombers. In June, P–51s flew escort all the way to Poltava in the Ukraine, (1,700 miles from base) where bombers and fighters landed.

Beginning in August 1944, the combat boxes of the bombers became smaller and columns longer. Fighter groups were split into two 24–aircraft units, each having its own air commander. This afforded flexibility of escort, allowing a combination of close support and sweeping tactics that could be carried on simultaneously. This was too much for the weakened Luftwaffe to fight against. Consequently, it confined its attacks to bombers that were lost, though on occasion exposed bomber groups were heavily assaulted, with severe losses. By December 1944 the whole VIII Fighter Command was operating P–51s, except for the 56th Fighter Group which retained P–47s. This range extension was the final phase in the transformation of a fighter force, having chiefly a protective escort function, into a much more versatile one possessing offensive and harassing capabilities as well.

Evaluating the Strategic Bombing Campaign in Europe

The strategic bombing campaign has long been a subject of intense controversy and may well remain so for years to come. Certainly the moral issue will be debated as long as morality itself lacks a confirmed definition. What actually happened to the war-supporting structure of Germany as a result of strategic warfare? How far did actual operations depart from the strategic plans?

Although the evidence is still interpreted in various ways, the question as to what actually happened to the war-supporting structure is well documented. Before the end of the war, Maj. Gen. Muir S. Fairchild initiated and General Arnold carried out a bold and statesman-like proposal. General Arnold requested that a special high-level civilian committee make an immediate and thorough investigation of the effects of bombing in Germany. He asked that it be headed by a citizen of unusually high repute who was untainted by philosophical leanings toward any type of warfare, in order that the report might be as objective as possible. The committee should be commissioned by the President himself and should report directly to him. It should be dominated by civilians throughout and should use military men solely to the extent it found their professional experience to be necessary and helpful. Arnold persuaded Adm. Ernest J. King that the Navy should be represented in the survey. Finally, General Arnold specifically requested that the committee's findings not be divulged to him or to the senior commanders and staff of the Army Air Forces until the report had been completed and submitted to the President.

As a result, the United States Strategic Bombing Survey was established by the Honorable Henry L. Stimson, Secretary of War, on November 3, 1944, pursuant to a directive from the President. The Bombing Survey was headed by Franklin D'Olier as Chairman and Henry C. Alexander as Vice Chairman. Directors included: George W. Ball, Henry L. Bowman, John K. Galbraith, Rensis Likert, Frank A. McNamee, Paul H. Nitze, Robert P. Russell, Fred Searls, Jr., and Theodore P. Wright. Charles C. Cabot acted as Secretary.

These men, all with well-established reputations, set up an organization calling for 300 civilians, 350 officers, and 500 enlisted men. Headquarters were established in London, and teams operated literally on the heels of advancing Allied armies. Several hundred German plants, cities, and industrial areas were examined. Hundreds of Germans were interrogated, among them the top German government officials and the managers of the German industrial plants and systems. Documents and reports were studied and analyzed. War records were relentlessly ferreted out. Some 200 detailed reports were made. It was a stupendous undertaking and a superb accomplishment.

First the bombing efforts were measured against the plans and objectives. In 1941 the enemy's armed forces appeared to be far too powerful to be defeated by the Allies unless the state supporting them could be fatally weakened by strategic air attack. The aim of our strategic air plans, AWPD–1 and AWPD–42, was to destroy the industrial fabric buttressing the military power and social order of Germany. The purpose was to defeat the Third Reich by destruction or paralysis of the vital organs of the state body, without invasion if possible, or with it if need be. The original plans called for six months of uninterrupted air attack to fatally weaken the Nazi state. This was to take place before the final decision on whether to invade. The full effect should be achieved *before* the invasion. Then, if necessary, two months of preparatory air attack would follow in direct preparation for it.

The Casablanca Directive, approved by the President and the Prime Minister in January 1943, expressed the purpose of the air assault, as a part of Allied grand strategy: "To bring about the progressive destruction and dislocation of the German military, industrial, and economic system, and the undermining of the morale of the German people to a point where their capacity for armed resistance is fatally weakened."

The air plans called for providing and operating air forces that could defeat the German fighter forces as an *intermediate (counterforce) objective*, and then achieve their principal purpose by destroying and dislocating the countervalue system. The system encompassed transportation, electric power (later dropped from the primary target list by actions of the Committee of Operations Analysts), as well as petroleum, ball-bearing, and various munitions factories (including tank, rubber and chemical plants), and certain vital bases).

The air offensive by bombers and accompanying fighters attained the *intermediate objective*—defeat of the German Air Force—during Big Week in February 1944. This made possible the invasion at Normandy in June. But the strategic bomber offensive suffered critical delays that postponed the major air effort against some of the primary targets until four months *after* the invasion. Obviously the grand strategy had missed its timing. Instead of six months of air attack with the force at full strength *before* the invasion, just two months of strategic air attack were permitted before the invasion, then six months of air support for the invasion and ground campaign. Not until mid-September 1944 was the strategic air offensive resumed, and even

EUROPEAN CAMPAIGN

PLANNED TIME PHASING - VICTORY PROGRAM

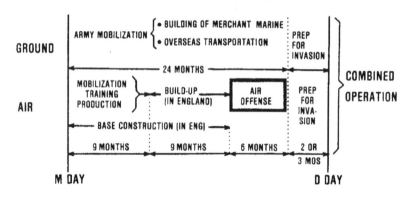

TIME PHASING - ACTUAL CAMPAIGN

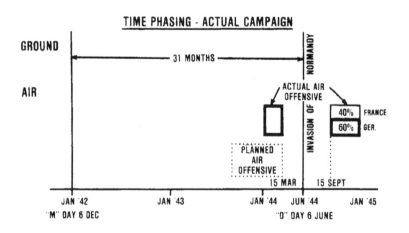

then forty percent of the bomb tonnage was delivered against targets in support of the ground forces in France, instead of approved strategic primary targets in Germany. The strategic air offensive, in spite of delays and diversions, completed the "fatal weakening" of Germany before a single Allied soldier had set foot on German soil. The combined strategy would have better served the Allied cause if the original plan had been followed. The effect of the bombing upon the selected industrial and economic systems was catastrophic. The strategic air forces finally returned to their primary objectives in October 1944. In the next four months, the strategic air forces completed all the remaining strategic objectives originally proposed.

Effects of the Strategic Air War against Europe

The brief digests that follow examine the effects of the Allied air strategy against Germany. They include pertinent extracts from the report of the U.S. Strategic Bombing Survey.

The German Air Force

The long and bitter battle for control of the skies over Europe culminated in victory in the spring of 1944. There was no German air opposition to the landings in Normandy, and the strategic air forces struck targets deep in Germany at will. The defeat of the German Air Force was the consequence of many factors: destruction of manufacturing plants, combat attrition, disruption of training, and the loss of aviation gasoline from attacks on the Rumanian oil fields and the synthetic plants in Germany. (Synthetic production of aviation gasoline suffered drastically.) The intensity of the bitter fighting in the air was reflected in combat losses. Excluding the Russian front, the Germans lost more than 22,000 fighters. The U.S. losses came to over 12,000 bombers and a like number of fighters.

Ball Bearings

The target was right but the bombs were too small and the campaign was intermittent. There were two attacks in the fall of 1943. Factory buildings were demolished, but heavy machinery on the

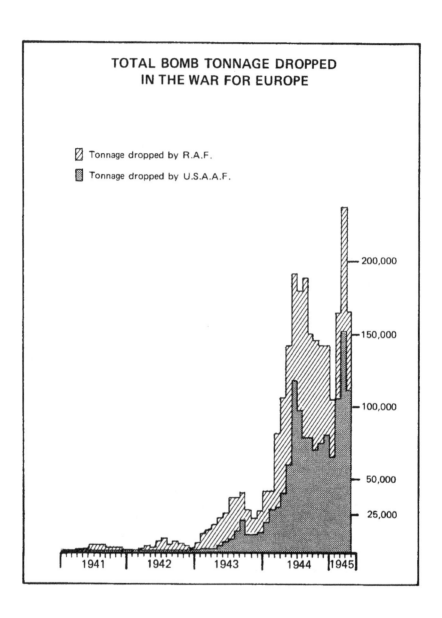

TOTAL BOMB TONNAGE DROPPED
IN THE WAR FOR EUROPE

Tonnage dropped by R.A.F.

Tonnage dropped by U.S.A.A.F.

200,000

150,000

100,000

50,000

25,000

1941   1942   1943   1944   1945

ground floor survived. The bombs should have been heavier (2,000–pounders instead of the 1,100–pounders and 500–pounders) and the fuzes should have been set for longer delay so that the bombs would reach the ground floor. And the attacks should have been followed up more frequently to attain lasting effect.

Albert Speer, the German Minister of Armaments Production, was asked after the war what would have happened if there had been concerted and continuous attacks on the ball-bearing industry with heavier bombs. He replied: "Armaments production would have been crucially weakened after two months and after four months would have been brought completely to a standstill. In those days, we anxiously asked ourselves how soon the enemy would realize that he could paralyze the production of thousands of armaments plants merely by destroying five or six relatively small targets."

Synthetic Petroleum

This target system received 13 percent of total bombs dropped, almost all of it in late 1944 and early 1945. However, the system was extremely sensitive. An attack on 7 plants by nearly 1,000 bombers on May 12, 1944, sent German synthetic fuel production plummeting from 380,000 metric tons a month to 80,000 metric tons in July and to 27,000 metric tons in September—a reduction of 93 percent. Although there was a brief recovery to 80,000 tons again in November, subsequent attack brought it to nearly zero by March 1945. Total gasoline was reduced in like manner.

The oil campaign affected both the German air forces and ground forces. Gen. Omar N. Bradley, interviewed for the USSBS, commented:

> With the debut of the German gamble in the Ardennes, lack of oil, which the strategic bombing campaign had enforced upon the enemy, told handsomely. The withdrawal of Sixth SS Panzer Army, begun in daylight on January 22, 1945, was marked mainly by successes of US fighter-bombers against its tanks and trucks. These successes, however, took place against a background of painfully exiguous oil reserve—with supply trucks being drained to fill the tanks of fighting vehicles—and a long pull to the distant loading

stations. When the Allied breakthrough west of the Rhine followed in February, across the Rhine in March, and throughout Germany in April, lack of gasoline in countless local situations was the direct factor behind the destruction or surrender of vast quantities of tanks and trucks and of thousands upon thousands of enemy troops.

The effect spread to the Eastern Front as well; German forces restricted by lack of gasoline were unable to cope with the Russian onslaught. At the Baranov bridgehead, 1,200 German tanks, massed to hold the position, were immobilized because they had no gasoline and were overrun by the Russians. Even Marshal Joseph Stalin agreed that the strategic air offensive against the oil resources played a vital part in making possible Russian victories in the East.

Rubber

Synthetic rubber production, which relied upon nitrogen from the synthetic gasoline production plants, suffered similar catastrophic decay.

Ammunition

Ammunition production, which also relied upon the synthetic petroleum plants for nitrogen, showed a similar precipitous decline. The Germans had a huge increase in ammunitions requirements in mid–1944, just after the Allies' successful D–day landings at Normandy and reversals in Russia. Allied bombing of oil-chemical plants brought the explosives industry to almost a complete standstill. The USSBS reported:

> By February 1945 German explosives production, exclusive of extenders, had been reduced drastically to 8500 tons per month. This decline came at a time when the Germans were fighting on two fronts and consumption was at a peak. Stocks which were ample in mid–1944 evaporated. Thousands of finished shell casings remained unfilled and the Germans were forced on occasion to use as high as 70 percent rock salt to stretch the small supply of explosives.

Transportation

This system received thirty-two percent of the total bomb tonnage

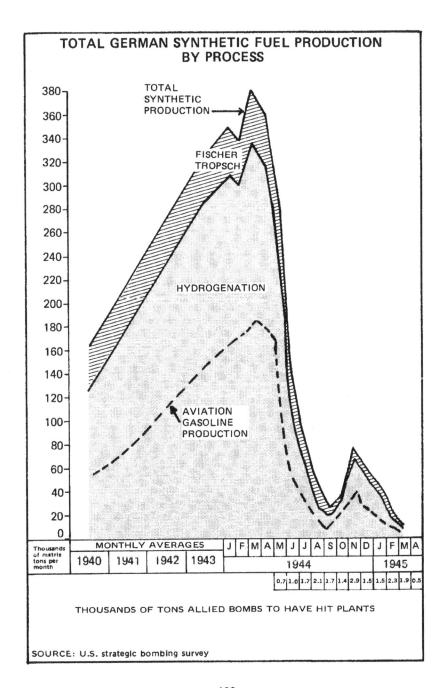

TOTAL GERMAN SYNTHETIC FUEL PRODUCTION BY PROCESS

TOTAL SYNTHETIC PRODUCTION →

FISCHER TROPSCH

HYDROGENATION

← AVIATION GASOLINE PRODUCTION

Thousands of metric tons per month	MONTHLY AVERAGES				J	F	M	A	M	J	J	A	S	O	N	D	J	F	M	A
	1940	1941	1942	1943	1944												1945			

					0.7	1.0	1.7	2.1	1.7	1.4	2.9	1.5	1.5	2.3	1.9	0.5

THOUSANDS OF TONS ALLIED BOMBS TO HAVE HIT PLANTS

SOURCE: U.S. strategic bombing survey

123

GERMAN EXPLOSIVES PRODUCTION

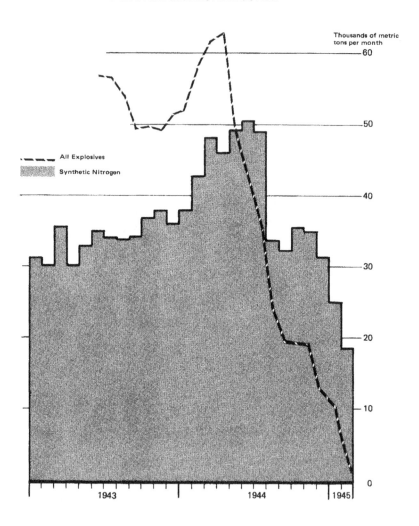

dropped in Europe. Although the attacks came late in the war, they were decisive. The USSBS described the situation:

> After the September and October [1944] attacks, it became entirely impossible for the railroad system to meet . . . transportation requirements. The evidence indicated that the supply of critical components in the hands of manufacturers was quickly exhausted, with a resulting severe impact on virtually all munitions and other finished products at roughly the same time in late November and early December.

Since the loss of transportation facilities completely disorganized the flow of basic raw materials and components, production of semifinished materials was no longer possible. The effects of the strategic air attacks upon rail and water transportation were almost exactly as envisioned in AWPD–1 and AWPD–42. Coal could not be moved to the steel plants and power stations, and the coal shortage interfered with rail movement. Component parts could not be moved to the assembly plants, and the plants themselves could not operate. The industrial fabric of the whole German state was ripping and unraveling.

This was not caused by foreign armies occupying German soil, for in January 1945 the German frontiers were still intact. It was caused by the air offensive, and the plunge in transportation capacity was lethal and irreversible. Transportation is just as vital to the corporate life of an industrial state as the flow of blood is vital to the life of the human body. The level of coal stocks for the railroads dropped to 18 days in October 1944 and to 4½ days in February 1945. Under these conditions, orderly production for civilian as well as military usage was now impossible. The steel industry, for example, dropped its output 89 percent in the first quarter of 1945 as compared with its production of 9 million tons in the first quarter of 1944. Destruction of German transportation had undermined the whole industrial and economic structure of the state. The U.S. Strategic Bombing Survey stated:

> The attack on transportation beginning in September 1944 was the

most important single cause of Germany's ultimate economic collapse. From December 1944 onward, all sectors of the German economy were in rapid decline. Even if the final military victories that carried the allied armies across the Rhine and Oder had not taken place, armament production would have come to a vital standstill by May; the German armies, completely bereft of ammunition and motive power, would almost certainly have had to cease fighting by June or July.

John K. Galbraith, Harvard economist and a Director of the Bombing Survey, presented a totally false picture when he said the strategic air offensive against Germany was a failure and that German industry actually thrived on bombing. German industry did thrive for two and a half years before the bombing really began in force. Under the genius of Albert Speer, German production of munitions actually tripled between 1942 and mid-1944. But when the heavy bombing of Germany finally began in September 1944, the output of munitions plunged dramatically. This effect reached a climax in four months of heavy bombing. But even then about two-fifths of the bombs dropped by strategic air forces between mid-September 1944 and mid-January 1945 were diverted to targets outside Germany.

Combat munitions included aircraft, ammunition, weapons, tanks, and ships. As shown on the chart, after the bombing of German targets rose from about 40,000 tons in August to a peak of nearly 200,000 tons in February, the index of combat munitions production dropped steeply from about 315 to about 140 on its way to zero 2 months later.

Strategic Bombing Survey Conclusions

The Strategic Bombing Survey gave as one of its major conclusions:

> The attack on transportation was the decisive blow that completely disorganized the German economy. It reduced war production in all categories and made it difficult to move what was produced to the front. The attack also limited the tactical mobility

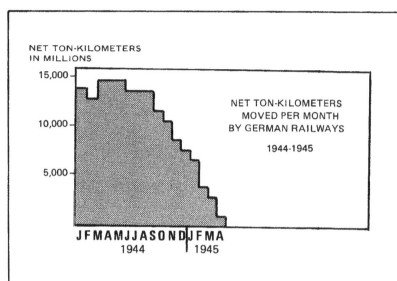

NET TON-KILOMETERS
IN MILLIONS

15,000 –

10,000 –

5,000 –

NET TON-KILOMETERS
MOVED PER MONTH
BY GERMAN RAILWAYS

1944-1945

J F M A M J J A S O N D J F M A
1944   1945

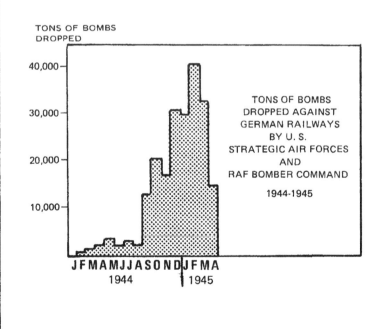

TONS OF BOMBS
DROPPED

40,000 –

30,000 –

20,000 –

10,000 –

TONS OF BOMBS
DROPPED AGAINST
GERMAN RAILWAYS
BY U. S.
STRATEGIC AIR FORCES
AND
RAF BOMBER COMMAND

1944-1945

J F M A M J J A S O N D J F M A
1944   1945

COMBAT MUNITIONS PRODUCTION IN GERMANY (USSBS)

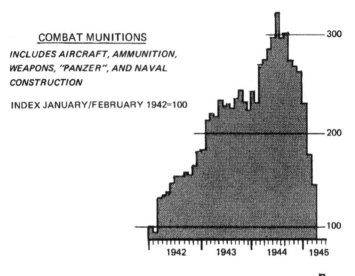

COMBAT MUNITIONS

INCLUDES AIRCRAFT, AMMUNITION, WEAPONS, "PANZER", AND NAVAL CONSTRUCTION

INDEX JANUARY/FEBRUARY 1942=100

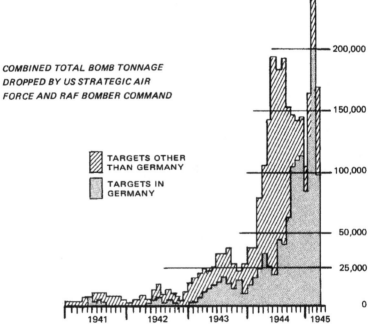

COMBINED TOTAL BOMB TONNAGE DROPPED BY US STRATEGIC AIR FORCE AND RAF BOMBER COMMAND

TARGETS OTHER THAN GERMANY

TARGETS IN GERMANY

of the German Army.*

By the beginning of 1945, before the invasion of the homeland itself, Germany was reaching a state of helplessness. Her armament production was falling irretrievably, orderliness in effort was disappearing, and total disruption and disintegration were well along. Her armies were still in the field. But with the impending collapse of the supporting economy, the indications are convincing that they would have had to cease fighting—any effective fighting— within a few months. Germany was mortally wounded.

Even if the final military victories that carried the Allied armies across the Rhine and the Oder had not taken place, armament production would have come to a virtual standstill by May. The indications were convincing that the German armies, completely bereft of ammunition and motive power, would have had to cease fighting—any effective fighting—within a few months. In the actual case—as in most others in the history of wars—the collapse occurred before the time when the lack of means had rendered further resistance physically impossible.

The creation of this condition was the intent of all the strategic air plans and should have been achieved before the 1944 invasion of the Continent. The diversion of the strategic air effort, with the subsequent delay in effect, was a tragic mistake.

In his report to Hitler on March 15, 1945, Albert Speer stated flatly: "The German economy is heading for an inevitable collapse within four to eight weeks." Some time later, looking back at the strategic air assault, the U.S. Strategic Bombing Survey also concluded: "Allied airpower was decisive in the war in western Europe." Noting that air power might have been employed more effectively at various times and places, the Bombing Survey's final report still stressed: "Its power and superiority made possible the success of the invasion. It brought the economy which sustained the enemy's armed forces to a *virtual collapse* [emphasis added], although the full effects of this collapse had not reached the enemy's front lines when they were overrun by Allied forces." The survey might have noted that the collapse of interior Germany led to the ensuing chaos and incipient

---

*USSBS Summary Report: European War, Sep 30, 1945, p 12.

anarchy. This condition, which typified interior Germany in mid-January 1945, had been brought about by strategic warfare. Germany's frontiers were still intact at that time, and the U.S. air offensive had been superbly effective while causing minimum loss of civilian lives. "The capability of the armed forces to fight," the "will to resist" of the people, and the functioning of vital systems and structures of the German state had been fatally weakened, and inevitable surrender was already assured. The tremendous power of strategic air attack against industrial systems, using conventional bombs dropped with reasonable accuracy against well-selected targets, was clearly demonstrated.

Other Potential Target Systems

Among the errors of omission which characterized our strategic air assault, two target systems stand out: grinding wheel manufacture and the German electric power system.

Grinding Wheels

In an introductory essay for *Impact,* an official AAF photographic magazine published during the war and reprinted in 1980, Albert Speer said:

> Every organism has certain vital nerve fibers: sever these and complete paralysis can result. For example, one, inconspicuous item, for lack of which the entire armaments industry would have been crippled, was the production of abrasives. Only eight small plants manufactured the indispensable grinding wheels without which no gun barrel, no crankshaft, no shell could be turned out. Those eight factories were easy to find; the glow of the big carborundum smelting furnaces could be seen far into the night. Given the tedious processing involved in the making of abrasives, destruction of these factories would have halted production for a year, but after only half a year the manufacture of virtually all armaments would have come to a standstill.

The Committee of Operations Analysts had been correct in predicting precisely what Speer said. They listed grinding wheels in fourth priority, right after the German aircraft industry, ball bearings, and petroleum. We operating people in the Eighth Air Force, who prepared the plan for the Combined Bomber Offensive, were at fault in passing over this target system. To be sure, we lacked target intelligence that would have let us make operational plans for this system. However, we could have requested the gathering of this information, which we failed to do.

Electric Power

As for German electric power, it was unfortunately eliminated as a target by the Committee of Operations Analysts, on the grounds that its paralysis was beyond the capability of the strategic air force. It was dropped from second priority to thirteenth.

In the same essay, Speer commented on the German electric power systems:

> Our production of electricity was being used to the limit, and there was no reserve capacity. Every loss meant reducing production by a corresponding amount. Possibly there would have been great difficulties in knocking out the hydro-electric plants,* as the attacks on the Mohne Valley dam showed, but the loss of some twenty major power plants would have constituted the final catastrophe. If in addition the transformer stations, such as Braunweiler, Herbertingen and Ernsthofen, among others, had been put out of action, this worst bottleneck in our industry would have been doubly shattered, for, as we discovered to our alarm, both the steam-power plants and the transformer stations were extremely sensitive even to accidental bomb hits. And ultimately, to note a third crucial factor, it would have been possible to attack the over-land transmission lines, which stretched for thousands of miles. These could scarcely have been protected from low-flying planes. With all the other essentials, such as fuel or rubber or ball-bearings, there was always a reserve stock, not to mention what was already in the pipe line to insure smooth distribution. Thus in all such cases we could have stretched our supplies for many months, even if production were halted. *Electricity alone could not be stockpiled*, and we need only

---

*The hydroelectric plants were an unreliable and inconstant source of dependable power, since their output varied with the seasonal flow of water from the Alps. They provided only about eleven percent of power and were used to meet peak loads when they were available.

remember the consequences of a blackout in New York City that lasted just a few hours!

Finally Speer had this to say on the subject:

According to the estimates of the Reich, a loss of sixty percent of the total power production would have sufficed to lead to collapse of the entire network. The destruction of the power plants would be the most radical measure, as it would at once lead to a breakdown of all industry and support of public life. Destruction of fifty-six targets would produce this effect.

Would it have been possible to paralyze the German electric power system besides accomplishing the other results that were actually attained? A postwar analysis, using actual bombing performance demonstrated by the Eighth Air Force, shows clearly that this would have been possible if the strategic air forces had been applied for two and a half months against the primary targets in Germany proposed in AWPD–1 and AWPD–42 immediately after defeat of the German Air Force, rather than applied in large measure against targets in France in preparation for the invasion and in support of the ground campaign. The subject is treated in some detail in the Appendix, but the conclusions are summarized below.

The task of knocking out the electric power system actually was much less difficult than knocking out the synthetic oil production— and keeping it out. The tonnage of bombs required, to provide a 95–percent probability of knocking out 2/3 of the electric power system (65 targets), came to 35,000 tons. This was a relatively small portion of the total effort available in March, April, and May of 1944—before the invasion. During this period the U.S. strategic air forces flew over 60,000 bombing sorties and dropped 150,000 tons of bombs, of which only 6,080 tons was directed against petroleum targets. Thirty-five thousand tons would have been 23 percent of the tonnage dropped by these forces on targets predominantly in France during this period. The tonnage actually dropped, exclusive of the oil targets in Germany, between March 1 and May 15 was sufficient to have caused paralysis of the German electric power system before the invasion, and still have left 15 days of operations in May for attack of rail transportation in France to the extent of 96,000 tons.

I believe the answer to the question "could the German electric power system have been paralyzed before the invasion?" to be "yes." In combination with the attacks on German transportation and synthetic petroleum systems, the result would have been even more catastrophic to the "will" and "capability" of Germany to continue the war. Whether the German electric power system could have been paralyzed before the invasion is questionable in view of General Eisenhower's vehement support of the air attack on rail transportation in France. But it certainly could have been accomplished immediately after the invasion. German electric power had been No. 2 priority (next after the defeat of the Luftwaffe) in AWPD-1 and No. 4 priority in AWPD-42.

The chief electrical engineer in charge of design of the system volunteered this information: "The war would have been finished two years sooner if you concentrated on the bombing of our power plants."

A DIRECT HIT AT THE MUSASHINO AIRCRAFT EN-
GINE PLANT dug this crater and destroyed half of the
industrial target, located on the outskirts of Tokyo.

Chapter IV

Planning the Strategic
Air War against Japan

Grand strategy for the Pacific began to receive formal reexamination at the Quebec (Quadrant) Conference of the Combined Chiefs of Staff, held at Quebec in August 1943. The conclusions of the conference made no mention of a specific bomber offensive against Japan. However, there was agreement on the overall strategic objectives for the prosecution of the war:

    1. In cooperation with Russia and other Allies to bring about at the earliest possible date the unconditional surrender of the Axis in Europe.

    2. Simultaneously, in cooperation with other Pacific Powers concerned, to maintain and extend unremitting pressure against Japan with the purpose of continually reducing her military power and attaining positions from which her ultimate surrender can be forced. The effect of any such extension on the over-all objectives to be given consideration by the Combined Chiefs of Staff before action is taken.

    3. Upon the defeat of the Axis in Europe, in cooperation with other Pacific Powers and, if possible, with Russia, to direct the full resources of the United States and Great Britain to bring about at the earliest possible date the unconditional surrender of Japan.

There were two specific agreements made at Quadrant that would affect the air operations in the Far East.

> We are agreed that the re-orientation of forces from the European Theater to the Pacific and Far East be started as soon as the German situation, in our opinion, so allows.
>
> General Stilwell will be Deputy Supreme Allied Commander South East Asia Theater and in that capacity will command the Chinese troops operating into Burma and all US air and ground forces committed to the South East Asia Theater.
>
> The plan for defeat of Japan would be taken up at the Sextant Conference [held at Cairo, Egypt, in the late November–early December 1943].

President Roosevelt headed the U.S. delegation at the Cairo (Sextant) Conference. With him were his personal military aide, Maj. Gen. Edwin M. "Pa" Watson; the Joint Chiefs of Staff (Gen. George C. Marshall, Adm. Ernest J. King, Gen. Henry H. Arnold); Adm. William D. Leahy; Maj. Gen. Muir Fairchild, AAF, from the Joint Strategic Survey Committee; Maj. Gen. Laurence S. Kuter, Deputy Chief of Staff, AAF; the Joint Plans Committee; and the Joint Logistics Committee, among others. The Joint Staff planners consisted of Brig. Gen. Frank N. Roberts, USA; Rear Adm. Bernhard H. Bieri, USN, formerly of the Joint Strategic Committee; and myself, recently returned from the Eighth Air Force. For this occasion Admiral Bieri, the senior member and chairman, chose to consider there were just two legitimate members of the Joint Plans Committee, one representing the War Department, the other the Navy Department. He considered me, if he noted my presence at all, as a sort of junior consultant to Frank Roberts on air matters.

Because Admiral Bieri would not bring himself to recognize my existence, he could not very well argue against the items I presented and supported. The chief air objectives I supported were: (1) Consolidating our strategic air forces under unified air command and control, both in Europe and in the Pacific; (2) Recognizing strategic air warfare as a principal, war-winning strategy, and its acceptance as such in the war against Japan; (3) Obtaining air base sites from which strategic air warfare could be waged against Japan. General Roberts was cooperative, and I was able to get the Joint Plans Committee to agree to all of the important things affecting the air forces.

Long before the proposed invasion of Normandy, General Arnold had sought to strengthen the strategic air forces opposing the European Axis powers, through merger and establishment of a unified air command. The Eighth Air Force in England and the Northwest African Strategic Air Force should have been directed in a coordinated attack against the selected targets in Germany. But they were separated by command barriers. The strategic air forces in England operated under the direction of the Combined Chiefs of Staff, with Air Chief Marshal Sir Charles F. A. Portal as executive agent. The strategic air forces in the Mediterranean were under the theater commander in that area, an Army general. They were being used to support theater objectives. General Arnold endeavored to correct this fault by merging the command of the U.S. strategic air forces in both areas under a single U.S. strategic air commander, who would have authority to direct all European strategic air operations.

As the Army Air Forces' air planner, I succeeded with some difficulty in putting the issue through the Joint Plans Committee of the U.S. Joint Chiefs of Staff. As the American air member of the U.S.-British Joint and Combined Plans Committee, it was my job to put it through that committee at the Cairo Conference. It met stiff opposition from the British members. They pointed out that the strategic air forces in the Mediterranean were wholly dependent upon theater agencies for logistic support and administration. Our contention was that unity of command and concerted cooperation in the *target* area were more important than unity of command of logistics and administration in the *base* areas. The British, who had the overall command of all air forces in the Mediterranean, were quick to oppose a change that would rob their senior air commander in the Mediterranean of a large block of his air power. They stressed the complexities of logistic support and the fact that the U.S. strategic air forces in the Mediterranean were completely dependent upon the common logistic facilities. A separate operational command would still be at the mercy of the logistic allocations and capacity. Why not leave the command chain as it was and direct the U.S. strategic air commander in the Mediterranean to cooperate and coordinate with his opposite number in England? This would, of course, leave the strategic air forces in the Mediterranean under the command of the local theater commander, who could use them as he deemed necessary and leave the arguments to be settled later.

In the final confrontation we prevailed, asserting that the RAF did in fact have unity of command of its own air forces through the Air Ministry, and that this practice bridged the boundaries between theaters. Why should not the American strategic air forces have a similar structure and unity of command?

The argument and agreement that unity of command and control over air operations to be exercised at the *target* areas was more important than that covering the *base* areas later served us in good stead when the Twentieth Air Force was created. The outcome of the issue at the Cairo Conference was the creation of the U.S. Strategic Air Forces in Europe and the organization of the Fifteenth (Strategic) Air Force in the Mediterranean as the second component (along with the Eighth) of that strategic force.

Even this consolidation could not prevent frequent diversion of strategic air forces from their primary mission to the support of local ones. Without this unified command, however, the diversions would have been far worse. Airmen grew distrustful of the powers of surface theater commanders. When the time for organization and command of air forces in the war against Japan came up for consideration, the fight was renewed on a broader scale. But command of strategic air forces in Europe was not the only air issue at Cairo.

I had returned from England to become the U.S. air member of the Joint Plans Committee just about four weeks before departing for the Cairo (Sextant) Conference in November 1943. During my preparation for the conference, I was surprised by one paper I came across. It was the outline of the proposed Joint War Plan for the conduct of the war in the Pacific. The opening statement of basic strategy, prepared by the Far East War Plans Group and endorsed by the Joint War Plans Review Board (which contained an Army Air Forces general officer), said in effect:

> It has been clearly demonstrated in the war in Europe that strategic air forces are incapable of decisive action and hence the war against Japan must rely upon victory through surface forces, supported appropriately by air forces. Final victory must come through invasion of the Japanese home islands.

There was no dissenting voice from the air members of the committee and the review board. The draft plan had been sent to the various members of the Joint Plans Committee in October 1943. To be sure, the bombing offensive against Germany had not yet shown decisive capability. It had not yet been launched in strength and would not reach full power and application against primarily strategic targets in Germany for almost another year. And nothing had been demonstrated either for or against the potential of that strategic air offensive. But it was clearly evident the Far East War Plans Group and the Joint War Plans Review Board had written off the possibility of victory over Japan through final reliance on air power and were dedicated to victory through invasion. I knew that the Army and Navy members of the Joint Plans Committee would welcome this conclusion. With much difficulty I succeeded in amending that statement of basic strategy and establishing a provision for an initial potentially decisive strategic air offensive against the Japanese home islands. It was agreed preparations for invasion should proceed concurrently, in case such an air offensive should not be decisive. Strategic air power barely attained a reprieve, and strategic air forces gained a temporary stay against dismemberment and apportionment to various theaters for support of surface operations. But final reliance on surface invasion of the Japanese home islands was indelibly imprinted on Allied grand strategy, at least so far as the U.S. Army and Navy were concerned.

At Cairo I succeeded in making a very substantial change in the original statement of a grand strategy for the Pacific. The Combined Chiefs of Staff accepted and approved the "overall plan for the defeat of Japan" as submitted by the Combined Staff planners on December 2, 1943. The new description of grand strategy stated:

> Our studies of the subject (of grand strategy) have taken account of the possibility that invasion of the principal Japanese islands may

GENERAL ARNOLD AND HIS AIR STAFF at the Cairo (Sextant) Conference of November 1943. The delegation was led by (front row, left to right) Brig. Gen. Hansell, Maj. Gen. Muir S. Fairchild, General Arnold, Brig. Gen. Laurence S. Kuter, and Col. Willard R. Wolfinbarger.

GEN. GEORGE C. MARSHALL (right) and General Arnold meet with the Combined Chiefs of Staff at Cairo's Mena House Hotel, December 4, 1943.

not be necessary and the defeat of Japan may be accomplished by sea and air blockade and intensive air bombardment from progressively advanced bases. The plan must, however, be capable of expansion to meet the contingency of an invasion.

At another point the Combined Chiefs agreed to this overall objective among others: "To obtain objectives from which we can conduct intensive air bombardment and establish a sea and air blockade against Japan and from which to invade Japan proper if this should be necessary."

I also succeeded in inserting a sentence in a paragraph of "Specific Operations for the Defeat of Japan, 1944," which was approved by the Combined Chiefs of Staff on December 3, 1943. The paragraph read:

> Central, South, and Southwest Pacific. The advance along the New Guinea-Netherlands East Indies-Philippines axis will proceed concurrently with operations for the capture of the Mandated Islands (by then the Central Pacific). A *strategic bombing force will be established in Guam, Tinian, and Saipan for strategic bombing of Japan proper.* Air bombardment of targets in the Netherlands East Indies-Philippine Area and the aerial neutralization of Rabaul will be intensified.

The strategy underlying the bombing of Japan proper was similar to that applied against Germany: to defeat the enemy air force and to so weaken the Japanese capability and will to fight as to cause capitulation or permit occupation against disorganized resistance; failing this, to make invasion feasible at minimum cost.*

The position of air strategists regarding the air offensive against Japan was very weak in November 1943. B-29s were beginning to come off the line, but essential bases for their operation against the Japanese home islands had not yet been provided. General Arnold and his Air Staff were determined to employ B-29s against the Japanese homeland. We were extremely apprehensive lest they be apportioned to theater commanders for local operations. Once assigned to such

---

*The expression "occupation," as distinct from "invasion," was deliberately inserted by the airmen in Sextant discussions.

control, it would be hard to extricate them and concert their efforts against the prime targets in Japan.

Operation Matterhorn

An outline plan was prepared in August 1943 by the Air War Plans Division of the Air Staff for use of the B–29s from bases to be built by the forces of Chiang Kai-shek in China. It was the only way we could find to start using these aircraft (however ineffectively) against Japan proper, prior to the capture of the Marianas.

The idea of basing strategic bombers in China was not entirely new. At the Casablanca Conference in January 1943, President Roosevelt discussed with Prime Minister Churchill the possibility of air operations out of Chinese bases against the Japanese. General Marshall endorsed General Arnold's view that Japanese industry was very vulnerable to bombardment from the air. The President added that periodic bombing of Japan would have a tremendous effect upon the morale of the Chinese people. He suggested sending 200 to 300 planes to China, including heavy bombers (B–24s), and proposed that the bombers be based in India and staged through advanced bases in China.

The President had gone so far as to wire Chiang Kai-Shek that he was sending General Arnold to Chungking to discuss U.S. aid because he was "determined to increase General Chennault's air force* in order that you may carry the offensive to the Japanese at once." However, this reference was evidently to the Japanese in China, not to Japan proper. In August 1943, a new outline plan for using B–29s based in India and staged through China to attack the Japanese home islands was first presented to the Combined Chiefs of Staff by General Arnold at the Quebec (Quadrant) Conference. The plan was tabled there for study by the Joint Logistics Committee and restudy at the Cairo (Sextant) Conference in November.

AWPD–42 had listed "iron and steel" as a primary target system

---

*Brig. Gen. Claire L. Chennault was commanding the newly created AAF Fourteenth Air Force, stationed at various airfields in China. At the same time, he was air advisor to Chiang Kai-shek and Chief of Staff for Air of the Chinese Air Force.

in the air offensive against the Japanese home islands. The Committee of Operations Analysts agreed that iron and steel were vital, both to the war-making capabilities of Japan and to the economic structure of the state. Steel production was in short supply and was running about 9.5 million tons per year. The consumption was divided equally between military and civilian usage. The following table shows the extent to which steel was vital in both categories:

Consumption Group	Tons (Thousand)	Percent	
Military and Naval			
Aircraft	190	2.02	
Armored fighting vehicles	142	1.51	
Ammunition	1,800	19.15	
Artillery & small arms	190	2.02	
Miscellaneous field equipment	998	10.62	
Shipbuilding	950	10.11	
Buildings & works	430	4.57	
Subtotal	4,700	50.00	
Industrial and Civilian			
Buildings & works	430	4.57	
Storage & transport	380	4.04	
Mining & quarrying	470	5.00	
Carbonization industry	190	2.02	
Agricultural machinery	95	1.01	
Machinery, equipment, tools	475	5.05	
Railways	1,140	12.13	
Motor vehicles	190	2.02	
Chemical & electrical industry	380	4.04	
Miscellaneous	950	10.11	
Subtotal	4,700	49.99	(50.00)
Total	9,400	100.00	

The Committee of Operations Analysts found that in Japan the steel production was uniquely vulnerable, because of the heavy concentration of coke ovens upon which steel production depended. Six coking plants (3 in the Japanese southern island of Kyushu, 2 near Mukden in Manchuria, and 1 in Korea) produced 73 percent of

Japanese coke. The Committee of Operations Analysts said the destruction of these 6 coking plants would deprive Japan of 66 percent of her total steel output. Coke ovens were susceptible to shock and their replacement would take years. The Air War Plans Division proposed that B–29s be based in India and operated from advanced bases in China, within range of some or all of these coking plants. The vicinity of Chengtu, China, was the preferred forward base. The location, relative importance, and approximate distance of these plants from Chengtu were:

Plant Location	Percent of Production	Miles from Chengtu
Anshan (near Mukden, Manchuria)	34.5	1,350
Penchihu (near Mukden, Manchuria)	11.2	1,300
Kenjiho, Korea	3.6	1,400
Yawata (Kyushu, Japan) (1)	16.2	1,500
Yawata (Kyushu, Japan) (2)	3.9	1,500
Omuta (Kyushu, Japan)	3.3	1,475

Chengtu, China, was situated about 1,150 miles from Calcutta, India.

General Arnold directed Brig. Gen. Kenneth B. Wolfe, who was to command the first combat unit of B–29 bombers—the XX Bomber Command—to prepare an outline operational plan to carry out attacks on these targets. General Wolfe's plan was expanded by the Air War Plans Division and became Project Matterhorn.

The strategic purpose and concept of Project Matterhorn were sound. But the logistic requirements were staggering and the logistic plan was horrendous. Based in India, the B–29s would stage through advanced bases in China. Even if the Chinese could be persuaded to build the air bases, it would be necessary to support B–29 operations from the advanced bases by air supply over the Himalayas. The B–29s themselves would have to ferry bombs and gasoline over "the Hump," and supply would have to be supplemented by B–24s converted into tankers. The effective rate of the operations would be very low indeed. Their primary virtue would be in striking an important blow against Japan proper and in preserving the command-and-control structure,

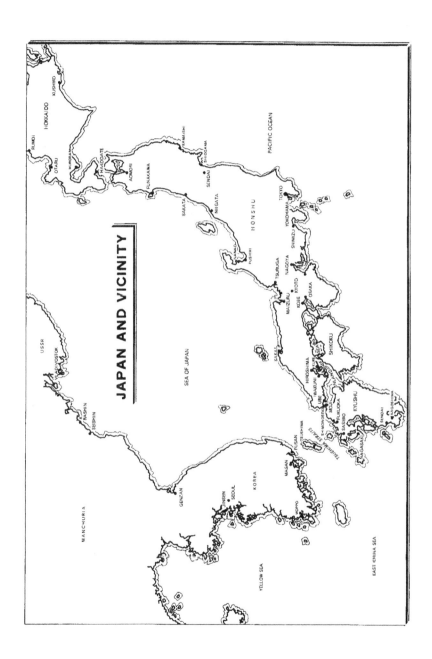

JAPAN AND VICINITY

145

pending a time when other Pacific bases could be captured and prepared for other B–29 forces.

Chiang Kai-shek, who was present at the Cairo Conference in November–December 1943, agreed to the base construction at Chengtu. He was as good as his word. The bases were hand constructed by hundreds of thousands of workers.

Actually, Project Matterhorn had a painful birth and a brief life span. Under General Kuter's supervision, the Air Plans Division of the Air Staff planned Matterhorn. General Arnold presented the final plan to the Joint Chiefs of Staff and, after some discussion, they, at General Arnold's request, referred it to the Joint Staff planners (before my arrival in that committee). These planners and the Joint Intelligence Committee seriously questioned if the concept was desirable and feasible. Nevertheless, it was sent to the Combined Staff planners for comment or agreement.

The overall objective of Matterhorn was to accelerate the destruction of selected systems of critical Japanese industry. This would reduce the industrial support of the Japanese war effort as a contribution to the overall strategic air plan. The plan, like that in Europe, contemplated an intermediate objective, the neutralization of the Japanese Air Force by combat and by destroying aircraft and engine factories. Then would come the destruction of primary targets whose paralysis would lead to fatal weakening (or collapse) of the Japanese will to resist and capability to continue the fight. Operations from Chinese bases would further this objective and reduce Japanese shipbuilding and naval resources. This would directly assist the later major air offensive from the Marianas. The plan called for 4 advanced bases near Chengtu to be furnished by the Chinese, and 4 main bases in the vicinity of Calcutta, India, to be provided by the British. Ten B–29 groups (28 aircraft per group) were to be ready by October 1944 for deployment to India and operation from China. Two thousand B–24s converted to transports were to support such operations over the Hump from supply bases around Calcutta. These 2,000 converted aircraft could be made available in the Calcutta area by October 1944.

The Combined Logistic Committee concluded on September 14, 1943, that the plan was not feasible from a logistic viewpoint. General

Arnold received this negative opinion of the Matterhorn proposal just before he departed for the Cairo (Sextant) Conference. Even so, he asked the Committee of Operations Analysts to give him a list of recommended targets in Japan for the final air offensive, and show which targets could be included in the initial operations from Chinese bases. The plan would embody the operations from other bases. Targets would be those suitable for air bombardment that would "knock Japan out of the War." Iron and steel were high on the list.

The operations analysts described seven industries which "now appear profitable aviation target systems," and listed thirteen others which "did not now appear to be profitable" but might become so. The seven preferred target systems were:

    a. Merchant shipping in harbors and at sea.

    b. Iron and steel production, to be reached through coke ovens (in Manchuria, Korea, and Kyushu, within range of Chengtu).

    c. Urban industrial areas vulnerable to incendiary attacks.

    d. Aircraft plants.

    e. The antifriction bearing industry, highly concentrated in six main factories.

    f. The electronic industry whose interruption would have immediate military effects.

    g. The petroleum industry.

The Committee of Operations Analysts contended, however, that the list was not in an order of desired priority.

In spite of all the criticism and opposition, Project Matterhorn was approved at the Cairo (Sextant) Conference. Chiang Kai-shek agreed to build the advanced bases at Chengtu. The British, who would have to build the bases in the Calcutta area, went along. But this did not end the argument. As late as February 15, 1944, the Joint War Plans Committee still believed the best use of the B–29s before deployment in the Marianas would be from Australian bases against shipping and oil. In that committee's opinion, Chengtu, China, was a very poor choice. Nonetheless, Matterhorn was approved at Sextant and proceeded as planned.

147

Allied leaders also agreed at the Cairo (Sextant) Conference upon two coordinated but semi-independent surface thrusts in the Pacific. One would be from the Southwest Pacific, under the command of Gen. Douglas MacArthur. The other would be across the Central Pacific, under the command of Adm. Chester W. Nimitz.

Conference in the Pacific Theaters

At the termination of the Sextant Conference at Cairo in December 1943, I was chosen to go with General Marshall to meet with our principal commanders in the theaters in the Pacific. Our flight plan took us to Karachi, India, then to Ceylon, and to Exmouth Gulf and Darwin in Australia.

Lt. Gen. George C. Kenney, General MacArthur's air commander, met us at Darwin. We next flew across the Arafura Sea to Port Moresby in New Guinea. The following day, General Marshall met with MacArthur at the latter's headquarters on Goodenough Island. Only four persons were present at the meeting: Marshall, MacArthur, Kenney, and myself. As a staff officer to Brig. Gen. Frank M. Andrews in the early days of GHQ Air Force, Kenney had made a major contribution toward creation of air power. He hit it off from the first with General MacArthur—and little wonder. He did things with air forces that left airmen gasping. MacArthur owed much of his brilliant success in the Southwest Pacific to General Kenney's imaginative performance.

It was Kenney's idea to establish advanced air bases, bypass enemy strongholds, furnish air support for forward movements, cooperate with the Navy in cutting off sea movements by isolated Japanese garrisons, and even to supplement important supply movements by air. He proposed to General MacArthur that, instead of inching slowly over the formidable Owen Stanley mountains in New Guinea, an airborne force be dropped and landed on the other side behind Japanese strongholds, and supplied initially by air. This would leave a Japanese force behind the invading force, cut off by the jungle, the terrain, and the sea. When one of General MacArthur's staff officers asked sarcastically what the troops were supposed to do

148

without wheeled vehicles, Kenney said he would move these too. He proceeded to cut trucks and other vehicles in two with acetylene torches, stuff the parts into air transports, fly them over the mountains, and have them assembled and welded back together. It worked! He also promoted low-level skip bombing on ships, armed medium bombers with multiple batteries of .50–caliber guns for strafing, and sponsored the mounting of a 75–millimeter cannon on a light bomber.

No air strategist or tactician showed greater imagination and inventiveness than George Kenney. And it speaks volumes for mutual trust and confidence that General MacArthur embraced the daring proposals of his chief airman and pursued his audacious program of "island hopping."

The meeting place was a shack that had been fitted up as a private war room for General MacArthur. Maps and charts covered the walls. MacArthur described the situation and his plans. He stood at various maps, strode back and forth, and talked for about two hours without notes of any sort. He had at his fingertips all the dispositions and recent actions of his troops. He seemed equally well acquainted with his enemy. He named Japanese organizations and their commanders everywhere and seemed well informed of their competence. MacArthur revealed his plans, culminating in the recapture of the Philippines and preparations for the next campaign, whether it be Formosa or the coast of China. In minute detail he defined the force requirements (land, sea, and air), the timing, the objectives, and the logistic flow. Throughout the presentation he employed wit and charm with devastating persuasiveness. Although I had from the first been an advocate of a "Europe first" strategy, with attendant delay against Japan, I simply melted under the persuasive logic and the delightful charm of the great MacArthur. By the time he had finished, I was anxious to find some way to give him what he had asked for.

General Marshall was of far sterner stuff, though his position left him reason for sensitivity or even embarrassment. In their relationship years before, General MacArthur had been Chief of Staff of the U.S. Army when Marshall was still a colonel. In World War I, MacArthur had been a general officer who had achieved an aura of fame from personal bravery on the battlefield, while Marshall was an able but little-known officer on General Pershing's staff. Now the tables were completely turned. General MacArthur, for all his great prestige, was really a supplicant for approval of the strategy which he had proposed with such élan. Those plans would have required the assignment to General MacArthur not only of the majority of the American forces arrayed against Japan, but also substantial diversion of forces destined for Europe.

This was seven months before the launching of the Normandy invasion. General Marshall had to tell MacArthur he could not have these forces and hence could not carry out the program he had described. This Marshall proceeded quietly to do. He reminded him that the basic grand strategy of defeating Hitler first, and of concentrating maximum forces to that purpose, was agreed upon and approved by the Combined Chiefs of Staff as well as by President Roosevelt and Prime Minister Churchill. Marshall stated quite calmly his own devotion to that scheme, of which in fact he had been one of the chief architects.

The meeting closed on the same level of punctilious courtesy on which it had commenced. If General MacArthur was chagrined and disappointed, he did not show it. We left for home via Hawaii where General Marshall met with Admiral Nimitz and his staff. There was a presentation of a plan for Central Pacific strategy that quite naturally advocated primary reliance on the U.S. Navy for progress toward Japan and for regaining base areas. General Marshall made no commitments that I know of, and we journeyed home.

Pacific Strategy

After our return from the Sextant Conference at Cairo, arguments on Pacific strategy rose. The next major strategic objective was depicted by General Marshall as the "Formosa-China Coast-Luzon" triangle, to be approached by General MacArthur from the Southwest Pacific and Admiral Nimitz from the Central Pacific. Proponents of the two thrusts presented their views to the Joint Chiefs of Staff, each proposing that the preponderance of effort and of forces be assigned to his axis.

On March 7, 1944, Admiral Nimitz, supported by his Deputy, Rear Adm. Forrest P. Sherman, appeared before the Joint Chiefs of Staff. They suggested bypassing the Japanese base at Truk and seizing the southern Marianas. From there they would capture Ulithi Atoll (about 360 miles southwest of Guam) for use as a fleet base, together with nearby Yap where airfields could be constructed to support Pacific naval operations. Nimitz's schedule called for capture of the Marianas in mid-June, Ulithi-Yap by September 1, and the Palau Islands by November 1. It would then be possible to invade the Formosa-China Coast-Luzon area by early spring 1945. He later amended the plan to specify the capture of Palau before Ulithi-Yap.

On the same day, Lt. Gen. Richard K. Sutherland, General MacArthur's Chief of Staff, tendered a plan for major support of an operation (Reno IV). This operation would be a push along the northern coast of New Guinea into Mindanao, Philippine Islands. In a covering letter, General MacArthur said: "The line of action presented in RENO IV will sever sea communications between Japan and the vital Borneo-Netherlands East Indies-Malaya region and will place our forces in the Luzon-Formosa-China Coast area at the earliest possible date under conditions that can be foreseen at this time."

Neither of these plans and presentations attached any importance to a strategic air offensive against Japan proper. When these proponents of rival strategies had reached the end of their presentations before the Joint Chiefs of Staff, General Arnold remarked that the Army Air Forces would like to present its views on Pacific strategy at the next meeting. As he was leaving the room, he turned to me and told me to prepare the presentation. I conferred with Generals Santy Fairchild and Larry Kuter and prepared an outline.

I went up to General Arnold's office to seek his approval or instructions and learned he had gone to the West Coast and would not be back for the next Chiefs meeting. Later I came to understand and appreciate this tactic, which General Arnold used several times. His position as a member of the Joint Chiefs of Staff was equivocal at best. The AAF was never accepted as an equal partner by the Navy. The

Navy Department did not openly try to quash the upstart air membership, but it worked quietly on the premise that there were by law just two recognized military departments—the War Department and the Navy Department. General Marshall was a tower of strength in supporting General Arnold and the Army Air Forces. Still, Arnold was a subordinate Army officer and he could never afford to openly oppose Marshall. The Army Chief of Staff was universally fair and unbiased, but the Army people as a whole tended to support MacArthur just as Navy people tended to back Nimitz.

General Arnold knew that we airmen would lean toward Nimitz's position and the Navy, if we could be assured of the capture of the Mariana Islands as base areas for B–29 strikes against Japan. If in Arnold's absence from the next meeting, General Marshall should disagree with this approach, the AAF Chief on his return could dismiss us in good grace on the ground that we had not been instructed to take this line and had exceeded our authority. The status of the Army Air Forces and the support of Marshall could thus be preserved.

But in fact General Marshall did not take exception to the air position as I presented it on March 9, 1944. The presentation was favorably received. Subsequently, the Joint Plans Committee and the Joint Logistics Committee proposed this schedule:

Objective	Command	Date
Hollandia	Southwest Pacific	April 15, 1944
Marianas	Central Pacific	June 15, 1944
Palau Islands	Central Pacific	September 15, 1944
Mindanao	Southwest Pacific	November 15, 1944
Formosa	Central Pacific	February 15, 1945

The question of Pacific strategy had not been clearly resolved, and both the rival strategies were endorsed. Achieved, however, were the capture of the Marianas as air bases and support for the B–29 operations in their air offensive against the Japanese home islands. This precipitated the vital question of how the B–29 force would be organized, commanded, and controlled.

Roles and Missions for Strategic Air Forces

The command of strategic air forces was thornier than the technical problems posed by the new bomber airplane. Unity of command was a cherished military concept in both the Army and the Navy. The Army attained this unity by designating a single commander with authority over all units within specific geographical boundaries. The Navy achieved it by retaining control of major combat naval forces under the ultimate command of the top naval echelon of the nation. Fleet units were rarely assigned to territorial command areas. When they were, it was always with the proviso they could be withdrawn at any moment for use elsewhere if the naval situation should so require.

Strategic air forces did not fit either concept, but their command characteristics resembled more closely those of the Navy than those of the Army. Often the long-range air force straddled several land commands. Its bombers might be based in many areas, each under separate Army or Navy jurisdiction. But bombers of the strategic air forces demanded unity at the target area, and they needed continuity of application if they were to accomplish their strategic mission. The very flexibility that was the cardinal virtue of strategic bombers was also their greatest vulnerability. There was a constant temptation to divert them from their long-range strategic war objectives to targets critical only to local area commanders.

The problem of unity of command grew more acute as primary attention turned to Japan and the B–29 force started to emerge. To apply this very heavy bomber force against Japan proper—its most important and potentially decisive role—plans were made to set up a number of bases within action radius of Japan. These bases were to be in China, the Marianas, Alaska, the Philippines, and Formosa or Okinawa.

Project Matterhorn called for bases in India and China. All U.S. forces there were under Gen. Joseph W. Stilwell, USA. He in turn was part of the Allied Southeast Asia Command headed by Adm. Lord Louis Mountbatten of the Royal Navy. (This command had been created at the August 1943 Quebec (Quadrant) Conference.) Although

Admiral Mountbatten was Supreme Allied commander, Southeast Asia, Chiang Kai-shek did not recognize any commander in China above himself. General Stilwell commanded all U.S. forces in the China-Burma-India Theater, which would include the B–29 forces. General Chennault commanded the U.S. Fourteenth Air Force and was at the same time Chiang Kai-shek's Chief of Staff for Air. Admiral Mountbatten had an Allied Air Commander in Chief, Southeast Asia Command, Air Chief Marshal Richard E. C. Peirse. Maj. Gen. George E. Stratemeyer was Commanding General, U.S. Army Air Forces in the India-Burma Sector, and Air Advisor to General Stilwell in China. Stratemeyer's command included the Tenth Air Force based in India. To further confuse an already complicated command arrangement, Stilwell gave Stratemeyer administrative command of the B–29 force (with its main bases in India) and also issued orders to the Fourteenth Air Force through him. General Stilwell proposed to exercise direct control of the B–29s, which he planned to use extensively in combined operations in China against Japanese ground troops. Admiral Mountbatten endorsed the initial operations entailed in Matterhorn, but planned to use the B–29s later in support of Southeast Asia Command objectives. In his capacity as Chiang Kai-shek's Chief of Staff for Air, General Chennault appealed to President Roosevelt directly requesting that all B–29s operating out of China be placed under his control. He made a similar request to General Arnold, asking that the B–29s operating from Chinese bases be put under the U.S. Fourteenth Air Force.

The Joint Staff planners proposed that ultimately four groups of B–29s be based in the Philippines. Those islands, when recaptured, would be under the command of General MacArthur. His chief airman, General Kenney, was already making vigorous demands for B–29s to be used in the Southwest Pacific campaign. Kenney wanted B–29s stationed in Darwin, Australia, for strikes on targets in the Netherlands East Indies. In addition, plans were actively being prepared for positioning B–29s in the Central Pacific and in Alaska. The Marianas, due to be captured chiefly as the Central Pacific base for the B–29s, would under existing circumstances be under the command of Admiral Nimitz. Alaska was still another command area.

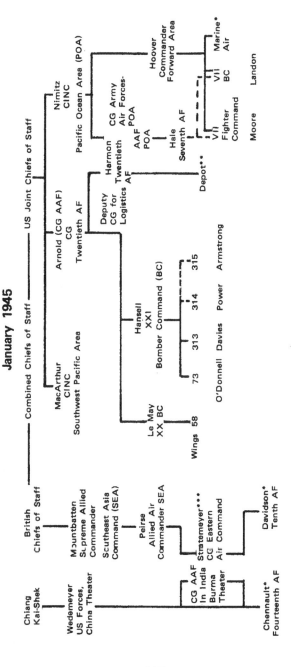

COMMAND, CONTROL, AND SUPPORT RELATIONSHIPS
TWENTIETH AIR FORCE
January 1945

* Responsible for Air Defense of B-29 bases
** Responsible for Depot Support of B-29s—Marianas
*** Responsible for Depot Support of B-29s—XXth Bomber Command

155

Every one of these base areas was under a separate theater commander, and these field commanders were powerful people. Each wanted to apply the B-29s to his own strategic theater purposes, and each resented any incursion into his area of control. Yet there was one area in which unity of air command and continuity of effort was imperative. That was the target area itself, Japan, which was under the control of none of them.

In March 1944 I presented to the Joint Chiefs of Staff the Army Air Forces concept of Pacific strategy. It envisioned a concerted bombing offensive against the Japanese home islands from the Marianas, to undermine the war-making capability of Japan. The plan also provided for the main B-29 force to be located in the Marianas. When the Philippines had been retaken, B-29 units were likewise to be situated on bases there within range of Japan. The B-29s in Chengtu, China, were to be moved forward when better base areas became available. A base was to be built in the Aleutian Islands as well.

Prior to the redeployment of the Eighth Air Force, the first plan for the final deployment of B-29s (and escort fighters when they became available) was as follows:

Chengtu, China	4 B-29 groups*
Mariana Islands	16 B-29 groups (3 squadrons each)
Ryukyu Islands	12 B-29 groups (3 squadrons each)
Philippine Islands	12 B-29 groups (3 squadrons each)
Aleutian Islands	4 B-29 groups (deployment questionable)
Iwo Jima Island	3 groups of long-range support fighters (type unspecified)
Ie Shima Island	2 groups of support fighters (type unspecified)
Kikai Island	2 groups of support fighters (type unspecified)
Okinawa Island	1 squadron of strategic reconnaissance aircraft (type unspecified)

*These groups, making up the 58th Bombardment Wing of the XX Bomber Command, were later transferred to the Marianas.

The main thrust of the plan was a unified and concerted air bombardment concentrated on a single list of targets in the Japanese home islands and coordinated through a unified air command.

Twentieth Air Force

Various schemes for centralizing control of the B–29s under the Joint Chiefs of Staff had been discussed ever since Sextant. Actually it was the similarity of this air problem to the traditional naval problem which finally was persuasive. At least, it was this resemblance which persuaded Adm. Ernest J. King to accept the idea of a strategic air force that would be assigned to none of the surface commands, but would report directly to the Joint Chiefs.

In retrospect, the way this significant agreement was reached seems almost trivial. I secured General Arnold's permission to discuss the subject with Admiral King. I found King and Arnold walking together down a corridor leading to the Joint Chiefs of Staff conference room. I asked Admiral King if I might have a word with him. I described briefly the problem of concerted command and control of the long-range bombers that would be attacking common targets in Japan, but would be operating from bases under the command of several separate theater commanders. I suggested a similarity with the problems attendant on control of the U.S. Fleet whose command was centralized under him as Commander in Chief, U.S. Fleet, as well as the Navy member of the Joint Chiefs of Staff. The U.S. fleets in the Pacific could be employed in concerted action against the Japanese naval forces under unified command, wherever the battle area might be and regardless of the geographical areas in which naval bases might lie. The B–29s had a like requirement. Would it not be sensible to concentrate the very long-range bombers arrayed against Japan in a strategic air force under General Arnold, Commanding General of the Army Air Forces? Unified operations against targets in Japan could be assured, notwithstanding the geographical areas in which the B–29 bases might be located. Under this arrangement, the B–29s would in fact fall under the control of the Joint Chiefs of Staff, with General Arnold serving not only as Commanding General, but as executive agent for the Joint Chiefs. The Joint Chiefs would furnish unified strategic air objectives. As in the case of logistic support for fleet units of the Navy, such support could be provided the B–29s through directive to appropriate area and theater commanders. Admiral King reflected for a moment and said, "I could find such an arrangement acceptable."

I prepared a brief memorandum to that effect, discussed it with Generals Kuter and Fairchild, and took it over to the War Department Operations Division. The struggle was only half won because General Marshall was dedicated to the concept of theater unity of command. He had even forced through the first Allied unified command, the ill-fated organization under British Gen. Archibald P. Wavell. This command embraced all the forces in a specified area, and was formally called the Australian-British-Dutch-American Command. Set up in January 1942 at General Marshall's insistence, it operated until the fall of the Netherlands East Indies to the Japanese in February. I gave the paper to Maj. Gen. Thomas T. Handy, Marshall's Deputy for Plans and Operations. Tom Handy was one of the finest and most able officers with whom I have been associated. He had General Marshall's great integrity and intellectual grasp, coupled with a fine sense of humor. He accepted the paper, read it carefully, and looked at me. "I'll tell you the truth, Hansell," he said, "I don't like any part of this paper. It violates the principle of unity of command in a theater of war. It inserts operational forces into a commander's area of responsibility but gives him no control of those forces. At the same time, the theater commander is expected to defend and supply and support those forces in competition with his own requirements. I don't like it." Then he grinned and said, "But I don't have a better solution. I'll buy it." I said, "Do you think General Marshall will buy it?" He replied, "General Marshall isn't here. But I know how he'll react. If General Arnold and Admiral King are agreed on it, he'll go along. As a matter of fact, I'll approve it in his name." That memorandum served as the basis for a paper presented to the

Joint Chiefs of Staff by the Joint Plans Committee, of which I was the air member.

The Twentieth Air Force was born on April 4, 1944, with General Arnold its first commander. It was designated the Twentieth to distinguish it from the other numbered air forces. On April 10 the Joint Chiefs of Staff accepted the Joint Plans Committee paper, and it constituted the formal charter under which the Twentieth operated. I have always believed the wartime establishment of the Twentieth Air Force was one of the most important events in United States Air Force history. If it had not occurred, we might be still parceling out our big punch in penny packets to numerous theaters and lower commands. And there might have been no United States Air Force.

The Joint Chiefs, in approving the creation of the Twentieth Air Force, directed:

> Commanders of the Theaters in which the Twentieth Air Force's XXth and XXIst Bomber Commands are based are directed to coordinate B–29 operations with other air operations in their Theaters, to construct and defend B–29 bases, and to provide logistical support and common administrative control of the B–29 forces. Should strategic or tactical emergencies arise requiring the use of the B–29 forces for purposes other than the missions assigned to them by the Joint Chiefs, Theater commanders are authorized to use the B–29 forces, immediately informing the Joint Chiefs of such action.

Admiral King's endorsement was vital because the bulk of the bombers would be in the Pacific Ocean Area, a naval command. General Marshall, with his typical breadth of vision, gave full support to the project.

The British Chiefs of Staff Committee plans called for participation of British bombers in the final air offensive against Japan. Also, the change in command relations would affect the Supreme Allied Commander, Southeast Asia, who operated under the Combined Chiefs of Staff with the British Chiefs of Staff Committee as executive agents.

The British Chiefs countered with the proposal that the air

offensive, including the Twentieth Air Force and later a British bomber contingent, be placed under the control of the Combined Chiefs of Staff rather than the U.S. Joint Chiefs of Staff. This would parallel the command relationship in the European Combined Bomber Offensive in which Air Chief Marshal Portal had been the executive agent of the Combined Chiefs. The Joint Chiefs demurred: The CBO in Europe was a British-American venture, while the air offensive against Japan was almost completely an American one. The British did not press the issue.

When General Arnold assumed command of the Twentieth Air Force and I became its first Chief of Staff, it was apparent we needed a staff for the new organization. But Arnold already had a staff—a large one—the Air Staff, or Headquarters Army Air Forces. He was loath to increase the "overhead" by creating yet another staff. I suggested to General Arnold that the Air Staff meet the needs of the Twentieth Air Force. He agreed somewhat reluctantly. The Air Staff was part of AAF Headquarters, the parent for all the numbered air forces. To single out the Twentieth as the special concern of the Air Staff—as an operational headquarters for a combat air command—would seem to slight all the others. But General Arnold did not want another headquarters staff in Washington, so he went along with my suggestion. Each of the Assistant Chiefs of Air Staff (Personnel; Intelligence; Training, Materiel, Maintenance, and Distribution; Operations, Commitments, and Requirements; and Plans) was told to wear two hats: one for Headquarters AAF and the other for Headquarters Twentieth Air Force. Each of these Assistant Chiefs selected one senior officer to represent him on Twentieth Air Force matters. General Order No. 1, Twentieth Air Force, assigned Col. Cecil E. Combs to the A–3 Division of the Twentieth as Chief of Combat Operations. I was designated a Deputy Chief of Air Staff as well as Chief of Staff of the Twentieth. On the whole, I thought the scheme worked reasonably well.

In many ways the Twentieth had unique features and problems. There was the need to draw up and approve tables of organization and equipment and to establish tactical doctrine and standing operating procedures. This would (1) permit the handling, control, and coordination of many aircraft and units, and (2) provide a basis for uniform training.

Air Staff members who served as principal staff officers for the Twentieth Air Force while I was the Twentieth's Chief of Staff and Deputy Chief of Air Staff included:

Brig Gen. John H. McCormick	A–1 (Personnel)
Col. Woodbury M. Burgess	A–2 (Intelligence)
Col. Cecil E. Combs	A–3 (Combat Operations)
Col. William F. McKee	A–3 (Operations, Commitments, and Requirements)
Col. Llewellyn O. Ryan	A–3 (Training)
Lt. Col. John W. Carpenter	A–3 (Crew Training)
Col. Samuel R. Brentnall	A–4 (Materiel, Maintenance, and Distribution)
Col. Sol Rosenblatt	A–4 (Supply)
Maj. Gen. Laurence S. Kuter	A–5 (Plans)
Maj. Gen. David N. W. Grant	Surgeon
Brig. Gen. Harold M. McClelland	Communications Officer
Col. Max F. Schneider	Air Inspector
Col. Guido R. Perera	Target Intelligence Officer and representative of the Committee of Operations Analysts

Arrangements had to be made for deployment to overseas bases and for logistic support. Personnel needed to be selected for key assignments. The top ones, of course, required General Arnold's approval, and he selected commanders at his own discretion. I anxiously watched the Materiel Command's progress in correcting a multitude of airplane and engine technical problems. I spent as much time as I could shepherding concepts and ideas through the Joint War Plans Committee, the Joint Plans Committee, and the Joint Chiefs of Staff and discouraging dismemberment of the force. At my request, the Committee of Operations Analysts was rendered responsive to the Chief of Staff of the Twentieth Air Force on matters relating to that command. I had to be ready at a moment's notice to answer General Arnold's questions, so he could be prepared to field those of the other

161

members of the Joint Chiefs of Staff, who were showing a lively interest in the new Twentieth Air Force.

One of the first challenges facing the Twentieth was communications—both command-and-control and administrative. The Joint Chiefs had approved our request to set up our own separate communications system. This was a sizable order seeing that we would have units and headquarters scattered over half the world. I briefed General Arnold on our communications requirements and watched with amusement as he applied his famous technique for attacking the impossible. He called in Brig. Gen. Harold M. McClelland, head of communications for the Army Air Forces. General Arnold said with caustic emphasis that he wanted:

> A net that would include Washington, Hawaii, the Marianas (which had not yet been captured), Calcutta, India, and Chengtu, China, with provision for extension to somewhere in the Philippines (when they were captured). He wanted TOP SECRET security with instantaneous coding and read-out by teleprinters. He wanted the net in operation twenty-four hours a day.

Fantastic, I thought! It couldn't be done. General McClelland didn't bat an eye. He said "Yes, sir," saluted and departed. It left Arnold a little flat and completely deflated me.

General McClelland had the last chuckle. He produced. Shortly after I had set up headquarters in Guam, (about six months after this conversation) the machinery was working. Within six weeks, I was sick of it. The machine worked twenty-four hours a day all right, without stopping. Most of the messages seemed to consist of questions I could not answer. I began to understand the meaning of the remark ascribed to the English statesman, Lord Palmerston, that the disintegration of the British Empire had begun with the invention of the telegraph.

During one of our daily staff meetings at Headquarters Twentieth Air Force, I got rather upset because supplies were not being provided for at a rate I thought satisfactory. The staff representative for materiel was Sol Rosenblatt, a temporary wartime colonel. I delivered myself of a somewhat intemperate diatribe. I mentioned that the U.S.

Navy always got the best of everything, with plenty to spare, while good fighting people in the Army—and the Army Air Forces in particular—made do on a song and a shoestring. The Twentieth Air Force was on its way to becoming the most powerful fighting force in the world, and it deserved the best and we were going to provide it.

I felt that I had expressed myself well and that the point was clearly understood—and I dismissed the subject from my mind for a while. But intemperance often breeds surprising results. It did so in this case. It was some time before I found out what a fire I had started. Colonel Rosenblatt took me seriously. He used not only my meager name and authority to churn the brew, but he used General Arnold's name and authority as well. I do not suppose we will ever find out the true level of supplies that were ordered for the Twentieth. I think it likely supplies were still being shipped to the Marianas long after the war was over and the troops had come home. Through his efforts I also acquired for a brief time my own personal "fleet" of cargo vessels. But that is another story.

During the period I served as Chief of Staff of the Twentieth Air Force, I had one particular experience which I well remember. The B–29s were coming off the production line, and there was increasing interest and speculation in the aviation press. We tried to keep a tight rein on security. The B–29s were destined for the major air assault on Japan. They would be operating at high altitude, unescorted. If the Japanese learned this and also discovered the salient elements of B–29 performance and defensive firepower, they would try by every means at their disposal to provide defenses against them. Security could be directly equated in terms of mission success or failure and in terms of the lives of American crewmen. We were deeply worried about news leaks. Of course there was wartime censorship, but skilled aviation writers who indulged in speculation could, and often did, hit upon the truth.

We had an exceptionally fine public relations officer in Twentieth Air Force Headquarters. His name was Rex Smith, and he was a wartime colonel in the Army Air Forces. He was a veteran newsman and had been at one time a foreign editor of *Newsweek* magazine. He came to me with a suggestion and recommendation. He said:

I know my people and my associates. They are as loyal and patriotic as any Americans you can find anywhere. They will respond to a gesture of faith, if they understand the issues and if they are treated fairly and equitably. I suggest we have a general meeting of all the professional aviation writers, tell them the truth, put them on their honor not to divulge, and assure them that, when the news can be released, they will all be told so at exactly the same time so that there will be no "scoops." Let them write their stories and file them with us. We will release them simultaneously at the earliest time that will not jeopardize our mission.

I was somewhat shaken by this bold suggestion. But I had a lot of faith in Rex Smith, and I realized I knew practically nothing about the press and news media. I bought the idea and then obtained General Arnold's agreement.

We had the meeting in a midwestern city. There were several hundred people present. The security arrangements were carefully prepared and carried out. We "spilled the beans" to a degree that left me quaking. But it worked like a charm. Reporters and writers filed their stories. When the first bombs released over Tokyo were still in the air, a message was flashed back to Guam and was automatically relayed to Washington. The President was the first recipient. But almost simultaneously, all the stories and reports Rex Smith had been holding were released to the press and the other news media. Whether this approach would work again, I do not know. But it worked once to perfection and every attendee at the conference proved completely trustworthy.

Original plans called for the Twentieth Air Force to eventually have three or four bomber commands: the XX Bomber Command in China-India; the XXI in the Marianas; the XXII in the Philippines or Formosa or Okinawa; and perhaps the XXIII in Alaska. The Twentieth's total aircraft would be 1,000 to 1,500 operational B–29s and such escort fighters as could be developed or modified.

The decision to concentrate the B–29s under Joint Chiefs of Staff control made possible the development of the concerted bomber offensive against Japan. However, it did not mark the close of the argument from the theater field commanders. They continued their efforts to gain control of the B–29 units in their areas. Requests from General MacArthur's headquarters were especially insistent. They were coupled with personal letters from General Kenney to General Arnold contending that B–29 operations out of the Marianas against the Japanese home islands were militarily and technically unfeasible.

The XX Bomber Command

The initial operations of the XX Bomber Command in India and China did not go well. Logistic problems had been expected, but the operational tactics were not yielding results even when the B–29s had sufficient gas and bombs to attack their targets. Brig. Gen. Kenneth B. Wolfe was using night operations exclusively. The coke oven targets (prescribed as first priority) did not present good radar images and were not easily seen at night. In consequence, the bombs were not being placed on their targets. As Chief of Staff of the Twentieth Air Force, I prodded General Wolfe to improve bombing results. I requested daylight bombing of the coke ovens in the Mukden area in Manchuria, where Japanese fighter defenses were not very effective. The available B–29 force was deemed by some to be too small to penetrate the air defenses of the Japanese islands themselves. Others of us believed it could be done. As a matter of fact, the XXI did pierce the air defenses of Tokyo in raids from the Marianas later in the year, with only one wing of B–29s—the same strength available to the XX. General Wolfe vigorously denied that his B–29s could fly in formations in daylight to these targets. He also categorically said B–29s could not reach their targets in daylight in formation from the Marianas. This assessment dealt a real body blow to the operational plans of the XXI. Wolfe was the only air commander having actual experience with the airplane, and he was the real expert and final authority on the technical aspects of the B–29 itself.

I directed Colonel Combs, Chief of Combat Operations for the Twentieth, to conduct practice tests to confirm or refute this contention that the B–29 had insufficient range to operate in formation as required. He went to Eglin Field, Florida, and set up a test run over the Gulf of Mexico simulating the flight from the

Marianas to Tokyo and back. Simulated bombloads of 8,000 pounds were carried as well as full loads of ammunition. Combs could muster but 3 B–29s for the test, but it was run with wartime combat tactics imitated as closely as possible, including the nature of the formation itself. That is to say, the test entailed initial assembly, loose formation en route, climb to 30,000 feet for the bomb run, tight defensive formation in the areas of potential fighter interception, and retention of that formation until beyond the range of enemy fighters, then return to base in loose formation.

The aircraft all returned successfully to the original base, Eglin Field, but gasoline reserves were admittedly too low. Though the operation was feasible, much remained to be learned about fuel consumption and daylight tactics if large formations were to be flown over those distances. Upon receiving the report of the test, General Wolfe still did not move from the stand he had taken. The B–29 was a magnificent engineering achievement, but it was new and different and it had new engines that we did not fully understand.

The XXI Bomber Command

The Twentieth Air Force was under extreme pressure to perform. One major slip and the critics would have their way—the Twentieth would have been dismembered and parceled out to the various theaters. An understanding of this tension and pressure is vital to an understanding of the XXI Bomber Command's early struggle to meet its commitments. We had pledged to launch an air offensive against Japan in November 1944. This proposed assault was tied into the carefully prepared plans for the Pacific campaigns of Admiral Nimitz and General MacArthur. The target date had to be met and the success of a highly controversial operation had to be shown, if strategic air power was to reach fruition in the Pacific.

The XXI Bomber Command was activated at Smoky Hill Army Air Field, Salina, Kansas, on March 1, 1944. At that time, the XX Bomber Command was stationed at Kharagpur, India, in the China-Burma-India Theater. The 73d Bombardment Wing, originally scheduled for the XX Bomber Command, had been transferred to the XXI when the XX was reduced from two wings (eight groups) to one wing, the 58th. The XXI Bomber Command was trained and staffed by the Second Air Force. Headquarters of the XXI was later moved from Salina, Kansas, to Peterson Field, Colorado Springs, Colorado. The XXI was to consist of 1,000 B–29s and it had to be given the necessary training.

In late spring 1944, General Arnold told me I was to have command of the XXI Bomber Command destined for the Marianas. My replacement as Chief of Staff of the Twentieth Air Force was Brig. Gen. Lauris "Larry" Norstad. His arrival was delayed because he felt he should "visit the troops" before becoming Chief of Staff, and he insisted on going to the India-China Theater. This took time so I could not get away until August to get a look at training and organize Headquarters XXI Bomber Command. When I finally assumed command of the XXI on August 28, 1944, the units of the 73d Wing were training for night radar bombing, along the pattern of the XX Bomber Command, of which it was to have been a part.

Due to its location, logistic troubles, and relationship to the chief target areas, the XX had been given target priorities different than those of the XXI. The force was thought to be too small to fight its way through the defenses of the Japanese homeland in daylight. And it could reach solely the southern portion of Japan from bases around Chengtu, China. The coke oven targets had proved unsuitable for night radar bombing. Other targets needed to be suited to radar bombing or situated in lightly defended areas. Aside from the coke ovens, this left little of real importance as targets for the XX.

The advice of the Committee of Operations Analysts was sought on the strategic targets of the Twentieth Air Force regardless of basing locations. The committee recommended using the B–29s against merchant shipping, steel production (through coke ovens), urban industrial areas, aircraft plants, the antifriction bearing industry, the electronics industry, and belatedly the petroleum industry. The committee repeated its conviction that the coke oven plants in Manchuria were highly vulnerable to bombing and were vital to Japanese steel production. It further pointed out the extreme vulnerability of Japanese urban areas to incendiary attack.

167

Memory of the Luftwaffe still fresh in its mind, the Air Staff advocated destruction or neutralization of the Japanese Air Force as an overriding priority for the XXI Bomber Command. The Joint Chiefs of Staff agreed. The aircraft and engine plants assigned as top priority targets to the XXI (based in the Marianas) were precision targets. Thirteen aircraft and engine plants were known to exist in Japan. It was estimated that eight of them turned out seventy percent of Japanese aircraft engines. The towns hosting these factories were known. Even so, the actual plants had not been pinpointed—a major task for the reconnaissance squadron of the XXI.

We had some general knowledge of the industry. Right after World War I, the Japanese had canvassed European and American aircraft and engine builders and had obtained production licenses. Three major Japanese producers emerged at that time: Nakajima, Mitsubishi, and Kawasaki. They had continued to dominate the Japanese airframe, engine, and propeller business. As the *U.S. Strategic Bombing Survey* later reported:

> While waves of Japanese technicians were studying American factories, America's top engineering schools were training men who, on their return to Japan, were to design the Zero fighter, Betty bomber, and other planes on which the Japanese bid for Pacific domination was to be based.
>
> By 1930, the Japanese Army and Navy had decided the industry should stand on its own feet, and established a policy of self-sufficiency, whereby only aircraft and engines of Japanese designs were to be considered. No more foreign engineers were to be hired. This was intended mainly as a sop to Japanese nationalistic pride, however, and did not prevent their technical missions from continuing to buy the best foreign models as starting points for Japanese designs. In 1935 Nakajima purchased licenses on the early Corsair from Chance Vought Corp., and it acquired designs of the Whirlwind and Cyclone engines from Wright Aeronautical Corp. in 1937. Mitsubishi purchased a French radial engine, which became the basis for their famous Kinsei series, and secured plans for a Curtiss fighter in 1937. Sumitomo Metals bought rights to the American Hamilton Standard and German VDM propellers. Kawasaki secured rights on the German Daimler-Benz engine, from which came the only Japanese liquid-cooled engine of the war. . . .

We knew that Japan had embarked upon a vast and hurried expansion of her military aircraft industry. We knew, for example, that the Japanese government had directed a near-doubling of the aircraft plants in 1941. Japanese newspapers bragged to the world that a great new airframe and assembly plant had been built at Musashino, near Tokyo, and another close to Nagoya was heralded as the second largest in the world. Kawasaki set up immense modern ones near Nagoya. However, the precise location and description of these plants was a mystery to us in the fall of 1944. We recognized that those concentrated in the vicinity of Tokyo, Nagoya, and Kobe would be extremely vital precision targets—if and when we discovered their precise locations and descriptions.

The aircraft targets could not be found, hit, and destroyed with the radar bombing equipment and the meager information we had. So the units of the XXI Bomber Command required crash retraining to do high-altitude, daylight precision bombing and to fly in formations not yet selected. We had to plan on reconnaissance after we had created a base on Saipan. The airplane and engine factory targets were at the extreme limit of the B–29 radius of action as it was then understood. Formations flying always reduces range, and it made completion of our missions (marginal at best) even more of a problem. In fact, it took several months of actual operation to master the techniques of fuel control that would give the B–29 its design capability.

There was spirited dispute at the time over this change in bombing tactics. The dispute persists, but the reasoning is not hard to trace. Our only real experience in massive bombing operations was over Europe. Had we not learned a painful lesson there? In Europe the whole concept of American air power—the selection of vital targets on the ground and their destruction through precision bombing—had faced the possibility of disastrous failure. The ability of massive bomber formations to fight their way through enemy defenses and reach remote targets, without intolerable losses, came dangerously close to being disproved. If the German fighter forces had been left free to expand, the price might have been too high. And if it had been, the air offensive would have failed and with it any hope of surface invasion.

In Europe the bombers of the Eighth and Fifteenth Air Forces were directed against the sources of German fighter development and strength—aircraft and engine factories, air bases, and sources of aviation fuel. These comprised the targets of the "intermediate objective:" the enemy air force. As soon as possible, the penetration capability of the bomber formations was supplemented by escort fighters. This experience in Europe obviously weighed heavily in establishing target systems in Japan. The aircraft and engine factories and to a lesser degree the oil resources were designated the intermediate objective in the war against Japan. They were to receive first priority in point of time. Dangerous as unescorted daylight missions might be, they had to be undertaken against Japanese aircraft and engine plants lest the Japanese air force grow strong enough to make our missions too costly to sustain.

The other lesson of European air combat could not be applied initially to the Twentieth Air Force. The range of the B–29 prevented escort fighters from accompanying the formations from the Marianas, though steps were taken to secure a very-long-range escort fighter. Until Iwo Jima could be captured and a fighter base set up there, the bombers would be completely on their own. This was really the most controversial point of all. Seasoned experts on every hand assured us the B–29s would simply be shot out of the air. But it was a risk that had to be taken if the strategic purposes were to be achieved. And the B–29s had some factors working for them—greatly improved defensive firepower and high-altitude performance.

Early in September 1944, I issued orders for converting the 73d Bombardment Wing to daylight tactics, and I established tactical doctrine for daylight operations including a standard formation. Opposition to this change was severe, especially from the 73d Wing. Training was intensive. But training missions from Kansas to Cuba, simulating the mission from Saipan to Japan, left bombers down all over the Gulf States. Meanwhile, the pressure to commit the command to combat rose. Final practice missions were flown. Groups of the 73d flew two long-range missions that stressed takeoff, assembly, rendezvous, formation flying, and simulated frontal weather penetration. Still, it was simply impossible to train bombardiers to an acceptable precision accuracy in the time remaining. Training would have to be completed in the Pacific.

Capture of the Marianas as a base for B–29 operations stemmed from the Army Air Forces' initiative and insistence. However, the decision was arrived at before the crews had enough flying experience with the B–29 to know what its performance truly was. Early experience in the training areas revealed that the round trip from the Marianas to Tokyo was marginal for the B–29, even on paper and without opposition. Depending on the location of the base and the target, the distance could be as much as 1,550 miles one way. Clearly there would be no land-based escort fighters for the first part of the campaign, prior to the capture of Iwo Jima. Apart from the marginal range of the B–29, nearly 1,500 miles of hostile water separated the Marianas from Tokyo.

When the first units deployed to Saipan six weeks later, the crews had averaged less than a hundred hours of total flying time in the B–29. The average high-altitude formation flying experience was under twelve hours. Moreover, the B–29's engines developed a mean tendency to swallow valves and catch fire. The magnesium crankcases burned with a fury defying all extinguishing. Besides, gunsighting blisters were either blowing out at high altitude or frosting up so badly that the gunners could not see through them. But there was not time to fix them properly.

The burning out of exhaust valves was finally solved by fitting a goosenecked pipe that sprayed cool air directly on the valve housing, and by putting cuffs on the props to pump more air through the engine cowling. Oil flow through the exhaust valve housing was also improved. The other problems—frosting of panes in the cockpit and of plastic bubbles at gunners' scanning stations—were solved by running hot air hoses to the affected areas. With the cockpit blanked out, it obviously would have been impossible to keep formation. And with the scanning bubbles clouded, the gunners could not see to shoot. These problems were solved at literally the eleventh hour.

I requested that the units of the XXI Bomber Command be flown in squadron formation to Saipan under Air Transport Command control. This would let them get needed experience flying in formation over considerable distances. The request was denied on the ground that the B–29 had not the range to fly in formation the 2,400 miles from Sacramento to Hawaii. The flight would have been without a bombload, in the face of no opposition, and with excellent communications, weather reporting, and base facilities. These same units, on arrival in Saipan, were faced with a round trip of about 3,000 miles, with bombloads, in the face of expected enemy opposition, and with no weather data or communications.

Two bases, each with two 8500–foot paved runways and 80 hardstands, necessary shops, housing, fueling facilities, and other essentials were supposed to be ready on Saipan. The bases were to have been built by the Central Pacific Area Command, but stubborn interference by the Japanese garrisons in the Pacific and competition from U.S. Navy construction work had set the schedule back by several months.

I paid a departing visit to General Arnold and General Marshall in Washington in mid-September. In response to his inquiry, I assured General Marshall we would carry out our pledge to attack Japan in November. Departing on October 5, I took the first B–29 to the Marianas and started the flow which ultimately grew massive. I flew with the crew from the 73d Wing, the aircraft commander being a bright and capable young major named Jack J. Catton. Catton and I alternated in the pilot position; I took it from Sacramento to Hawaii; he took it to Kwajalein; and I flew the last lap to Saipan. We took off from Mather Field near Sacramento. The original design gross weight of the B–29 was 120,000 pounds. Wright Field reluctantly permitted an overload weight to 128,000 pounds. With our spare engine in the bomb bay and the various kits we carried, we weighed in at about 130,000 pounds.

When we reached Hickam Field in Honolulu, Admiral Nimitz, Commander in Chief, Pacific Ocean Area, greeted us as did Lt. Gen. Millard F. "Miff" Harmon, Deputy Commanding General for Administration and Logistics, Twentieth Air Force. General Arnold retained direct control for operations as Commanding General of the Twentieth as well as executive agent for the Joint Chiefs of Staff. I asked Admiral Nimitz and General Harmon for an opportunity to discuss my mission and my requirements. Meeting with Admiral Nimitz the next morning, I explained my mission and its peculiar command relationships. That is, I would be completely dependent on him for construction of bases in the Marianas, for movement and delivery of all supplies by surface transportation, and for defense of the bases. At the same time, I would be independent of his authority in operational matters, except for serious emergencies.

This command relationship had apparently not been clearly spelled out or explained to Admiral Nimitz, because he expressed surprise on some counts. I, for my part, was surprised too. General Kuter had made a trip to Hawaii in late March or April for the express purpose of describing these relationships. On his return, a staff unit, headed by Maj. Gen. Walter H. "Tony" Frank, in a followup visit, had spent a week reaching accord on the principal details. Colonel Combs represented Headquarters Twentieth Air Force on this mission. The results were favorable indeed.

Thinking the Joint Chiefs-approved command relationship had been explained, perhaps I was undiplomatic in presenting my understanding of it. Fortunately I had the forethought to bring a copy of the Joint Chiefs of Staff agreement on the subject, which I produced. Admiral Nimitz studied it intently and said:

> I must say to you that I am in strong disagreement with these arrangements. If I had been aware of their extent I would have expressed this disagreement to Admiral King and the Joint Chiefs. I command all of US forces in the Pacific Ocean Area. This is an abrogation of the chain of command. However this is the decision of the Joint Chiefs of Staff, and I say to you again, I will give you all the help and cooperation in my capability. You have my very best wishes for success.

He was a good as his word. I had good reason to be grateful for his continued support. But he ended on an ominous note. He said: "You are probably in for a rough time. You are going out to the Forward Area where my commander, Vice Admiral John Hoover, breaks my admirals and throws them overboard without the slightest compunction. God knows what he is going to do to you." When I got

173

to know Admiral Nimitz better, I recognized the vein of merry humor that flowed beneath a sometimes stern visage. But at the time I was somewhat shaken.

When I finally arrived at Saipan, I called upon Vice Adm. John H. Hoover, Commander of the Forward Area. He could not have been more cordial and helpful. I kept him constantly advised of my problems and progress, and I enjoyed his strong support. I made it a point to follow his advice and suggestions whenever I felt I could.

My movement to Saipan had been conducted in supposed secrecy. When I left my wife in San Antonio to return overseas, I did not even tell her which ocean I was going over—Atlantic or Pacific. The night of our arrival in Saipan, "Tokyo Rose" broadcast a welcome to Saipan for "General 'Possum' Hansell" over the Japanese radio network. This may have seemed amusing to many, but to one it was almost tragic. Col. Richard H. Carmichael, commander of a B–29 group operating from Chengtu, was shot down over Japan and captured. He was hauled before a Japanese investigator who demanded to know why I was called "Possum." When he professed ignorance, he was beaten unmercifully. This went on for days, until the Japanese finally concluded he really didn't know—which was all too painfully true. Years later at a cocktail party, he asked my wife, Dotta, why I was called "Possum." She said she had found an old prep-school annual bearing my likeness at age thirteen with the explanation, "He is called 'Possum' because he looks like one." I have been steadfast in a minority dissent on this report ever since, to no avail.

A survey of conditions on Saipan caused dismay. Of the two bases under construction, one could not be used at all by B–29s. The other had one runway 7,000 feet long (5,000 feet of it paved), a taxiway at one end only, about 40 hardstands, and no other facilities whatever except for a bomb dump and a vehicle park with gasoline truck-trailers. It was hardly ready to receive the 12,000 men and 180 aircraft of the 73d Wing. Ground crews put up borrowed tents in what was surely one of the most disorderly military encampments of the war, but they worked day and night to meet the demands for the first strike.

Chapter V

Early Operations

The base on nearby Tinian Island had hardly been started. Those on Guam, where the main Headquarters of the XXI Bomber Command was to be located, had not even been laid out. Communications were completely inadequate. The aircraft of the 73d Wing arrived rapidly on Saipan after mid-October 1944 and had to be double parked on hardstands. In the meantime, a shipload of supplies reached Guam, destined to become a depot. The ship had been carefully loaded so the supplies could be unloaded in reverse sequence and stacked at the depot in "combat-loaded" order. The procedure was a new and elaborate one that would give us an operating depot in a matter of weeks. Actually, fighting was still going on in Guam when the depot ship arrived, and confusion reigned supreme. The harbor master said, "I'll give you twenty-four hours to get that goddamned ship out of here."

Before I learned what was happening, the supplies were dumped in the jungle. They were never recovered. We had to provide aircraft supplies for the B-29s (themselves new and unfamiliar) by air from Sacramento, California—8,000 miles away! The in-commission rate of the B-29s was astonishingly high—considering the circumstances.

As indicated earlier, the strategic concept was for the defeat or neutralization of the Japanese air forces as an "overriding intermediate objective." Thereafter, the major strategic air offensive was to be

BRIG. GEN. HAYWOOD S. HANSELL, Commanding General, XXI Bomber Command, briefs pilots before a mission over Tokyo.

176

launched against the war-supporting and economic systems of Japan. These systems were the "primary objectives." The plan of operations against them contemplated the destruction of certain major industrial facilities by selective target bombing.

The overriding intermediate objective and its associated target system, assigned to XXI Bomber Command by agreement of the Joint Chiefs of Staff, gave first place to Japanese factories building airplanes and aircraft engines. This assignment was not lightly conceived, for it had been learned in Europe that air superiority is essential to strategic air operations as well as to surface operations and invasions. The Joint Chiefs had been persuaded to back the air offensive, but they were looking over the shoulders of the airmen at the invasion shore.

The primary targets, to be destroyed after the Japanese aircraft industry, were of two kinds: selected targets, to be destroyed by precision bombing; and urban targets, to be destroyed by incendiary attack. Precision bombing of selected targets was the preferred method. But it was believed that small, "home-shop" type production facilities were distributed in the great cities of Japan. Those cities were known to be highly flammable. Incendiary attack of urban areas was listed high among approved target lists because of these urban shops and also because the cities were the focal points of Japanese "will to resist." The targets initially assigned the XXI Bomber Command were aircraft and engine factories supporting the intermediate objective, and they had overriding priority. They were selected targets requiring precision, daylight attack. Japanese shipping was also high on the target priority list.

It must be remembered that the Twentieth Air Force had won its right to exist only by becoming a creature of the Joint Chiefs of Staff. Strategic air leaders believed the war could be won by air power, but the official war plans of the Joint Chiefs contemplated invasion, and the Twentieth could not divorce itself entirely from that ultimate concept. Certainly that was wise in the early stages. Air power alone had never before been sufficient to force capitulation of a major nation still in full control of its own military means. What if the strategic air offensive should not be effective? The Chiefs simply had to have a backup plan. To be sure, there was some skepticism of air power, but

177

even if there had not been, it would have been unwise not to furnish a backup. Actually, the Joint Chiefs of Staff did give the Twentieth Air Force a priority second-to-none in the creation and launching of the air offensive, and they did direct the capture of the Marianas as a base of operations for the XXI Bomber Command.

The pattern of B–29 operations against Japanese targets was not conditioned by the limited concept of airpower's role, as a preparatory bombing operation preliminary to the basic strategy of defeating Japan by surface invasion. The first target list had as its purpose the defeat of the Japanese Air Force. This, like the defeat of the German Air Force, was an intermediate objective, a necessary preliminary to ensure and enhance the effectiveness of strategic bombing operations. No doubt that goal also helped assure the success of future ground and sea operations. But the initial primary air aims were practically the same as those in Germany—the paralysis of the military, economic, industrial, and social structure supporting the will and the ability of the Japanese nation to wage war.

First Strikes

Plans for the maiden bombing of Japan from the Marianas called for a combined first strike with the Navy, so carrier-based aircraft would divert and absorb some of the Japanese fighter defenses. For the rest, the B–29s would have to rely upon high altitude and speed (their chief advantage) and their own defensive gunfire. The B–29 was designed as a high-altitude bomber, the first with pressurized crew compartments. It had turbosupercharged engines, was reasonably fast at high altitudes, and was heavily gunned. By operating in formation, it was expected to fend for itself against enemy fighters which would be operating at their ceiling and have little, if any, margin of performance superiority.

The first aircraft and crews to touch down on Saipan were given a little training in the Pacific area. Six short training missions were flown against Truk and Iwo Jima. In spite of all the obstacles, the XXI Bomber Command declared itself ready to meet combat commitments exactly on time—by the middle of November.

In early morning of November 1, 1944, an F–13A (a photo-reconnaissance version of the B–29) took off from Saipan to become the first U.S. plane over Tokyo since the Doolittle raid in April 1942. The crewmembers, led by Capt. Ralph D. Steakley, insisted upon an immediate mission, even though they had just arrived from the United States. I advised a rest but they were persistent. Thank God they were. They found clear skies over Japan—a phenomenon. Called "Tokyo Rose," the aircraft flew above the Japanese capital at 32,000 feet, photographing a complex of aircraft and engine plants just west of Tokyo and another on the outskirts of Nagoya. They shot over 7,000 excellent photographs. Before the first strike on Tokyo on November 24, 17 sorties had been flown over Japan by F–13s. Many of the missions were hampered by bad weather, but sufficient information on the location of aircraft factories was secured for the first bombing missions. Copies of the photographs were sent to General Arnold for the Joint Chiefs of Staff and to Admirals Nimitz and Halsey. Mosaics were made, strips laid out, and initial points and target approaches selected. Every crew was required to trace its photo map, mark landmarks and target runs, and then redraw them from memory—over and over.

As the day for the combined operation against Japan approached, the Navy found itself in serious combat trouble in its involvement with the Japanese fleet and movement into the Philippines. It therefore announced it could not take part in the planned combined air operation against Japan. The Navy recommended postponing the joint strike against Japan and grounding the B–29s until it could participate. I got word of this recommendation and notified General Arnold we would be ready to conduct the air attack in November as planned, without Navy support. I did not like the idea that the B–29s could operate only with Navy assistance. If that were the case, the B–29s might better be turned over to Admiral Nimitz. However, I did have our limited number of B–29s loaded up with 2,000–pound bombs and put on alert to support the Navy in the battle of the Philippine Sea, which was then raging. I told Admiral Hoover we stood ready to offer such assistance as he might request, and we would welcome Navy officers to go with us as recognition experts. I did this for two reasons:

We were still too weak to attack Japan but genuinely wished to help. And I was worried lest Admiral Nimitz invoke the emergency clause and take command of the B–29s. He might take a long time to release command. By volunteering our services I hoped to forestall his official action. We were not called upon, but I think the gesture was appreciated and was effective.

The first planned strikes were labeled San Antonio I and II. I was to lead the first, and Brig. Gen. Emmett "Rosey" O'Donnell, Jr., 73d Wing Commander, was to lead the second. These plans were reported to Washington in detail. To my surprise, General Arnold ordered me not to lead the mission. I presumed it was because of my extensive knowledge of the Pacific campaign plans. It was concern for just this possibility that had prompted me to make a special request about a month or so earlier. Just before leaving for the Pacific, I had been summoned to Washington to be briefed on a highly secret matter. I presume it was either on the atomic bomb or Ultra. I asked if the knowledge I was about to receive would keep me from flying combat missions. The answer was, "Yes." I asked to be excused from receiving the information, because I felt it imperative that I be free to lead my command if the going got rough. This request was honored and I proceeded without the briefing.

Now, it seemed to me, was the time when I should lead. The going was likely to be rough, and there was deep concern in the command about the chances of successfully performing the mission. I decided to ignore instructions, lead the mission, and hope for the best. My hope was short lived. Two or three days after advising Washington of our plans, I was called upon by a Navy lieutenant and a petty officer who had a copy of the message and demanded a written acknowledgment of its receipt. The message had been sent through Navy channels.

At the time I thought the decision was arbitrary and ill taken. Of course, I did know of the strategic plans for the Pacific war, but plans are constantly changing, and I had only a rudimentary knowledge of the atomic bomb. But there was another factor I overlooked at the time and did not think of until much later: I was thought to be privy to the existence of supersecret intelligence and, what was much more important, to the sensitive source of such information. The story is out now after thirty years of secrecy. It is told in fascinating detail in *The Ultra Secret* by the man responsible for it, Gp. Capt. Frederick W. Winterbotham, RAF. It is the story of the breaking of the most secret codes of the Germans and the Japanese. I was aware of the breaking of the Japanese code but I was actually unaware of Ultra.

How I could have forgotten this item is incredible. It had been the source of daily agony as far as I was concerned. For several months before I took over the XXI Bomber Command, General Arnold required Generals White and Kuter and me to meet in his inner office every morning. We were admitted at 0730. At 0715, General Arnold received the daily verbatim translations of high-level, secret German and Japanese messages. Before we entered, we were each familiar with the U.S. secret messages exchanged during the night. We were therefore prepared to present and discuss events pertaining to our several interests and responsibilities. However, we did not get Ultra messages directly. General Arnold would reveal the information he had just been given and demand to know what we were doing about it. We were not doing anything about it; we did not know about it. Even so, this did not save us from withering comments about our competence. Doubtless, General Arnold enjoyed this game, but it was pretty rough business to be on the receiving end.

Now that same supersecret intelligence I did not receive was returning to bite me again. There was an Allied agreement, without deviation of any sort, forbidding recipients of Ultra information and those who knew of its source from exposing themselves to capture. This may well have been the clinching argument in my case. The message from General Arnold could no longer be ignored. I designated General O'Donnell to lead San Antonio I.

I faced a very serious command dilemma. As Commanding General, XXI Bomber Command, I found myself in a severe predicament. Three nearly simultaneous events combined to make my position difficult. First was the Navy recommendation that the mission be canceled or indefinitely postponed until the Navy was ready to participate. If I accepted this, it would clearly show that the XXI Bomber Command could not operate independently but must do so solely in close concert with the Navy. If this were true, why have a

STRATEGIC BOMBING MISSIONS OVER JAPAN are reviewed on a B-29 base in the Marianas by (left to right) Brig. Gen. Emmett O'Donnell, Jr., Lt. Gen. Millard F. Harmon, and Brig. Gen. Haywood S. Hansell, Jr.

WRECKAGE of JAPANESE DIVE BOMBERS lines the runways on Tinian in the Marianas, March 1945.

separate Twentieth Air Force chain of command? Since coordination would be needed, and it could be furnished only by the Commander in Chief of the Pacific Ocean Area, Admiral Nimitz, why not place the XXI Bomber Command under his control? This would almost certainly destroy the strategic air war against Japan as a war-winning grand strategy—one in which I and my fellow airmen fervently believed. I had hastened to notify General Arnold that the XXI Bomber Command stood ready to discharge the mission without Navy assistance. Any equivocation now would place the Twentieth Air Force and the strategic air war against Japan in serious jeopardy.

Second, I received a disturbing message from General Arnold. Members of General Arnold's staff and at least one top-level AAF field commander, to whom my plan (San Antonio I) had been passed for comment, voiced grave doubts that we could carry out our mission. Gen. George Kenney predicted the planned operation would result in disaster. General Arnold forwarded these expressions of doubt and wrote in his own hand the comment that he was inclined to agree with the skeptics. The contention was that the airplanes lacked the necessary range and furthermore the Japanese would "shoot them out of the air." General Arnold did not direct me to abandon or modify the mission. Rather, he put me on record as having been warned. He concluded with the statement that he had high respect for the critics of the mission, but said if I were convinced of its feasibility and were determined to carry on, then I was at liberty to do so. He left the decision up to me and said if I chose to go ahead, he wished me luck. The effect was chilling. The warning was coming from the very people from whom I had expected firmest support.

Third, I received a handwritten letter from my senior wing commander, General O'Donnell, stating that he, too doubted if his unit could fulfill the mission. He suggested abandoning the daylight attack and substituting a night one against some area target. In a private meeting with him, I pointed out that the night operation he proposed would not accomplish the mission with which I was charged. I was determined to see the mission through, and if he was unwilling to lead his wing in this operation, I would turn it over to someone who was. (Brig. Gen. Roger M. Ramey, my Deputy, was anxious to head it.) O'Donnell assured me he was willing but had felt constrained to vent his doubts and worries. I recognized his right and obligation to give me, in private, his honest opinion. If the mission failed and he had not warned me of his true convictions, I would have been justified in reproaching him. On the strength of this, with his agreement I destroyed his letter. I explained that if the mission succeeded, the letter would be a black mark on his record that would be hard to live down. If we failed, the onus would be entirely on my head, since I had been warned from other quarters.

It was quite true that until the time for takeoff of San Antonio I, the XXI Bomber Command had never flown a formation as large as a squadron, a distance as far as Tokyo and back, and had not flown against any enemy opposition. But the potential impact of the mission on Pacific strategy and the future of the Air Force extended far beyond the XXI. The Army Air Forces, at the Joint Chiefs of Staff planning and command level, had been advocating primary reliance upon the decisive effectiveness of the air offensive, with provision for an invasion of the Japanese mainland only if the air offensive proved inconclusive. This viewpoint did not mesh with Army and Navy planning. To admit at this late juncture in November 1944 that the air offensive could not even attack its intermediate objectives, would have grave repercussions indeed. The whole command structure of the Twentieth Air Force as a worldwide command, reporting directly to the Joint Chiefs in a role parallel to that of the U.S. naval fleet, was in delicate balance. To subject it to reexamination resulting from a major degradation of capability would have had serious after-effects. To those who believed the air offensive was not only the most effective avenue to victory in the Pacific but also the cheapest in terms of American lives, abandoning the planned mission would be a disaster almost as great as the tactical disaster of failure might have been. Still, there was no denying that the decision to carry out the plan was extremely risky.

I thought I understood why General Arnold had sent me this message. Disaster on the first mission of the XXI Bomber Command would have altered Pacific strategy and would have delayed recognition of coordinate air power by many years. Since it seemed highly probable such a disaster would ensue, the ill effects would be less severe on the future of the Army Air Forces if the responsibility were borne by a subordinate field commander. Arnold had warned me, and I had chosen to go ahead in spite of the warning. His was not an unreasonable precaution to take under the circumstances. I decided to go on with the mission and so notified him.

Rosey O'Donnell asked for a change in the operational plan. I had set up two initial points, on opposite sides of the target, and planned for two converging bombing runs to confuse and divide the enemy air defenses. It called for a complicated maneuver. Rosey suggested the plan be simplified by using only one axis of attack, with Fujiyama volcano, west of Tokyo, as the initial point. I approved the change.

During preparation for the first strike, a delegation of congressmen visited my command. I was extremely busy. We seemed to be operating under one of Murphy's laws, "Anything that can go wrong will go wrong." I quartered the visiting congressmen in my own pyramidal tent, perched on a promontory jutting out into the sea. I issued each of them a mess kit and invited them to join me in the chow line and to wash their own kits afterward as I was doing. I must admit the chow was simply awful, but we were living on a shoestring and spending all our energies on training and preparation for the mission. I devoted as much time to the visitors as I felt able and told them of our general plans, problems, and expectations. I did not go into the details of operations and tactics. We kept those pretty close to the vest because security leaks would endanger our success and cost lives among our combat crews.

The group went back to Washington and wrote a scathing denunciation of my administrative arrangements. They also had interviewed members of my command who were from their home districts. Most of the responses were understandably flavored with apprehension about the forthcoming campaign. This problem was a forerunner of the massive difficulties that were to fall upon future American commanders in the field during the Korean and Vietnam Wars.

The first mission was laid on for November 17. At the final briefing before dawn, I made a short talk to the crews:

Stick together. Don't let fighter attacks break up the formations. And put the bombs on the target. If the bombs don't hit the target all our efforts, risks, worries, and work will be for nothing. That's what we're here for. If we do our job, this is the beginning of the end for Japan. Put the bombs on the target. You can do it.

Crews took their stations in the early dawn. The long line of B–29s formed up on the taxiway that led to one end of the runway. To extend our range, we were carrying an extra tank of gasoline in the front bomb bay [gross take off weight was about 140,000 pounds]. At the last moment, the wind, which had consistently blown down the runway, died down. We needed that wind badly to get off with our heavy loads. Then the wind reversed direction and freshened. It was impossible to taxi to the other end of the runway because the long line of B–29s could not be reversed. We could not use the runway itself to taxi down and then take off by successive airplanes, because the taxi time would have been excessive, causing long delays in assembly, and burning up too much of our precious fuel.

There was no choice. I had to call off the mission. I hated to do so. We had built up to a psychological climax. Delay would play on fears and apprehension. It was one of the hardest decisions I had to make, but it was one of the luckiest. In a few hours, a typhoon hit Saipan and lasted six days. Then it traveled north toward Japan on our route to our targets. It left our base a shambles and a sea of mud. If the typhoon had arrived a few hours later, we would already have taken off—and found no way to make a landing on return. The B 29s sat on their hardstands, two deep, fully loaded, for a week. The orders had been distributed. The thought of a security leak was a nightmare. A daily weather flight followed the typhoon northward. To my great grief, one of them was lost and never heard from again.

On November 24, 111 B–29s of the 73d Bombardment Wing, XXI Bomber Command, took off on the trip toward Japan. They represented over 90 percent of the B–29s on Saipan. Some of the crews had arrived less than a week before, and their first takeoff was for Tokyo. Each lift-off was an ordeal. As noted earlier, the B–29 was originally designed for a gross weight of 120,000 pounds. By urging and pleading, we had convinced the engineers at Wright Field to raise the

ORDNANCE SPECIALISTS LOAD BOMBS on a Boeing Superfortress on Saipan, Marianas, November 1944.

BOMBER CREWS LISTEN ATTENTIVELY to the pre-mission briefing for the XXI Bomber Command's first mission to Tokyo, November 1944.

A TWENTIETH AIR FORCE B-29 SUPERFORTRESS runs up its engines before taxiing out for take-off on a mission over Tokyo, December 1944.

GROUND PERSONNEL WATCH A BOEING B-29 take off on the first bombing mission from Saipan to Tokyo, November 1944.

allowable gross takeoff weight of the B–29s to 132,000 pounds. Now, to carry every gallon of gas that could be pumped aboard, they were taking off at 140,000 pounds! A faltering engine would spell the end for any aircraft.

Primary target for the B–29s on San Antonio I was the Musashino aircraft plant of the Nakajima Aircraft Company on the outskirts of Tokyo. The secondary targets and "last resort" areas were the docking facilities and urban areas of Tokyo. A total of 277.5 tons of bombs was delivered. Seventeen bombers turned back because of fuel problems, and 6 missed their bombing runs due to mechanical troubles. Flying between 27,000 and 33,000 feet, the bombers picked up a 120–knot wind over Japan, giving them a ground speed of 445 miles per hour. Twenty-four planes bombed the Nakajima plant on the outskirts of Tokyo, and 64 unloaded on the Tokyo dock areas. Only 1 B–29 was lost in combat. U.S. gunners claimed 7 enemy fighters destroyed and 18 probables. Final count for the XXI Bomber Command listed 2 B–29s destroyed, 8 damaged by enemy action, 1 man killed, 1 missing, and 4 injured. After the war, records indicated that 48 bombs had hit the factory area: 1 percent of the buildings and 2.4 percent of the machinery were damaged; 57 persons were killed and 75 injured.

The weather at the target had been far from favorable, and the bombing results left much to be desired. But losses were small, and the operation was completed despite the hazards and obstacles. Not the least of the hazards was the return flight to base. The mission lasted twelve to fourteen hours. Landing was at night with no runway lights and only smudge pots along the single runway strip. The next nearest landing strip was at Kwajalein, over a thousand miles away. If a B–29 splattered itself on the runway, the rest of the aircraft behind it, with nowhere to land, would be all through.

Perhaps in hindsight, the decision to launch the offensive in the face of such adverse conditions and recommendations seems reckless, and the results the product more of good luck than sound judgment. But this first great gamble proved the feasibility of the assault. Momentum, confidence, and improved efficiency would come with experience and numbers. In my opinion, if the decision had been to "stand down" San Antonio I and substitute a night attack against some urban areas, the result would have been catastrophic, particularly as regards confidence in and continuation of the Twentieth Air Force.

San Antonio II was staged on November 27 with the same target objectives. The crews of the eighty-one B–29s that flew the mission found Tokyo completely covered by clouds, so the bombs were dropped by radar on the secondary targets. The Japanese were provoked into trying to halt the bombing. From Iwo Jima they made one-way suicide air raids on Isley Field, our base on Saipan, destroying some B–29s. The Japanese had realized that their home islands were indeed susceptible to sustained attack and that their fighters could not turn back the B–29s.

Improving Successive Missions

The accomplishment of these first two missions, with very light losses, was an achievement in itself. The fact that bombing results were only fair could be overlooked in view of the proof that the force could indeed reach its targets and return to base. But succeeding missions made it clear that bombing accuracy would have to be greatly improved. Two methods were adopted to achieve that end—training in visual bombing techniques and the introduction of radar to assist and even substitute for optical bombing in attacks against selected precision targets.

A "lead crew" school was set up, and one B–29 from each squadron was set aside for training. This was rather a drastic move. We were desperately short of B–29s, and withdrawing at least twelve B–29s for training out of about one hundred aircraft in operational condition was critical weakening of the force. But there was no use sending bombers to Japan at all if they could not destroy the targets.

The other method to improve bombing simply made good sense. The AN/APQ–13 radar bombing equipment was used to supplement the bombing run with the Norden optical sight. Initial points were chosen that afforded good radar images. As each formation approached the initial point, the turn to the bombing run was made from observations by the radar-bombardier. He next conducted a radar bombing run, using the target if possible, or an offset aiming point if necessary. The radar-bombardier could then assist the optical-bombardier in setting up his bomb run. In this manner, it was possible to set into the optical sight the drift angle and rate of ground speed and to have the crosshairs of the optical sight aligned approximately on the target. Then if the target became visible through breaks in the clouds, only minor adjustments of the optical sight were needed. Although the bombs could be released on the radar sight if the clouds obscured the target from visual adjustment, the accuracy was inferior to visual sighting. For acceptably accurate radar sighting, we would have to prepare radar maps of the targets and determine precise locations of targets with reference to good offset aiming points.

Several events with a sobering impact on me occurred during the first ten days of operations. The first of these took place when Japanese fighters commenced strafing attacks on our Saipan air base and parked B–29s. They had come down from Iwo Jima on a one-way suicide mission and were completely undetected by the Marine outfit that was supposed to furnish our air defense. One such attack began around noon on November 27. I jumped in my jeep with Col. John B. Montgomery, my Chief of Staff, and headed for the field. As we came up a rise onto the flying field, I found myself looking straight into a Japanese fighter that was strafing the area. I brought the jeep to a halt and sought shelter under it. Quick as my reaction had been, it still was not quick enough. Colonel Montgomery was already there.

Fortunately, the wing was out on a mission over Japan and there were only a few B–29s on the ground. But several of these B–29s were bombers which had aborted the mission and were on the hardstands fully loaded with bombs and gasoline. The main warning radar, which the Marines should have installed on a hill, was still in crates. There had been ample time for installation, but the Marines simply did not expect suicide attacks. General Arnold was understandably outraged. He had warned of this possibility but suitable action was not taken to provide defenses.

Another incident had to do with Operation Memphis One, which was returning to Saipan when an intense tropical storm hit the island. It was about 2030 and the rain was so heavy that, standing in the improvised tower, I could not see the dim smudge pots outlining the single runway. Over eighty B–29s were approaching the field. The air was full of calls saying, "number such-and-such B–29, I am approaching Saipan. Visibility zero. I am out of gasoline. Request instructions." The tower operator was a noncommissioned officer who earned my highest admiration. He was calm and issued instructions without a hint of panic. The only thing we could do was hope the storm, which had arrived suddenly, would depart with equal dispatch, and that the fuel gauges which read zero did not really mean it. We were fortunate. The storm did clear. The B–29s landed in rapid succession. I realized then that I really was quite helpless. The real Commander of the XXI Bomber Command was a noncommissioned officer who was functioning superbly as the tower operator. The best help I could give him was to keep out of his way and avoid interfering with him.

In another incident one evening, an air raid warning sounded and all lights were doused. A Japanese twin-engined bomber made a couple of passes. Roger Ramey, my Deputy Commander, and I were standing on the runway watching the antiaircraft bursts when the bomber suddenly reappeared at very low altitude. A couple of B–29s had been hit and were burning brightly. They lit up the sky, and the oncoming Japanese aircraft was clearly visible. I think we noted something about it at just the same instant, because we took immediate and identical action. It was making a low-level strafing attack down the runway we were standing on. There was no place to go. We hit the pavement with great force at just the same time. Tracers from the ground defenses were pouring into the Japanese bomber but it continued on course. Then, as it approached the end of the runway, it swerved slightly and plowed into the ground. The pilot evidently had been killed. The bomber hit with a roar about a hundred yards from us and was engulfed in flames. Just as we were rising to our feet, there was a violent explosion. Evidently it still had bombs aboard.

That evening was replete with mental impressions as well. As soon as the attack started, the base was aswarm with thousands of men eager and determined to see what was going on. They were completely beyond control. Two B–29s were burning like torches, and there were other B–29s nearby. Men pushed and pulled to get the other sixty-ton monsters away from the fire. The B-29s were fully loaded with gasoline. Some of them had bombs aboard in preparation for tomorrow's mission. No one seemed to know which of them had bombs and which had not. Succor came from an unbidden and unexpected source: the engineers. They appeared on the scene with their massive bulldozers and earth-moving equipment. They pushed the flaming carcasses aside, piled dirt on them, and rode over them until they had crushed out the fires. It was the most amazing sight I have ever seen. No one knew for sure that there were not bombs in those flaming masses. Fifty-caliber ammunition was going off like firecrackers. The scene was an animated illustration out of Dante's *Inferno*. Engineers were riding in bulldozers through flames reaching high in the air; enormous monsters of steel were burying other monsters which threatened to lash back and blow up at any moment. I still do not know whose idea it was for the engineers to take this action. It certainly was not mine. I really think it was a spontaneous reaction from the engineers themselves. I have always regretted that I did not get them a unit combat citation. It certainly was heroism far beyond the call of duty.

The next three months (November 1944 through January 1945) were frustrating, to say the least. Schools worked hard to train the lead crews, determined to improve bombing accuracy. Enormous efforts were made to upgrade maintenance. The depot had to start all over again, and in the meantime the air supply from Sacramento had to be improved. More missions were run against Japanese engine and aircraft factories. But the weather was a terrible opponent, and there was no intelligence of its movements. Japanese fighter opposition was desperate but not deadly, at least in comparison with German fighters. Air kamikaze-ramming tactics were tried with some success. Morale was a critical problem. The airplane engines were still unreliable. Aircraft disabled from combat or other causes were 1,500 miles from friendly territory. The crews had the choice of drowning or bailing out over Japan, to be executed by maddened Japanese. The U.S. Navy contributed tremendously to morale by stationing rescue submarines at intervals along the route. Their performance was superb. One submarine entered Tokyo Bay in daylight and picked up a B-29 crew

A B-29 FLIES OVER THE HARBOR OF SAIPAN—headquarters of the XXI Bomber Command.

WITH NO. 4 EN-
GINE FEATH-
ERED, a Superfor-
tress lands on Saipan
after a successful
mission against To-
kyo.

A REINFORCED
CONCRETE
STRUCTURE at the
Musashino aircraft
engine plant escaped
the brunt of the AAF
bombing attacks,
which severely dam-
aged the weaker
buildings.

BRIG. GEN. HANSELL visits with Col. Seth S. Terry of XXI
Bomber Command.

DESPITE THE THREAT OF EXPLOSION, aviation engineers ram their bulldozer into a burning B-29, pushing dirt over the flames. The near-disaster was caused by a low-level Japanese attack on the Saipan airfield, November 1944.

A BULLDOZER PULLS THE TAIL OF A SUPERFORTRESS away from the burning wreckage following the Japanese raid on Saipan, November 1944.

right under the guns of the Japanese. From November 1944 to August 1945, 600 Twentieth Air Force flyers were saved in open-sea rescues. The system involved Navy flying boats, B–17s (Dumbos) carrying droppable lifeboats, B–29s (Superdumbos), and submarines, all under Navy control. The system was largely the achievement of my Navy Liaison Officer, Comdr. George C. McGhee.

On December 13, 1944, 74 B–29s of the 73d Wing received credit for doing significant damage to Japanese aircraft plants. Most of the bombers carried 500–pound general purpose bombs, while others were loaded with incendiary clusters. The primary target was the Mitsubishi engine plant at Nagoya. Photographs failed to show all the damage. Later reports disclosed that engine assembly shops and auxiliary buildings were destroyed or damaged. A total of 246 people were killed and 105 injured. Aircraft engine production capacity was reduced from 1,600 to 1,200 per month. The Mitsubishi No. 4 Engine Works no longer made parts. The Japanese also began transferring plant equipment to underground facilities. It was the most destructive mission to date for XXI Bomber Command.

The order for succeeding missions was for maximum strikes against top-priority targets by high-altitude precision bombing when weather was acceptable. When it was not, secondary targets were to be hit and time was also given to single-aircraft night operations, collecting weather data, and radar bombing. Bombing results remained hard to assess due to cloud cover, and were deliberately played down by XXI Bomber Command Headquarters. I wanted to build a reputation for credibility in the XXI's reports to counterbalance the known tendency to exaggerate. Our whole energy was devoted to improved effectiveness and accuracy.

During November and December 1944, forty-nine photo missions were flown and, by January 1945, thousands of photographs of Japanese targets had been taken. These missions performed five functions for the XXI Bomber Command: photo reconnaissance for target and strategic intelligence, weather reconnaissance, radar scope photography, lead-crew training, and nuisance raids.

The Aerial Mining Campaign

Preparation for aerial mining operations against shipping in Japanese home waters was likewise started during this early period. Later, Dr. Frederick M. Sallagar, while with the RAND Corporation (but a member of my 4th Operations Analysis Section in 1944), completed a postwar study, *Lessons From an Aerial Mining Campaign (Operation STARVATION)*. Dr. Sallagar showed clearly that the aerial mining of Japanese inland waters by B–29s of the Twentieth Air Force's XXI Bomber Command was a tremendous success and contributed enormously to the fall of Japan. He further noted a reluctance on the part of senior Air Corps officers to enter into this operation with the enthusiasm it deserved. As Commanding General of the XXI Bomber Command, I was one of those reluctant leaders. But there were reasons for my reluctance.

Army Air Forces leaders, including me, remembered what had happened in Germany. AWPD–1 committed the American bomber units to the factories, industrial systems, and enemy air bases in Germany. But these units were split apart and half assigned to the Allied forces invading North Africa in Operation Torch. This afforded a bitter lesson: Theater commanders, accustomed to seeking victory through surface warfare, would demand and get strategic air to support their ground campaigns at the expense of strategic air objectives. The Eighth Air Force had hardly recovered from this nearly mortal blow, when the ordeal was again endured in preparation for and during the invasion of Normandy. Strategic targets in Germany were neglected far too long while air power was tied down in ground operations. Consequently, the appeal for aerial bombing of Japanese waterways found a cool reception in the first months of the XXI's operations. It looked like one more diversion to the local needs of a ground commander, and away from primary industrial targets leading to defeat of the enemy air force. So the mining program, which proved to be one of the principal achievements of the Twentieth Air Force, met with initial opposition.

Mining of rivers and harbors in the Netherlands East Indies by the B–29s of the XX Bomber Command had been one of the first operations conducted by that command from bases in Ceylon. However, Admiral Nimitz's staff proposed a much more extensive campaign for XXI Bomber Command in Japanese home waters. In fact, the Navy's first proposal would have absorbed the total capacity of the XXI for the first three or four months of its operations. I objected to this on the ground that it was another major diversion from the chief purpose for which the command had been created and deployed. The objection was not directed against the idea of mining itself, but to the magnitude of the diversion at a time when utmost endeavor was needed to develop our primary capability.

I was not, of course, in a position to change the directive issued by the Joint Chiefs of Staff. But when General Arnold sought my recommendations on Admiral Nimitz's request, I opposed the application of so much of the XXI Bomber Command at that time to aerial mining. I recommended postponement until the force had grown and suggested that one group be charged with developing the technique and with limited initial operations. The problem was settled when General Arnold issued a directive calling for a somewhat postponed mining effort at a much reduced initial level.

Even as the problem was being discussed at high level, steps were taken to prepare for a mining campaign of some intensity. I directed the 313th Bombardment Wing, whose aircraft began to arrive on Tinian in December, to develop tactics and techniques for aerial mining. One group of the wing was designated to do this work. The XXI Bomber Command owed a debt of gratitude to the Navy personnel who assisted in adapting Navy mines to installation in B-29s and in helping develop dropping techniques and tactics.

When Maj. Gen. Curtis LeMay later took over the XXI Bomber Command,* his decision to launch a massive mining operation was a sound one. Adequate forces had been assembled. Tactics and techniques had been worked out (many of them by LeMay). Since mining was not dependent on weather, it was possible to achieve continuity of operations. I think General LeMay did not view mining at night as

---

*General LeMay succeeded me as Commanding General of the XXI on January 20, 1945.

199

abandonment of selective targeting. Moreover, the night mining, like the night urban bombing, could be carried out regardless of cloud cover at the target. It is quite clear I could have endorsed mining as an aspect of strategic bombardment against the Japanese transportation system rather than as an auxiliary aspect of the sea blockade. I probably could have persuaded General Arnold to stretch my target priorities as prescribed by the Joint Chiefs to include aerial mining when sufficient aircraft became available. I doubt if I could have, or should have, devoted most of the command's air power to this purpose in the initial phase of strategic attack against Japan, when first priority was prescribed as destruction of the Japanese aircraft industry.

In retrospect, the actual evolution of events was probably about right. The XXI Bomber Command did attain the "overriding intermediate objective of undermining Japanese aircraft production." It did preserve its identity and structure as a separate command even though operating in an area under Navy jurisdiction. And it did retain unity of effort while subjected to constant pressure to become subordinate to other commanders and staff agencies. These achievements might have been jeopardized or at least delayed if the XXI Bomber Command had initially devoted its capacity to aerial mining, and the independence of the XXI might have been compromised or lost.

The aerial mining campaign as pursued by General LeMay succeeded beyond anyone's expectation. Fleet Admiral Nimitz said, "The planning, operational, and technical execution of the Twentieth Air Force aircraft mining on a scale never before attained had accomplished phenomenal results and is a credit to all concerned." And as Dr. Sallagar stated in his *Lessons From an Aerial Mining Campaign*:

> The campaign was outstanding in many respects. More mines were laid in five months (over 12,000) than were dropped by all the other aircraft in the Pacific in more than two years (9,000). The "phenomenal results" mentioned by Admiral Nimitz included at least 70,000 (and possibly as much as 1,250,000) tons of Japanese shipping sunk or severely damaged. Perhaps more important, much of the surviving ship tonnage was bottled up in mined harbors for

prolonged periods while waiting for the mines to be cleared, which led to a virtual paralysis of Japan's essential maritime traffic.

We have gone somewhat ahead of the story. Yet, in view of the later undeniable success of the aerial mining campaign, I must explain my reluctance to begin an all-out campaign while I commanded the XXI Bomber Command.

Problems Faced by XXI Bomber Command

Our new equipment presented some technical problems affecting combat operations. I asked for three fixes which were attempted at Wright Field but did not materialize in time to be useful. They pertained to gunnery, weather penetration, and rescue at sea.

The gunnery equipment of the B–29 was new, formidable, and complex. Experience in operating without fighter escort in Europe had made defensive gunfire important. I had been instrumental in changing the top turret of the B–29 from a two-gun, .50–caliber pair to a set of four such guns, to meet the most dangerous of fighter attacks—those from the front. All the guns were remotely operated from sights placed in transparent sighting blisters. A master gunner operated from a master-gunner's position in a top blister from which all the guns except the two tail guns could be controlled and fired. The gunsights and controls were ingenious and sophisticated, but highly complex. The sight was swiveled by the left-hand grip control, both laterally and in height. The range of the approaching fighter was automatically fed into the sight computer by a right-hand grip control by which the gunner sought to keep an illuminated ring in the sight adjusted to the wingspan of the approaching fighter. Each hand had to work simultaneously with, but independently of, the other. To complicate the problem further, the messages fed into the computer were accepted in terms of "rate." The "rate of turn" of the controls established the velocity, rate of turn, and rate of approach of the target. If a gunner failed to manipulate his sight smoothly and moved with a series of jerks, these rapid jerks told the computer that the velocity of the target was accelerating or decelerating wildly.

I asked that a device be designed to determine range and rate of approach by radar and feed it directly into the sight computer. Such a device was available for the tail guns which had a somewhat limited field of fire. This would have relieved the gunner of at least half his burden. Actually, it would have provided far more relief than that. It certainly is far easier to do one thing at a time than to do two separate things simultaneously.

Another fix that I desired had to do with "stationkeeping" by radar. I worried about penetrating heavy weather fronts flying in formation. It was essential that the formations be able to reassemble easily after penetration of a weather front to furnish mutual protection. It was possible to use the APQ–13 bombing radar for this purpose to a limited degree, but I was not content about it. Finally, I asked for a floating transponder that could be tossed into the sea just as a damaged airplane "ditched." This would permit rescue aircraft to home on the transponder and quickly locate the position where the plane had gone down and, hopefully, where the crew would be rescued from their rubber rafts.

We had tactical problems as well as technical ones. In the early stages of operations, before we learned how to get the most from our engines, we were seriously constrained in terms of range. To save fuel, the first 1,000 miles or so were flown at low altitude. The climb to penetrating altitude was begun after the airplane had become lighter by the weight of the expended fuel.

General Arnold was understandably concerned about the large number of losses due to "ditchings" and failures to return for unknown reasons. I felt that losses must be expected in a highly risky wartime operation that gave promise of being decisive. Nevertheless, I undertook extensive measures to reduce them. The actual combat losses were not extreme, considering the nature of the operations and the desperate severity of the defenses. Even so, we could cut those due to inadequate maintenance and to equipment malfunction. We simply had to do everything within our power to overcome our deficiencies.

One measure, besides better maintenance and inspection, was lightening of the airplane by removing items that could be spared. A lighter aircraft had a much better chance of returning to base after battle damage or equipment failure. We stripped the plane itself of

1,900 pounds and removed one of the bomb-bay gas tanks for another 4,100, giving a total weight reduction of 6,000 pounds. Then, too, our operations were still confined to narrow deviations from the direct route to Tokyo and Nagoya. Mission after mission had to follow the same path. Our aircraft were therefore detected upon passing Iwo Jima (until its capture) and a few reporting ships. They gave warning in plenty of time for the Japanese defenses to concentrate at Tokyo or Nagoya.

The daily "command decision" whether to launch a mission the next day and against what target hinged upon the weather forecast more than any other factor. Our weather information came chiefly from a nightly B–29 flight to Japan. I had a meteorological officer who did a magnificent job under almost impossible conditions. His name was Col. James Seaver; I had known him in England. He knew perfectly well that my decision to "go" or to "stand down" depended directly upon his forecast. He also knew that his estimate was going to be better than mine, so he stated it without equivocation. He said what he thought would be the case, without hedging it with subjunctive clauses. Sometimes he was wrong, but more often he was right. I relied upon him heavily and was careful never to criticize when the weather forecast did not pan out.

The XXI Bomber Command had no special liaison unit (SLU) to receive Ultra information—a grievous omission. I cannot understand why. Group Captain Winterbotham in *Ultra Secret* drops the casual statement:

> In Brisbane (Australia) many of our main signals now came from Delhi, but radio blackouts were frequent. Sometimes signals came via the Australia Post Office cable, or even radio from Bletchley (England), and Japanese weather reports came up from Melbourne by teleprinter, so the SLU at Brisbane had a bit of a job sorting out what was going on.

What Colonel Seaver would have given for those Japanese weather reports! Weather over Japan was our most implacable and inscrutable enemy. Such reports received through Ultra were of great value in the strategic air war against Germany; they would have been priceless in the air war against Japan. It seems simply incredible that no one "in the know" recognized our need, especially for Japanese weather reports, and took steps to supply me and later General LeMay with an SLU.

Chapter VI

Other Operations

The first B–29 bomber commander was Brig. Gen. Kenneth B. Wolfe, who took the XX Bomber Command to India and China and initiated operations against Japan with Operation Matterhorn. The XX Bomber Command was formed at Marietta, Georgia, where the B–29s were being built. General Wolfe was designated to head that command in November 1943. A production genius and a first-class aeronautical engineer, he literally mothered the first phases of production and modification of the B–29. Some 2,000 changes were made in the engine alone.

The XX Bomber Command Headquarters later moved to Salina, Kansas. The Second Air Force supervised its training. The 58th Bombardment Wing, commanded by Brig. Gen. La Verne G. "Blondie" Saunders, was the first element to reach operational status, and the 73d Bombardment Wing under Brig. Gen. Emmett "Rosey" O'Donnell, Jr., was scheduled to follow. On arrival in India in preparation for operations from Calcutta and advanced bases in Chengtu, China, the XX Bomber Command came under the jurisdiction of Lt. Gen. Joseph W. Stilwell. He commanded all U.S. Army forces in the China-Burma-India Theater until activation of the Twentieth Air Force. First units of the XX Bomber Command arrived in that theater during April 1944. After the XX was established there, the command conducted a "shakedown" operation on June 5, 1944,

BOMBS BURST AT THE KAWASAKI AIRCRAFT PLANT—a strategic target located north of Tokyo. January 19, 1945.

against Bangkok from bases in India. On June 15 the XX launched a night attack from bases at Chengtu, China. The target was the Imperial Iron and Steel Works at Yawata on the Japanese home island of Kyushu.

Meanwhile, the B–29's mechanical and technical problems persisted. So in July 1944, General Arnold finally sent for the man in whom he had the most confidence, General Wolfe, who took over the Materiel Command with the primary mission of expediting production and improvements of the B–29. He was briefly succeeded at XX Bomber Command by General Saunders, and in turn Maj. Gen. Curtis E. LeMay replaced him on August 29. The original plans had earmarked LeMay for the XXI Bomber Command. However, recall of General Wolfe altered the plans, sending LeMay to head the XX Bomber Command and giving me command of the XXI Bomber Command, then in training in the Midwest.

When I first entered the Pacific Ocean Area, I was apprehensive about my command relationship. It was a Navy domain, dominated by strong-minded Navy commanders who could hardly be expected to welcome an intruder from the Army Air Forces who was independent of their operational control. But I got along well with the Navy commanders, due chiefly to the broad-minded support of Fleet Adm. Chester W. Nimitz, Commander in Chief of the Pacific Ocean Area, and the personal attitude of the Commander, Forward Area, Vice Adm. John H. Hoover whose flagship *Curtiss* was based at Saipan. I was uncomfortable in my relations with the senior AAF generals under Admiral Nimitz. They, quite understandably, resented this break in the chain of command. Lt. Gen. Millard F. Harmon was the senior AAF general in the Pacific Ocean Area and, under Admiral Nimitz, commanded all land-based aviation in that area—Army, Navy, and Marine Corps. He naturally wanted control of the XXI Bomber Command too. General Arnold had sought to smooth over the situation by appointing him Deputy Commanding General for Administration and Logistics, Twentieth Air Force. But General Harmon wanted full command, including operational control—or at least inclusion in the chain of command from Arnold to me. I had resisted this arrangement in Washington, when I was Chief of Staff of the Twentieth Air Force, and I continued to resist it. If the Twentieth was to exist as a unified strategic air force under the direct and unbroken command of General Arnold, and with a primary strategic mission, the chain of operational command from the Joint Chiefs of Staff through Arnold to the XXI Bomber Command had to be kept direct and uncluttered.*

Under General Harmon was another senior Army Air Forces officer, Maj. Gen. Willis H. Hale, who commanded our land-based air forces in the Forward Area. Whereas my relationship with General Harmon had been tolerably agreeable, if somewhat formal, that with Willis Hale deteriorated after a confrontation on Saipan. When the second air base built for the 73d Wing of the XXI Bomber Command on Saipan proved technically unsuitable for B–29 operations, I based the entire wing at Isley Field, Saipan. I agreed to turn the other base over to General Hale's units since it was suitable for operations by other types of aircraft. When I arrived on Saipan with the first B–29, I found a half-completed base and over a hundred of General Hale's airplanes on Isley Field. Several times I requested Hale to clear the field for my impending operations. He agreed to do so but failed to move his planes. Finally, in desperation, I forced a showdown; the situation had become intolerable and threatened to prevent our first strike. Admiral Hoover offered to clear up the matter with a direct order to General Hale. But I thought it would be better if two air officers settled their problem between them. Hale moved his aircraft, then went straight back to Washington to complain to General Arnold about my "arrogant attitude." General Arnold backed me up, but I suspect the incident did me no good.

Change of Command

About mid-January 1945, a delegation from General Arnold's office arrived at my headquarters at Guam. Brig. Gen. Lauris "Larry" Norstad, Twentieth Air Force Chief of Staff, bore a message from

---

*General Harmon respected but never really approved this arrangement. He was on his way back to Washington to try to have it changed when his airplane was lost without a trace in late February 1945.

Arnold: There was to be a major change in organization and command. Combat elements of the XX Bomber Command were to be transferred to the Marianas as soon as bases could be made available and operations from Chengtu could be discontinued. Though I had known of the plans for movement of the XX Bomber Command out of China, I was not aware of its imminence. The urgency stemmed in part from the insistence of my old friend Lt. Gen. Albert C. Wedemeyer, USA, who had replaced General Stilwell as the new commander of U.S. forces in the China-Burma Theater. Wedemeyer, strongly urged by General Chennault, requested that the B–29s be withdrawn from China as soon as possible. The XX was absorbing supply tonnage urgently required by the Fourteenth Air Force and other forces in China. The repeated requests were directed to the Joint Chiefs of Staff who gave them a sympathetic ear. General Arnold agreed.

There were other reasons for expediting the change. The XX Bomber Command was operating under numerous disadvantages. It expended about one-seventh of its flying hours in attacks against the enemy and absorbed the other six-sevenths in furnishing its own logistics, that is, transporting gasoline and bombs over the Hump from India to the forward bases in China. Furthermore, the China-based B–29s could not reach the most vital targets in Japan.

When General LeMay had taken over the XX Bomber Command in India, he quite independently arrived at the same decision that motivated me in retraining the 73d Bombardment Wing. He set about transitioning from area night bombing to daylight precision bombing from defensive formations. He also began lead crew training just as I had done in the Marianas. But his logistic problems were so severe that it was almost impossible to establish effective operations against Japan itself. The radius of action limited strikes to the southern island of Kyushu, Japan.

The XX Bomber Command, while headed by General Wolfe, had attacked the Imperial Iron and Steel Works at Yawata on Kyushu in a night raid on June 15, 1944. Only forty-seven of seventy-five B–29s arrived over the target, and damage was not extensive. Shortage of fuel at the advanced bases prevented the launching of another full-scale strike for several weeks. On July 7, a force of eighteen B–29s launched a small night raid against a number of targets in Japan, including Sasebo, Nagasaki, Omura, and Yawata. On July 29 the XX Bomber Command attacked the coke facilities at Anshan in Manchuria. Twentieth Air Force had directed a daylight precision attack with at least one hundred B–29s. In carrying out the operation, only sixty of the Superfortresses got over Anshan, and the effects were not satisfactory. The next operation was shifted to the oil refinery at Palembang, in the Netherlands East Indies, from advanced bases in Ceylon.

This attack, launched on August 10, 1944, entailed a 3,800–mile round trip. Results, unfortunately, were poor. On the same date, the XX Bomber Command sent a small force to attack the Nakajima engine works on Kyushu. The night attack was unsuccessful. B–29s struck Yawata in daylight on August 20. The losses from combat and operational causes were heavy: 14 out of 61 B–29s. Again, the outcome was disappointing. On August 29 the XX Bomber Command sent 108 B–29s against Anshan, under General LeMay's command and with his participation. This time there was considerable damage. The attack was repeated on September 26 in daylight using 12–plane formations, but cloud cover obscured the target. The logistic troubles grew so severe that the XX had to confine its operations mainly to targets outside Japan itself. Among them were: Okayama aircraft assembly plant on Formosa, October 14 and 16; Einansho Airdrome, Formosa, October 17; Omura aircraft factory, Kyushu, October 25; Rangoon, Burma, marshaling yards, November 3; Singapore Naval Base, November 5; Omura aircraft factory, November 11 (Nanking, China, was actually attacked because of weather at the primary target); and Omura on November 21, in daylight. The overall effectiveness was disappointing, caused by an intolerable logistic situation, unfavorable weather, and early training problems with a new and untried airplane.

On December 18 the XX Bomber Command conducted an operation that was significant from several points of view. Prompted by General Chennault, General Wedemeyer directed the XX to attack a theater target: the port facilities at Hankow, China. General LeMay objected, citing his command relationship as a part of the Twentieth Air Force. General Wedemeyer then appealed to the Joint Chiefs of Staff, citing the provision for emergency use of the Twentieth Air Force by the theater commander as a matter of urgency. The urgency existed all right. The Japanese were launching a major but unsuccessful drive toward the B–29 base areas. The Joint Chiefs agreed, and General LeMay performed the mission, dropping incendiaries from medium altitude. Eighty-four B–29s dropped more than 500 tons of incendiaries on Hankow, setting huge fires that burned for 3 days. General Chennault, who urged the use of incendiaries against the city, described the attack as "the first mass fire-bomb raid" by the B–29s and contended it was the precursor of the massive urban incendiary attacks against Japanese cities.

By year's end, neither the XX nor the XXI Bomber Command had shown real results or approached the destructive power inherent in the B–29. But in considering the future, there was a vast difference between the XX in China and the XXI in the Mariana Islands. The XX could never hope to reach true effectiveness, so long as it had to fly all its fuel, bombs, and supplies over the Hump from India. The XXI had enormous potential. Given time to perfect its tactical performance and the growing might of the mounting accretions of new wings, it held tremendous portent for the future. I believe that portent could have been attained either through selective targeting or incendiary urban destruction, if given time for training in bombing intelligence collection and for the arrival in quantity of APQ–7 radar bombing equipment.

Night incendiary attacks on Japanese industrial areas in 1945 were contemplated in the original plans for deploying the XXI Bomber Command. However, such operations were to be undertaken solely as a last resort, and only if precision bombing proved unfeasible or failed to do the job. And the night attacks were initially scheduled to take place after selected bombing had knocked out the Japanese aircraft and engine factories and had destroyed the vital industrial targets. The complication of conducting selective bombing in daylight over targets obscured by cloud cover was expected, and the greatly improved radar bombsight (AN/APQ–7) was rushed to completion. It was hoped it would permit all-weather bombing of selected targets (day or night). Since the sights were not instantly available, their use would take time. One of the XXI's wings, the 315th, had been equipped with this new bombsight, allowing more accurate day or night bombing in spite of cloud cover. The rest of the XXI's units used the less efficient AN/APQ–13, and they were partially trained for radar bombing of those area targets that rendered a good radar return.

Time, however, was not on the side of the XXI's Commander. General Arnold wanted and demanded measurable results at once. His judgment was heavily influenced by bomb tonnage instead of target destruction. Actually, many more tons of bombs could be dropped at night using radar bombing than in daylight. By day the force had to fly in formation and operate at high altitude to defend itself against Japanese fighters. These strictures reduced the bombload. Moreover, the rate of opportunity for daylight operations was heavily restricted by weather over the targets, which was very hard to forecast. Bad weather was the rule, and cloud obstruction was about the only weather feature that could be anticipated with any degree of assurance. At the start of the campaign, target locations were hard to determine and radar maps had not yet been prepared. Hence, the radar bombing was not adequate to put the bombs on selected industrial and economic targets.

In all fairness to General Arnold, he cannot be blamed for his impatience and his inclination to measure strategic air attacks in terms of tonnage and sorties. He was under constant pressure and criticism from his associates on the Joint Chiefs of Staff and from higher authority to explain what his Twentieth Air Force was accomplishing. It is exceedingly difficult to measure and evaluate the results of selective target bombing; in fact, we were unable to assess the real effectiveness of such operations both in Germany and Japan until after the war. To be sure, it is possible to report the destruction of a factory, but it is hard to estimate that destruction in terms of depletion of enemy industrial support for a specific set of economic or military needs. There is always the chance the enemy has found some substitute method of meeting those needs. It took the tremendous efforts of the U.S. Strategic Bombing Survey immediately after the war to evaluate those effects in Europe and in Japan. On the whole, these survey reports showed that selective targeting was far more destructive than we thought at the time of attack.

On the other hand, statistics of tons of bombs dropped and of sorties flown are easily compiled, seem factual and specific, and are impressive. Photographs of burned-out cities also speak for themselves. And "time" had become an obsessive compulsion—the time for invasion of Japan. Washington placed great stress on a quick end to the war, emphasizing that this carnage must not go on a single week longer than necessary to achieve victory. There were obvious weaknesses in this thought. The "carnage" would be enormously increased by an invasion. Casualties on both sides would be immense. Was it worth it? Was time itself all that important? Or were the casualties the more momentous consideration, once victory was assured? Some of this fixation on time mirrored the military habit of thought. And some of it doubtlessly stemmed from restless impatience among the American people and a desire to get this war over with and resume normal living.

The overriding priority of targets assigned to the XXI Bomber Command called for destruction or neutralization of the Japanese aircraft engine and airframe factories. One of the ironies of war is that in the early months of its operations the XXI actually did accomplish this mission, though the results were not then apparent. Its performance was surprisingly good, but unfortunately we could not prove it until after the war. I am sure General Arnold did not understand what the XXI Bomber Command had gone through or had achieved.

Since the XX Bomber Command was to be discontinued from Chinese bases, Arnold wanted to change the command and deployment setup at once. The proposed change appealed to him as a sensible step to greatly enhance B-29 performance, as well as to relieve the pressure from General Wedemeyer. The China Theater Commander was vigorously protesting to the Joint Chiefs that part of the Air Transport Command Hump tonnage was going to the XX at a time when he and the Fourteenth Air Force needed it all.

General LeMay, now senior to me, would take over the XXI Bomber Command within the month. I was offered the XX Bomber

Command scheduled for transfer to the Marianas; thereafter, I could become Vice Commander under LeMay. I did not wish to accept. I knew and respected LeMay as an able and competent bomber commander. I did not think he needed another bomber commander as deputy. I returned to the United States on January 20, 1945.

I was fortunate in having gifted and able associates in the Twentieth Air Force. Brig. Gen. Roger M. Ramey, my deputy, was not just a fine military associate but a fine friend. There were others who filled this dual role, among them being Col. Cecil E. Combs, Col. John B. Montgomery, and Comdr. George C. McGhee, USN. Such associations and friendships are a priceless boon that helps compensate for the pains and disappointments of wartime duty. Colonel Combs, who had been my Chief of Combat Operations in Washington, became Deputy Commander of the 58th Bombardment Wing when it arrived at Tinian. On my urgent recommendation, Colonel Montgomery, my Chief of Staff of the XXI Bomber Command, served General LeMay in an important capacity. Montgomery was a fine planner and manager, an expert pilot and navigator, and one of the best bombardiers in the Army Air Forces. Monty and I flew practice bomb runs against the Japanese-occupied island of Rota, to improve my understanding of the bombing technique and its problems. I was glad it was I who made out Monty's efficiency report on bombing, not the other way around.

Commander McGhee, a reservist, was my Navy Liaison Officer. The Navy repeatedly offered to replace him with senior, more experienced, regular professionals, but I resisted all offers. I knew I had an exceptional man. George was a competent Navy officer with interests and knowledge that covered a very broad range. I found his judgment invaluable in discussions of many facets of our problem in the Pacific. His responses and observations were stimulating and perceptive. He was that priceless combination—a practical intellectual. After the war, George McGhee became a member of the State Department Policy Planning Council and later Ambassador to the Federal Republic of Germany.

There was another military associate for whose friendship I am especially grateful. When I assumed command of the XXI Bomber

Command I started searching for an aide. I set forth my specifications to the Chief of Personnel. I said I wanted a young first lieutenant or captain who was intelligent, alert, hardworking, good-humored, tolerant, courteous, loyal, and trustworthy. Besides, he should be a top-notch four-engine airplane pilot with enough guts to keep his hands off the controls when I was flying. Personnel produced 2d Lt. Ray L. Milne, who filled every one of those specifications. He was a perfect aide so far as I was concerned, and he became a cherished friend.

I made my decision to resist remaining with the XXI Bomber Command as Vice Commander under the stress of surprise and emotion. But I still think it was the proper step. I had every confidence in General LeMay. He had been the outstanding group commander when I headed the 1st Bombardment Wing in the early and crucial days of the Eighth Air Force. When I returned from England to the United States to be the Air Staff member of the Joint Plans Committee of the Joint Chiefs of Staff, LeMay stayed on, was promoted, and became senior to me. I knew him well enough to realize he needed no second string to his bow. He did not need a second in command, and I would have been unhappy as a figurehead. Furthermore, it is not a good thing to replace a commander and leave him in a subordinate position in his own outfit.

The first three months for the B–29s in the Marianas helped lay the groundwork for the much larger bombing offensive against Japan during 1945. If it is conceded that initial periods are likely to be the most difficult ones, then that of the XXI Bomber Command was marked with reasonable success. It can not be denied, however, that such success was accompanied by a full measure of good fortune. It might so easily have been a period of disaster, seeing that our first operations were from uncompleted bases. If our aircraft had returned to find our single, partially completed runway blocked by a crippled B–29 (or the base closed by one of those intense tropical storms that came our way), the whole force could have been lost. All in all, I think it was a good beginning. Its predominant pattern was woven on the theme of selective target destruction.

215

Operations

In November 1944, the Joint Chiefs of Staff issued a new target priority list setting forth target systems for the XXI Bomber Command in this priority: (1) Japanese aircraft industry, (2) Japanese industrial areas, and (3) Japanese shipping. Our schedule of operations—all against aircraft and engine factories, except shakedown missions against Iwo Jima—were as follows:

Tokyo	November	24*
Iwo Jima	December	7
Nagoya	December	13 & 18
Iwo Jima	December	24
Tokyo	December	27
Nagoya	January	5
Tokyo	January	9
Nagoya	January	14
Akashi	January	21

Thirteen missions were flown in fifty-six days, or an average of one every four and one-half days, counting Iwo Jima.

Seven of the ten primary targets prescribed by the Joint Chiefs of Staff were specific aircraft and engine factories. Then an urban area system was prescribed, followed by "shipping." After these three top priorities were three secondary target systems: coke, steel, and oil. It is surprising that these vital selective target systems should have been assigned a priority below Japanese urban industrial areas.

When I left Washington as Chief of Staff of the Twentieth Air Force, a change in strategic policy set in. The policy I had espoused, and which I believe was generally accepted, was in this vein:

a. *Strategic Objective*: To force Japan to acknowledge defeat and to accept our terms of surrender.

b. *Primary Air Strategy*: To achieve the strategic objective by applying strategic air power. More specifically:

(1) To destroy the effectiveness of the Japanese Air Force to the degree

---

*Three times more by December 3; an initial rate of four missions in ten days.

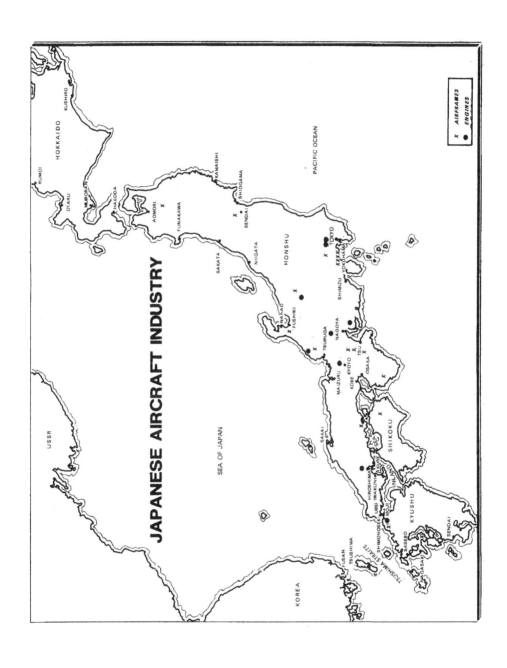

JAPANESE AIRCRAFT INDUSTRY

USSR

KOREA

SEA OF JAPAN

HOKKAIDO

KUSHIRO

RUMOI

OTARU

MURORAN

HAKODA

AOMORI

FUNAKAWA

SAKATA

NIIGATA

NANAO

FUSHIKI

TSURUGA

SAKAI

MAIZURU

KOBE

KYOTO

OSAKA

TSU

NAGOYA

SHIMIZU

YOKOHAMA

TOKYO

HONSHU

SENDAI

SHIOGAMA

KAMAISHI

PACIFIC OCEAN

SHIKOKU

HIROSHIMA

IWAKUNI

KURE

UBE

SHIMONOSEKI

MOJI

INLAND SEA

SASEBO

NAGASAKI

KYUSHU

SENDAI

TSUSHIMA STRAITS

TSUSHIMA

FUSAN

x AIRFRAMES
● ENGINES

where it should be incapable of offering a serious threat to our own bases and forces, or of offering effective hindrance to our strategic air offensive. To approach this objective by destroying Japanese sources of air power, using selective targeting and precision bombing.

(2) Through precision bombing, to destroy the war-making industrial structure of Japan by demolishing selected targets and systems vital to the war effort.

(3) Again, through precision bombing of selected targets, to destroy and undermine the social and economic structure of the Japanese state, by selection and annihilation of essential structures and systems indispensable to the organic functioning of the Japanese nation.

(4) To prepare for and, if necessary, to carry out urban incendiary attacks as a last resort.

c. *Secondary Air Strategy*: To support a surface invasion of the Japanese home islands if the air offensive failed to achieve its purpose.

I was in full agreement with this emphasis on selective targeting and precision bombing. I had been one of the authors of this policy at the Air Corps Tactical School. I had seen it work well in Europe and had devised the plans for it in that theater. I believed in it. But, after I left Washington to prepare and direct the XXI Bomber Command to carry out this strategic concept, a switch in strategic interest became apparent. In the communications I received from Washington, there was repeated reference to and stress upon incendiary urban attack. I do not know if this change was brought about by General Norstad, General Arnold, or the Committee of Operations Analysts.

Perhaps it was General Arnold. Unknown to me, Arnold harbored a lively interest in incendiary urban attack. On April 5, 1944, he wrote General Spaatz about the proposed U.S. Strategic Bombing Survey and included these remarks: "Of particular interest to me would be some idea as to the most effective mixture of high explosives and incendiaries against heavily built-up areas." At any rate, the Committee of Operations Analysts gave incendiary urban attacks a high priority.

On December 18, the day of our first reasonably successful attack on the aircraft facilities at Nagoya, I received a directive to launch a full-scale incendiary attack on Nagoya. This was a blow. I had been sweating blood in my efforts to make the 73d Wing a respectable precision bombing outfit, with very moderate success. We were just beginning to overcome the predilection for night area bombing, and we were just starting to show some improvement in bombing accuracy, both visual and radar. Now we were ordered to reverse our painfully achieved progress in accuracy and turn to area bombing. It was no good trying to attain real accuracy with the incendiaries. Their imprecise ballistic characteristic precluded any accuracy in delivery even if the sighting performance should be perfect.

Though in General Arnold's name, the directive had been signed by General Norstad. I protested directly to Arnold. I pointed out I had "with great difficulty implanted the principle that our mission is the destruction of primary targets by sustained attacks using precision bombing methods both visual and radar." I did not contend we had achieved an acceptable measure of success in this attempt, but I did assert that diversions from our determined efforts would impede a progress that was beginning to be encouraging for the future. General Norstad replied for General Arnold that the aircraft industry still had overriding priority and the fire raid was "simply a special requirement resulting from the necessity of future planning."

Future planning? Was the switch to area urban bombing already under way? The change to area urban incendiary attack, when it finally came, can not be laid directly at General LeMay's door. Its initial support came from Twentieth Air Force Headquarters. And it had begun with the selection of urban targets, after a revised report on Far East economic objectives was written and issued in October 1944 by the Committee of Operations Analysts. By that time, I had departed Washington for Saipan and was no longer in a position to influence strategic target selection. The report listed these cities as vital Japanese urban industrial areas to be considered for incendiary attack: Tokyo, Yokohama, Nagoya, Kobe, Kawasaki, and Osaka.

The Committee of Operations Analysts contended that the air offensive against Japanese urban areas would cut deeply into Japanese war production by (1) direct physical damage to major and feeder plants, (2) destruction of finished items and materials in process, (3) disruption of internal transportation and services, and (4) reduction of labor efficiency. Cities were specified as preferred targets, superseding economic and industrial systems. This list showed a sharp departure from earlier strategy. The selected industrial "primary targets" still contained aircraft factories. But iron and steel (to be disrupted by attacking coke ovens) and oil (the petroleum industry) were all dropped to "secondary targets," below urban areas. Shipping (presumably to include aerial mining) remained a top priority as it had been in the Committee of Operations Analysts' recommendation a year before. However, antifriction bearings and the electronics industry had been dropped, for reasons that I do not to this day understand. And the electric power and rail transportation systems had not been revived from their first rejection.

Since I had not yet accomplished my first-priority task—destruction of Japanese aircraft and engine plants—I was not immediately affected by this change. I continued to pursue selective bombing.

Refining Pacific Strategy

On December 1, 1944, the Joint Chiefs of Staff issued a revised memorandum describing U.S. Pacific strategy. It read:

> The United States Joint Chiefs of Staff have adopted the following as a basis for planning in the war against Japan. The concept of operations for the main effort in the Pacific is:
>
> A. Following the Okinawa operations to seize additional positions to intensify the blockade and air bombardment of Japan in order to create a situation favorable to:
>
> B. An assault on Kyushu (Island)—in order to establish a tactical situation favorable to:
>
> C. The decisive invasion of the industrial heart of Japan through the Tokyo Plain.

General Marshall was generally acknowledged to be the author and proponent of this strategy.

Dr. Sallagar reviewed the U.S. Pacific strategy in *Lessons from an Aerial Bombing Campaign.* He discovered that:

> To the Army, the JCS endorsement of naval blockade and strategic

bombardment merely meant that the Navy and the Air Force should be allowed to apply their favorite methods of warfare, provided that these preliminary operations were used to soften up the enemy in preparation for the invasion and did not interfere with the major objective.

But my chief aim as Commanding General, XXI Bomber Command, was unchanged. That is, the "intermediate objective of overriding priority" was still the Japanese aircraft industry. Moreover, the overall statement of military strategy for the strategic air war did not specifically countermand the initial statement of the strategic air objective—to destroy Japan's capability to support the war.

In January 1945, we planned a variation from the steady stream of air attacks on factories in the Tokyo-Nagoya area. The Kawasaki Aircraft Industries Co., Ltd., was the third largest aircraft production company in Japan. It had a new engine and airframe complex at Akashi, about 12 miles west of Kobe and around 100 miles west of Nagoya. Besides being the biggest facility of the company, Akashi was also the headquarters of the Kawasaki engine division. There was another engine plant at nearby Futami, approximately 8 miles west of Akashi, and one at Takatsuki (about halfway between Kyoto and Akashi), nearly 20 miles from Akashi. Akashi was, however, the key installation in the engine complex. There was an additional Kawasaki airframe plant at Kagamigahara (Gifu), just north of Nagoya. The Akashi and Futami plants were on the coast of Harimanada, an arm of the Inland Sea, and adjacent to prominent landmarks that showed up well on radar. The targets, the plants of the Akashi engine and airframe facility, were about 2 miles from the town of Akashi. The engine plant occupied 1,287,700 square feet of productive floorspace, and the adjacent airframe plant occupied 1,047,000 square feet. The total target area was slightly over 3,300,000 square feet.

Kawasaki was one of the oldest and most experienced engine manufacturers in Japan. It started under French license in 1919, progressed through various German licenses for in-line engines, and culminated in the Daimler-Benz design designated Ha–60 (Model 22) of 1,150 horsepower, the Ha–40 of 1,175 horsepower, and the Ha–60 (Model 33) of 1,350 horsepower (purchased in 1937). These were used

BRIG. GEN. HANSELL AND HIS XXI BOMBER COM-
MAND STAFF plan a mission against Tokyo. Staff members
include: (clockwise from left) Col. John B. Montgomery, General
Hansell, Col. Ralph B. Garretson, Maj. D. P. Hatch, Lt. Col.
Alan F. Adams, Col. Willard R. Shephard, Col. Seth S. Terry,
Col. Albert T. Wilson, Jr., and Lt. Col. James T. Seaver.

B-29 ATTACKS INFLICTED HEAVY DAMAGE on the
Kawasaki aircraft factories in January 1945.

in Tony fighters which resembled the German Me–109. The Tony entered operational service in 1943 and at one time was the most potent of the Japanese army's fighters. Its service ceiling was given at 32,800 feet.

Akashi engine works also turned out Nakajima-designed air-cooled radial engines, the Ha–35 (Model 22) and the Ha–35 (Model 32), rated at 1,100 and 1,150 horsepower respectively. They were used in Oscar fighters. Akashi likewise produced a Mitsubishi-designed radial of 1,970 horsepower, the Ha–45 (Model 21) used principally in the army's Frank fighters, Ki–84–1a, thought by many to be the best Japanese fighter built in quantity during World War II. Bearing a resemblance to our P–47, it was smaller and much lighter. Its service ceiling was given at 34,450 feet.

The Akashi airframe plant made Nick, a twin-engined fighter with day or night versions. A two-seater for defense against the B–29, its service ceiling was put at 32,800 feet. The plant also assembled Randy, a twin-engined, two-slot, attack fighter much like Nick but with better performance. In both its main plants, between 1941 and the end of the war, Kawasaki put together 8,269 airframes. Overall, that company completed 10,274 engines during January 1941–August 1945. Kawasaki accounted for 12 percent of the combat engines manufactured in 1944 (the industry's peak year) and 17 percent of the combat airframes. All in all, the Akashi complex presented a lucrative precision target.

The mission of January 19, 1945, against the Akashi works contained a diversionary ruse and a tactical variation. The 73d Wing went up the well-beaten path to Nagoya, but just as it approached the coast of Honshu, the force split. Three aircraft of the lead squadron continued toward Nagoya and bombed Hamamatsu, southeast of Nagoya, at high altitude—35,000 feet. It dispensed "rope" to obscure enemy radar screens and to impart the belief the main force was bound for Nagoya. The rest of the force (56 B–29s) turned sharply to the left and approached Akashi. The axis of attack was selected to optimize radar bombing of the target should it be covered with clouds. Bombing altitude was dropped to 25,000/27,400 feet, about 5,000 feet below previous levels. This decision was made to improve bombing accuracy.

222

It diminished the problem caused by very high winds and extreme turbulence encountered above 30,000 feet and cut down on errors that tended to be proportional to bombing height. The lower levels entailed a calculated risk in terms of fighter opposition. I relied on the ruse to deflect most of the enemy aircraft—which it did. And I made the first move in a planned schedule of reducing altitude by successive steps to enhance bombing. This was based upon the discovery that Japanese fighter attacks, while bitter and reckless, were not as deadly against the B–29s as German fighters had been against B–17s and B–24s. I had intended to press this step-by-step lowering of altitude to sharpen bombing accuracy, until we reached a level where further reduction incurred too many losses from enemy fighters.

The January 19 mission was a magnificent success. The bombs were dropped between 1450 and 1524 in clear weather. A total of 610 500–pound bombs were dispensed on the primary targets; 275 (45 percent) hit within the plant areas, measuring roughly 1,200 feet by 4,000 feet for the engine facility and 900 feet by 2,400 feet for the airframe one. Every important building in the engine and airframe complex was hit. Nearly two-thirds of the bombs struck within the engine works. Production in both facilities dropped 90 percent and never recovered. Eleven Japanese fighters attacked, the bombers claiming 4 shot down. No B–29s were lost. The mission has been depicted as one of the most perfect examples of selective bombing in the entire war. It was among the best of which I had personal knowledge. An important side effect of the mission was to accelerate the dispersion of the aircraft industry—a drastic move from which it failed to recoup.

The mission was, in my opinion, of great significance, the selected target being virtually destroyed. But of far more consequence in the long run, the bombing accuracy showed substantial improvement and the bomb pattern was well concentrated. The analysis of bombing accuracy by the 73d Wing Intelligence Section revealed that 46 percent of the bombs actually released at the primary target fell within 1,000 feet of the aiming point, giving a circular error probable of 1,030 feet. Nevertheless this analysis, based on bomb craters identified in reconnaissance photographs, did not account for all the bombs that were carried to the target area. A damage report prepared by the U.S. Strategic Bombing Survey after the war painted a less favorable picture. Forty-five percent of the bombs landed in the principal target area, which exceeded 1,000 feet in radius.

As a broad approximation, the target area was closely equivalent to that within a circle of 1,490 feet radius, and 45 percent hits within a circle of that area gives a CEP of about 1,600 feet. This is not a demonstration of good bombing accuracy from 26,000 feet by the 73d Wing. Still, it was a marked improvement when compared with earlier strikes, and the bombing pattern showed a sufficient close concentration to destroy all elements of the target. Further training produced an average circular error probable of 1,250 feet, based on all bombers that did not abort for mechanical reasons.

To be sure, the visibility was excellent and local fighter opposition was minimal due to the successful ruse. Even so, the XXI Bomber Command had every reason to be elated. The intensive training program was paying off. It was clear to all, especially to the combat crews, that the XXI could destroy selected targets when weather conditions permitted visual bombing. It was an immense first step. The next would be the achievement of acceptable accuracy in radar bombing of selected targets. That, too, was on the way to attainment later in the war. This was the last mission that I laid on as Commanding General, XXI Bomber Command.

Since that time, I have assessed the situation in terms of the success of selected strategic bombardment in regard to the Japanese aircraft industry and war production industries. Using the U.S. Strategic Bombing Survey, the extensive postwar evaluation of the air war against Japan, I came to the conclusions set forth below.

The Japanese aircraft industry did comprise a selected strategic target system. Initial operations against the Japanese aircraft and engine factories were far more destructive that I judged them to be at the time. I was highly critical of our bombing accuracy. Nonetheless, that bombing was so devastating that the Japanese believed their industry doomed. They took the drastic countermeasure of dismantling their aircraft engine and airframe industry, dispersing it, and protecting it underground. The combined result of our destructive bombing and the precipitate Japanese dispersal effectively realized the purpose of the strategic air offensive against the sources of production and supply of Japanese aircraft. Japanese aircraft production never recovered. As Dr. Robert Frank Futrell, Air Force historian, observed in his *Ideas, Concepts, Doctrine: A History of Basic Thinking in the United States Air Force, 1907–1964*:

> Actually the B–29 attacks against the Japanese aircraft factories proved to be more effective than was realized. The U.S. Strategic Bombing Survey would discover that the damages caused by the B–29's were enough to convince the Japanese of a need to disperse their aircraft plants. The destruction inflicted, plus the confusion resulting from frantic dispersal efforts, reduced the pre-attack capacity of the aircraft engine plants by 75 percent, of airframe plants by 60 percent, and of electronic and communications equipment plants by 70 percent.

Japanese combat aircraft production peaked in 1944, before the B–29 attacks commenced in late November. Output for the year was 21,058, an increase of 662 percent from the 3,180 built in 1941. There were 9 producing companies. dominated by:

	Percent
Nakajima	37.1
Mitsubishi	23.0
Kawasaki	14.9

followed by:

	Percent
Aichi	6.9
Tachikawa	6.0
Total	87.9
Others	12.1
Grand Total	100.0

The primary and vital airframe and engine facilities were concentrated in the central manufacturing districts of these areas: Tokyo-Kawasaki-Yokohama; Nagoya; and Osaka-Kobe.

As shown in the chart, the drastic drop in actual aircraft

225

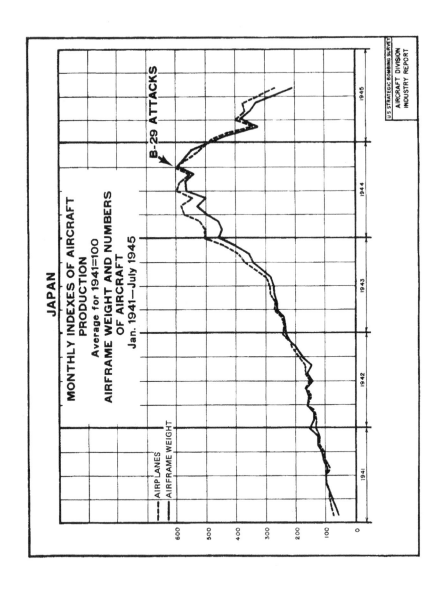

JAPAN

MONTHLY INDEXES OF AIRCRAFT
PRODUCTION
Average for 1941=100
AIRFRAME WEIGHT AND NUMBERS
OF AIRCRAFT
Jan. 1941—July 1945

B-29 ATTACKS

AIRPLANES
AIRFRAME WEIGHT

600
500
400
300
200
100
0

1941   1942   1943   1944   1945

U.S. STRATEGIC BOMBING SURVEY
AIRCRAFT DIVISION
INDUSTRY REPORT

production began in the third quarter of 1944. This reflects the air attacks on the Japanese aircraft industry by the XXI Bomber Command.

Later Operations

When General LeMay assumed command of the XXI Bomber Command, he "stood down" the groups briefly. He retained my training program and improved the Lead Crew School. He focused on the maintenance effort, keeping on my A–4, Col. Clarence S. Irvine, who had worked wonders with this terribly difficult problem. After loss of the depot at Guam, Colonel Irvine needed to improvise a maintenance system based on the depot at Sacramento, 8,000 miles away. He set up an air transport system of his own, and I was careful not to ask where he got the transport aircraft or the authority to use them. In addition, he set up a streamlined maintenance organization in the 73d Wing by consolidating the resources of the combat and service groups.

General LeMay retained most of my tactical methods, including the airplane formations. This was hardly surprising since we had worked together in the Eighth Air Force. The capture of Iwo Jima by the Marines in February 1945 (an operation advocated by the Twentieth Air Force in May 1944) provided an advanced air base that was a boon to the bomber offensive. The air base was of enormous significance from the standpoint of morale, the recovery of crippled aircraft, and the improvement of operations in general. Damaged B–29s returning from raids could land at Iwo Jima, and it served as a fighter base from which escort fighters could support the Superfortresses or make strafing and bombing attacks on their own. Finally, the capture of Iwo Jima removed the Japanese early-warning station that had been giving 2– to 3–hour warning to Japanese defenders. From March 4, 1945—when the first crippled B–29 touched down there—to the end of the war, 2,241 B–29s landed at Iwo Jima. Otherwise many of these would have been lost. Iwo Jima became the base of the VII Fighter Command.

For about six weeks, General LeMay carried forward the

operations I had started—with almost identical results. It was apparent our preferred strategy (destruction of selected targets through precision optical bombing) could not be sustained in the face of the almost continuous cloud cover over Japan. Furthermore, the APQ-7 radar was still unavailable. General Norstad paid LeMay a visit at the end of six weeks, bringing the expected news that General Arnold was far from satisfied with performance. The factor of time was taking on a new insistence. The invasion of the Japanese home islands—whose necessity had become an obsession with the Army planners—had been agreed upon. If air power was to end the war without a massive bloodletting on the ground, its application could not be delayed. A drastic reappraisal was in order. LeMay made it.

The cities of Japan were vital to the ongoing war effort. Small factories were extremely vulnerable to incendiary attack. Although the first priority objective (destruction of Japan's aircraft industry) had not been fully attained, it had been approximated. Night attack of Japanese cities with incendiaries and radar bombing with the APQ-13 could be conducted on a consistent schedule, regardless of the weather. Japanese air defenses against night or all-weather assaults were minimal or nonexistent. Since it would not be necessary to operate in formation or at high altitude, bombloads could be much greater (up to 20,000 pounds per aircraft).

LeMay decided to switch from chief reliance on daylight precision bombing of selected targets to night incendiary attacks of Japanese cities. The first incendiary attacks against six of Japan's greatest cities were very effective and most impressive. The tonnage of bombs dispensed was extremely high, losses were very low, the rate and frequency of operations were unconstrained by poor weather, and the devastation of urban and industrial areas was startling. This new type of operations, attacking at low and medium altitudes at night, represented a superb tactical and strategic decision, and a most courageous and fitting one. Though it was suitable to the specific situation and circumstances, it was not necessarily appropriate to all requirements for the future. General LeMay recognized this. He went on using selected targeting whenever the weather and his equipment permitted.

These operations induced interesting reactions. The Joint Target Group of the Joint Chiefs of Staff seized upon the new tactic with enthusiasm. As depicted in Craven and Cate's *The Army Air Forces in World War II*:

> The Joint Target Group, after studying reports of the blitz, concluded that there were no strategic bottlenecks in the Japanese industrial and economic systems except aircraft engine plants, but that the enemy's industry as a whole was vulnerable through incendiary attacks.

Set up in the Joint Chiefs of Staff organization to recommend Twentieth Air Force targets, the Joint Target Group began functioning in December 1944. The judgment on its part that "there were no strategic bottlenecks in the Japanese industrial and economic systems except aircraft engine plants" was wholly unwarranted, as intelligence studies had shown and the postwar Bombing Survey was later to prove. The Joint Target Group simply embraced a new tactic that was easier to perform and to measure.

In order of priority, the Joint Target Group listed twenty-two of the most vital Japanese cities from the standpoint of the important industries they contained. Based on these recommendations, the Twentieth Air Force on April 3 issued a new target directive. The leading aircraft engine manufacturers, Nakajima-Musashi in Tokyo and the Mitsubishi at Nagoya, were given top priority. Both were selected targets. Then the directive listed six priority urban areas: Tokyo, Kawasaki, Nagoya, and Osaka Urban Areas 1, 2, and 3. Again quoting Craven and Cate:

> The Joint Target Group based its recommendations on the assumption that the principal function of air attack was to pave the way for an invasion of the home islands. . . . But after studying the results of the March fire raids, LeMay came to the conclusion that with proper logistic support air power alone could force the Japanese to surrender—a view shared privately by some members of Arnold's staff.

Thus, one outcome of the first urban incendiary attacks was an

THREE LEADERS OF THE XXI BOMBER COMMAND: Maj. Gen. Curtis E. LeMay (left), Brig. Gen. Hansell, and Brig. Gen. Roger M. Ramey, Deputy Commander. Saipan, January 1945.

ORDNANCE MEN ON SAIPAN IS-LAND load B-29 with incendiary clusters. Fire raids on Japanese cities began in February 1945.

endorsement of this method to the near exclusion of selective targeting. There was also another reaction. Granting the obvious tactical advantages to single-plane night operations at relatively low altitudes, did it follow that selective targeting should be abandoned? Was it possible to apply these same tactics to selective precision targets?

General LeMay was ordered to find out, and he applied himself to the question with his customary zeal. There was every reason to believe he would have welcomed an effective tactic to destroy selective targets as well as urban areas. Even so, the bombing equipment on hand was of limited capability, and his crews were ill-trained in this technique. LeMay concluded that the APQ–13 radar was inadequate for precision bombing. This was almost certainly true, in the absence of good-quality radar maps and selected offset aiming points affording good radar returns. He chose to adopt and adapt the RAF night bombing technique that, late in the European war, had yielded surprisingly accurate bombing results. He ran four good-sized experimental missions.

On March 24, 1945, there were 251 planes of the 73d, 313th, and 314th Wings dispatched against the Mitsubishi plant at Nagoya. The RAF pathfinder technique was employed. Ten minutes before bombing time, 10 B–29s lighted the engine works area with M–26 flares. Five minutes later, another 10 Superfortresses dropped M–17 incendiary clusters to start marker fires. The main force then attacked with 500–pound, general purpose bombs—sighting visually with the optical sights on the fires started by the pathfinders. Nagoya, however, was obscured with clouds. Though 1,533 tons of bombs were dropped, the results were negligible.

On March 30 the 314th Wing sent a small force to bomb the same target, once more using pathfinder tactics. The bombers missed completely, again applying visual sighting with the Norden optical sight. On April 1 the 73d Wing dispatched 121 aircraft to strike Nakajima-Musashi. Of the 1,019 tons of bomb dispensed, there were just 4 hits. On the 3d of April, 3 attacks were conducted consisting of 1 wing each attacking Mitsubishi's Shizuoka engine plant, Nakajima's

Koizumi assembly plant, and the Tachikawa engine plant. Damage in each instance was slight.

The command was simply not equipped or sufficiently trained for night precision bombing. Specifically, it needed target marker bombs, such as the 1,000–pounders used by the RAF, and reflex optic bombsights. Lacking these, General LeMay abandoned the experiment at the time. However, with the arrival in May of the 315th Wing, equipped with the APQ–7 radar bombing equipment, he tried again with results that were satisfactory indeed, as described later.

When I commanded the XXI Bomber Command, I had hoped to use aircraft equipped with the APQ–7 as lead aircraft. This would have enabled the entire force to bomb in daylight in squadron formations through the undercast cloud cover. And it would have let individual aircraft fitted with the APQ–7 bomb at night. But arrival of the 315th Wing had been delayed, and there was slight chance to test this tactic. Interest in the continued application of selective targeting, and the directive to try it, may well have come from Maj. Gen. Laurence S. Kuter, General Arnold's Assistant Chief of Staff for Plans.

Methodically, General LeMay proceeded to destroy the urban industrial areas that had been prescribed for him. But he did not lose interest in selective targeting, and attacked Japanese aircraft and engine plants whenever the weather appeared favorable. He carried out such strikes on April 7, 12, 24, and 30; May 5 and 11; June 9, 10, 22, and 26—a total of 10 such missions in 3 months. Then he bombed selected targets again on July 24. From April 8 to May 11, 75 percent of the XXI Bomber Command's effort was diverted to tactical support of the invasion of Okinawa (Operation Iceberg), particularly to attacks on airfields in Kyushu to suppress kamikaze operations from there. After the B-29s were released from Iceberg, intensive incendiary attacks on Japanese cities were resumed at once.

Incendiary Strikes

During General LeMay's concentration on incendiary bombing of urban industrial areas, there were 17 maximum-effort attacks entailing

6,960 B–29 sorties and 41,592 tons of bombs. Losses were 136 B–29s or about 2 percent of the sorties. Thereafter, LeMay turned to the smaller cities on his list, eventually assaulting and devastating a total of 66 urban areas. The chronology of these incendiary strikes was:

May 14: Daylight incendiary attack on Nagoya, including the Mitsubishi plant area. 529 B–29s were dispatched, 472 dropping 2,515 tons of bombs from 12,000 to 20,500 feet. 3.15 square miles burned out.

May 16: Nagoya urban area assault at night. Of the 522 B–29s taking part, 457 dispensed 3,609 tons of bombs. 3.82 square miles burned out.

May 23: Night bombing of urban Tokyo. 520 of 562 B–29s reached the target, dropping 3,646 tons of bombs from 7,800 to 15,000 feet. 17 Superfortresses were lost. 5.3 square miles burned out.

May 25: Strike against Tokyo urban area at night. 501 B–29s were sent, 26 being lost to flak. 3,262 tons of bombs dropped. 56.3 square miles destroyed. 50.8 percent of city burned out.

May 29: High-altitude, daylight attack on Yokohama urban area. 517 B–29s were escorted by 101 P–51s. 2,570 tons of bombs dispensed. 6.9 square miles burned out.

June 1: Osaka urban area struck in daylight by 458 of 521 B–29s dispatched. Escort of 148 P–51s suffered heavily from violent weather. 2,788 tons of bombs released from 18,000 to 28,500 feet. 3.15 square miles burned out.

June 5: Kobe hit in daytime by 473 of the 531 B–29s airborne. 3,077 tons of bombs dropped from 13,650 to 18,000 feet. 11 Superfortresses lost. 4.35 square miles burned out.

June 7: Day assault on Osaka by 458 B–29s with an escort of 138 P–51s. Radar bombing was from 17,900 to 23,150 feet. 2,540 tons of bombs dispensed. 2.21 square miles burned out.

June 15: Attack on Osaka at night. 444 of the 516 B–29s dropped 3,157 tons of bombs. 1.9 square miles burned out.

The bulk of XXI Bomber Command's operations was devoted to urban industrial area incendiary attacks. In the entire period of its operations, the Twentieth Air Force applied its capacity as follows:

	Sorties	Tons of Bombs
Precision bombing attacks:		
Aircraft and engine targets	2,838	14,152
Petroleum targets	1,437	10,600
Assorted industrial targets	1,459	8,093
Total	5,734	32,845
Urban industrial area attacks	21,671	138,215
Aerial mining	1,750	
GRAND TOTAL	29,155	171,060

Thus, just 19 percent of the total effort in terms of both sorties and bomb tonnage was directed against selective targets; 80 percent went to urban incendiary attacks; and less than 1 percent to mining.

The somewhat precipitate decision of the Joint Chiefs of Staff to move the 58th Wing from China-Burma-India Theater to the Marianas had at least one ill effect. It postponed the deployment of the 315th Wing (equipped with the new AN/APQ–7 radar bombing system) from April to June 1945. So upon the 315th's arrival in the Marianas, it carried out fewer than two months of operations before the end of the war. The deployment delay, however, was put to good use by intensifying training, particularly to perfect radar bombing accuracy. Consequently, the 315th's performance with the APQ–7 was spectacular. It clearly showed that selected targets could be hit at night or when obscured from visual bombing.

The first group of the 315th touched down at Northwest Field, Guam, late in June. Only one runway was available, although the other was nearing completion. Many of the base facilities were not yet installed, for construction of the field had been seriously delayed. The decision of the Navy Commander in Chief, Pacific Ocean Area, to move his advanced headquarters to Guam had caused critical changes in construction priorities there. Roads and naval facilities enjoyed a higher priority than B–29 bases. As a matter of fact, Northwest Field was slipped to Priority 95 on the Island of Guam. It taxed General Harmon's great persuasive powers to get the project moving again.

By the time the 315th Wing arrived, Lt. Gen. Barney M. Giles was the Deputy Commander, Twentieth Air Force. General Giles

INCENDIARY BOMBS SHOWER on the dock area of Kobe, Japan, on June 5, 1945.

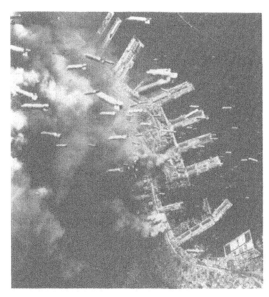

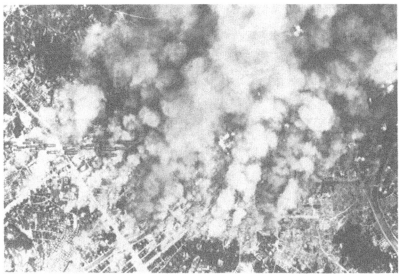

SMOKE BILLOWS FROM AN INDUSTRIAL SECTION OF YOKOHAMA, JAPAN, as B-29s continue to dump fire bombs during a daylight raid on May 29, 1945.

SCENES OF WIDESPREAD DESTRUCTION greeted the first Americans arriving a Yokohama harbor three days after the Japanese surrender on September 2, 1945.

A JAPANESE SURVIVOR AMONG THE RUINS of Yokohoma, now occupied by American forces.

KOBE, JAPAN, EXPERIENCED THE FURY OF INCENDI-
ARY ATTACKS IN JUNE 1945.

AMONG THE BURNED-OUT RUINS OF TOKYO, a survivor
drinks from a broken water pipe.

237

established his headquarters on Guam. He endorsed and supported General LeMay's decision to direct the 315th operations against a set of selected targets comprising the Japanese oil industry. These targets had been given in the 1942 Air War Plan (AWPD–42), and more recently strongly recommended as a consequence of the analysis contained in the recently completed Strategic Bombing Survey of the European Theater. General Spaatz, who became Commander in Chief, U.S. Army Strategic Forces in the Pacific, in mid-July 1945, strongly supported the decision. Because the destruction of oil refining was not specified as a top-priority objective in the current assigned target list, LeMay described the initial attacks as shakedown training operations.

The selection of strategic bombing objectives was being argued back and forth in the Joint Target Group in Washington. But more and more the picking of such objectives was being evaluated in terms of influence upon the proposed invasion of Japan. By April, however, the Strategic Air Intelligence Section in Washington was contending that the state of the Japanese petroleum industry was so critical that the destruction of facilities and storage in Japan would instantly influence the tactical situation. So the position of Generals Giles and LeMay had considerable backing. This fine decision by General LeMay afforded the opportunity to test again the feasibility of all-weather attack on selected targets by radar bombing, and at the same time to contribute substantially to the conduct of the war.

Between June 26 and the end of the war on August 14, the 315th Wing flew fifteen night missions against oil refineries or synthetic plants in Japan. These missions are listed below:

Date	Mission Number	Target
June 26/27	1	Utsube Oil Refinery at Yokkaichi
June 29/30	2	Nippon Oil Company at Kudamatsu
July 2/3	3	Maruzen Oil Company at Shimotsu
July 6/7	4	Maruzen Oil Company at Shimotsu (Repeat)
July 9/10	5	Utsube Oil Refinery at Yokkaichi (Repeat)
July 12/13	6	Mitsubishi Oil Company at

		Kawasaki
July 15/16	7	Nippon Oil Company at Kudamatsu (Repeat)
July 19/20	8	Nippon Oil Company at Kansai
July 22/23	9	Imperial Fuel Industry Company at Ube
July 25/26	10	Mitsubishi Oil Company at Kawasaki
July 28/29	11	Toa Fuel Company at Smimotsu
August 1/2	12	Mitsubishi Oil Company at Kawasaki (Repeat)
August 5/6	13	Imperial Fuel Industry Company at Ube (Repeat)
August 9/10	14	Nippon Oil Company at Kansai (Repeat)
August 14/15	15	Nippon Oil Company at Tsuchizaki (near Akita)

The missions were conducted by streams of single aircraft at night, bombing from 15,000 feet. The initial bombloads averaged 14,631 pounds per airplane but, with experience, this grew to 20,684 pounds. Only 4 planes were lost and 66 damaged in the entire campaign. The 315th Wing launched its first mission on the night of June 26/27, under the command of Brig. Gen. Frank A. Armstrong, Jr., who had been one of my wing commanders in the 1st Bombardment Division of the Eighth Air Force. Two groups attacked the Utsube Oil Refinery at Yokkaichi which was producing aviation gasoline. The mission was only partly effective.

The second mission was flown against the Nippon Oil Company at Kudamatsu on the night of June 29/30. This oil refinery was on the coast, west-southwest of Kure. Of the thirty-six aircraft airborne, thirty-two bombed the primary target. No B–29s were lost. The attack was but moderately successful, so the target was hit again on Mission No. 7 during the night of July 15/16, using seventy-one aircraft of which fifty-nine bombed the primary target. Again there were no losses. The cumulative results of both missions were damaging indeed.

On the night of July 2/3, Mission No. 3 struck the Maruzen Oil Company at Shimotsu (located on the coast, south-southwest of

THIS OIL REFINERY IN THE TOKYO AREA was a key
target during the final five months of the war against Japan.

ALL THAT REMAINS OF THE POWER AND GENERA-
TOR PLANT at the Imperial Fuel Industry Company at Ube,
after the bombing attacks of July and August 1945.

Osaka). Because the attack was not a complete success, the target was hit again on the night of July 6/7 by Mission No. 4. This time the outcome was superb as the mission reports attested:

Target: MARUZEN Refinery

Located immediately north of Shimotsu and 7 mi South-Southwest of Wakayama. The Plant produced aviation gasoline, lube oil, ordinary gasoline and fuel oil. It had extensive storage facilities. Crude capacity was 5000 barrels per day.

On Mission No. 3, 40 aircraft were airborne. 30 dropped 297 tons of general purpose 500 lb. bombs on the primary target (95.7 percent of the bombs which were airborne).

On Mission No. 4, 60 aircraft were airborne. 59 bombed the primary with 441 tons of 500 lb. general purpose bombs (98.2 percent of bombs which were airborne).

Damage from Mission No. 3 was just moderate, but photographs from Mission No. 4 disclosed that ninety-five percent of the installation was damaged. Only five large tanks and several small ones were left standing.

General LeMay, who never extended unearned praise, sent this message after photo reconnaissance and interpretation of pictures confirmed the mission report:

I have just reviewed the post-strike photography of your strike on target 1764, the MARUZEN Oil Refinery at Shimotsu, the night of 6/7 July. With a half-Wing effort you achieved ninety-five percent destruction, definitely establishing the ability of your crews with the APQ-7 to hit and destroy precision targets, operating individually at night. This performance is the most successful radar bombing of the Command to date. Congratulations to you and your men.

On the night of July 28/29, Mission No. 11 demonstrated the high degree of accuracy obtainable with the AN/APQ-7 Eagle radar bombing equipment. The target was the Toa Fuel Company at Shimotsu. Extracts from the mission report revealed:

An important refinery of crude petroleum with large and modern facilities and good shipping and rail connections, the target

241

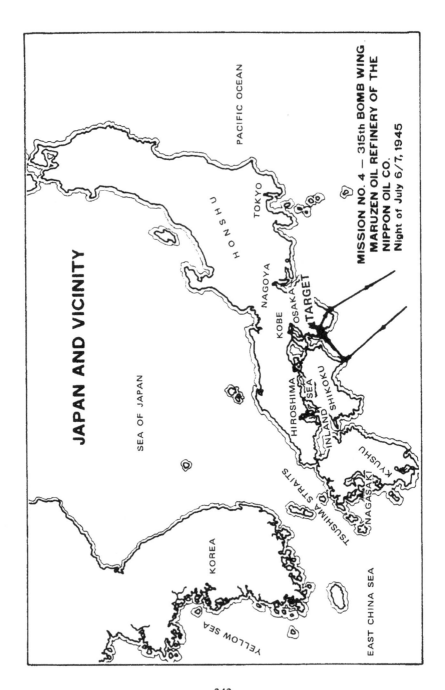

JAPAN AND VICINITY

MISSION NO. 4 — 315th BOMB WING
MARUZEN OIL REFINERY OF THE
NIPPON OIL CO.
Night of July 6/7, 1945

also had a tank capacity of about 600,000 barrels. It was roughly the shape of an equilateral triangle about 2,500 feet along each side. The storage area extended 1,000 feet beyond the northern top of the refinery area.

84 aircraft were airborne and 78 bombed the primary target, dropping 658.3 tons of 500 pound GP bombs. Opposition was light and there were no aircraft losses or crew member casualties.

Photos showed it was unnecessary to return to the refinery for in this one mission the target was almost completely destroyed. 927,000 barrels of the 1,245,000 barrel storage capacity was damaged while the 1,274,000 cubic foot gasometer capacity was almost completely destroyed. 69 percent of the 210,254 square foot group area was destroyed. The target was thoroughly saturated with bombs and obliterated beyond repair.

The target photo and interpretation showed the following distribution of bombing effort and impact of aircraft salvos:

Group	Number of Aircraft Bombing Primary Target	Percentage of Aircraft Dispatched Bombing Primary Target
16th	20	95
331st	13	93
501st	16	100
502d	15	91
Total	64	96

Centers of impact of 80 percent of salvos were identified in the photographs. Of these, 78 percent were in the target circle of 1,000–foot radius; 7 percent were over the target circle of 1,000–foot radius; and 15 percent were short of the target circle of 1,000–foot radius. Thus, 96 percent of aircraft dispatched bombed the primary target; 80 percent of the salvo centers were identified; and 78 percent of those identified were within 1,000 feet of the aiming point. This meant that 60 percent of the bombers dispatched placed their salvo centers within 1,000 feet of the aiming point, giving an average circular error probable of about 850 feet for salvo centers. This was an astonishing degree of accuracy for bombing at night from 15,000 feet through an undercast. It was actually much better than the average

CEP bombing distribution of XXI Bomber Command for visual daylight formation bombing (1,250 feet), though this was conducted at much higher altitude. Of course, one mission does not establish a CEP that can be taken as a reliable basis for forecasting and planning. Unfortunately, the other mission reports of the 315th Wing did not contain bomb plots.

The final mission of the 315th, flown on the night of August 14/15, was also remarkable. The mission report stated:

TARGET: NIPPON OIL COMPANY
REFINERY AT TSUCHIZAKI NEAR AKITA

This target was attacked on the 15th and last mission flown by the Wing, flown on the night of 14–15 August 1945 with bombs released only a few hours before the announcement by President Truman that the Japanese had accepted the United States terms.

The mission was the longest nonstop combat flight ever made, a distance of 3,740 statute miles from base at Guam to the target on the northern coast of Honshu island and return.

Postponed for several days by the peace negotiations, the mission took off, led by the Wing Commander (Brig Gen Frank Armstrong) at 1637 hours on 14 August. 143 aircraft were airborne and 134 dropped 953.9 tons of 100 pound and 250 pound GP bombs on the primary.

Results of photo-interpretation brought now familiar words: "Almost completely destroyed or damaged." Photographs disclosed that no portion of the target was untouched. The three refining units were a tangled mass of wreckage, the main power plant still standing but seriously hit. More than 66 percent of the tank capacity was destroyed. Lesser installations, including the worker's barracks, were destroyed.

Note: This mission was conducted by the Twentieth Air Force, after redesignation of the XXI Bomber Command, under the command of Lt. Gen. Nathan F. Twining.

[The figure for bomb size in the report is probably in error; it should have been 1,000–pound GP bombs rather than 100–pound GP bombs as reported.]

The operations of the 315th Wing showed conclusively that it was feasible to destroy selected targets by radar bombing when the target location was well known and the radar returns of the target itself were clear or its location relative to a prominent radar feature was well known. As suggested earlier, B–29s with AN/APQ–7 radar systems might have been used as lead aircraft for daylight selective bombing by formations of the other B–29s. This technique would have permitted employment of the entire force for daylight attack of selected targets even if those targets were obscured by clouds.

Effects of the Air Offensive

The U.S. Strategic Bombing Survey was able to report the effects of strategic bombing on the Japanese aircraft and engine target system, the aerial mining campaign, and attacks against selected targets in the iron, steel, and petroleum industries. On the other hand, it had trouble reporting the results of strategic bombing on Japanese war production and upon Japan's war economy, because no related system of targets was set up by the Joint Chiefs of Staff and the Twentieth Air Force as selective priority strategic targets. Nevertheless, the Bombing Survey submitted reports on a number of war production industries.

The Report on Japanese War Production Industries set forth the objectives of our strategic air force:

1. To bring about an overwhelming and immediate drop in war production.

2. To shut off output of certain specific high priority items of war production.

3. To accelerate the rate of the existing decline of overall war production.

4. To force a substantial cut in production of those military supplies of such high priority that they would otherwise withstand the effects of the current restrictive economic forces.

All four of these objectives were met to some degree. Strategic bombing did hasten and intensify the decline in war production, and prevented the Japanese from saving the production of high-priority items from the general decline. The report did not say from whence the objectives were derived; probably they were deduced from various statements by military leaders and from mission directives and orders. It chose to consider Japanese "war production" as comprising six categories: aircraft industry; army ordnance; naval ordnance; naval shipbuilding; merchant shipbuilding; and the motor vehicle industry. Of these, only the aircraft industry was subjected to selective air attack.

The effects of the strategic air offensive were catastrophic in the aggregate. They stemmed from a series of interacting results of air bombardment: direct damage from bombing; indirect results of bombing reflected in frantic efforts to disperse industry; loss of basic raw materials through blockade, including aerial mining; and absenteeism of workers whose homes had been destroyed and who had to forage for food and the essentials of life for themselves and their families.

The report gave this analysis of the selective bombing of the aircraft industry:

No figures are available for loss of production due to physical destruction of plant, machinery, and equipment. Loss of production capacity through unsuccessful attempts at dispersal (which resulted from fear induced by the early attack on airframe and engine plants) was:

Airframes	33 percent
Engines	57 percent
Propellers	42 percent

About 55 percent of the whole aircraft industry's facilities were out of production due to dispersal alone.

For other categories of war production, the overall drop in production capacity through physical destruction of plant, machinery, and equipment was:

Army ordnance	26 percent
Naval ordnance	28 percent
Merchant and naval ships	10–15 percent
Motor vehicles	negligible

The decline in production capacity due to unsuccessful attempts at dispersal (induced by the threat of bombing) was:

Army ordnance	12 percent
Naval ordnance	12 percent
Merchant and naval ships	small
Motor vehicles	sufficient to bring a complete collapse of production

The loss of production capacity by bombing was brought about by a combination of heavy urban area attacks and a relatively small amount of bombing (24,000 tons or 17 percent of total bomb tonnage) directed at selected targets. Strategic bombing alone did not reduce Japanese production. Loss of raw materials from shipping losses and blockade had an impact as well, especially in the case of steel. The report pointed out that:

The loss through ships sunk of 17 percent of all Army supplies shipped overseas (including food, clothing, fuel, and construction materials as well as ordnance) in 1943; 30 percent in 1944; and 50 percent in 1945 shows that increased production alone would not have been sufficient to provide adequate supplies for the Japanese Army overseas.

The report summed up its findings on the effect of strategic bombing of Japanese war industry production in these terms:

There was a 53 percent decline in war production between September 1944 (just prior to the launching of the air offensive) and July 1945—the last full month of production before the end of the war. The magnitude of the decline in output of each of the major categories of war production from peak levels to the July 1945 level is shown below:

Category	Percentage drop from peak production
Aircraft	57
Army Ordnance	54

Naval Ordnance	56
Merchant ships	82
Naval ships	53
Motor vehicles	96

There can be no doubt that the air offensive crippled Japanese war industries, even though only one of them (aircraft) was selected for direct attack. And the urban area incendiary attacks indirectly crippled other industry.

The Bombing Survey recognized another basic Army Air Forces strategic objective—one that had been clearly defined in AWPD-1 and AWPD-42, though it had been submerged by other considerations in later plans. This objective was not only to destroy the war-supporting structure, but the economic framework on which the Japanese state depended. The combination was meant to bring about surrender, when it became apparent to the Japanese they could no longer supply the basic needs upon which the population relied for its life and social survival.

The U.S. Strategic Bombing Survey issued a report on the effects of strategic bombing on Japan's war economy. It concluded:

> By July 1945 Japan's economic system had been shattered. Production of civilian goods was below the level of subsistence. Munitions output had been curtailed to less than half the war-time peak, a level that could not support sustained military operations against our opposing forces. The economic basis of Japanese resistance had been destroyed. This economic decay resulted from the sea-air blockade of the Japanese home islands and direct bombing attacks on industrial and urban-area targets.
>
> The urban-area incendiary raids had profound repercussions on civilian morale and Japan's will to stay in the war. Sixty-six cities, virtually all those of economic significance, were subjected to bombing raids and suffered destruction ranging from 25 to 90 percent. Almost 50 percent of the area of these cities were leveled. The area raids interrupted the normal processes of city life to an extent that interfered seriously with such production as the shrinking raw material base still permitted.
>
> The bombing offensive was the major factor which secured agreement to unconditional surrender without an invasion of the

home islands—an invasion that would have cost hundreds of thousands of American lives. The demonstrated strength of the United States in the B–29 attacks contrasted with Japan's lack of adequate defense made clear to the Japanese people and to the government the futility of further resistance. This was reinforced by the evident deterioration of the Japanese economy and the impact it was having on a large segment of the population. The atomic bomb and Russia's entry into the war speeded the process of surrender already realized as the only possible outcome.

The effectiveness of strategic air attack was limited by the concepts of its mission. Had the purpose of strategic air attack been primarily to force an independent decision rather than to support a ground-force invasion in November 1945, there would have been no occasion to attack oil, tetraethyllead, arsenals, or, after March, aircraft. Efforts could have been concentrated against food and fuel supply by attacks on internal transportation and against urban areas, thus striking solely at the main elements upon which continued Japanese resistance was based. Moreover, a part of the bombing effort merely duplicated results already achieved by blockade. Attack on the rail transportation system would have secured full coordination with the blockade program. The railroads were overburdened, defenseless, and had only limited ability to replace rolling stock or major installations.

The testimony was overwhelming that the air offensive against Japan—essentially an anti-Japanese Air Force operation followed by an urban-area strategy—was a magnificent success. The conclusion that the bombing effort should have been concentrated upon aircraft and engine production, transportation, and urban areas alone is interesting, significant, and worthy of further evaluation.

Debate over Grand Strategy in the Pacific

As the time for the Potsdam Conference drew near, President Harry S. Truman asked that the Joint Chiefs of Staff and the Service Secretaries meet with him to discuss Pacific strategy before his meeting with Prime Minister Churchill and Marshal Stalin. The Joint Chiefs immediately asked theater commanders for their views on strategy to defeat Japan.

General MacArthur had previously advocated invasion of Honshu at the plain of Tokyo. He had stipulated that Russia must be induced to enter the war, so as to tie down the million-and-a-half Japanese soldiers believed to be in Manchuria. Without this provision, MacArthur advised against direct invasion of the Japanese home islands. In a staff report of March 8, 1945, he was quoted as saying he was in complete agreement with the Army that the sole means of defeating Japan was by invading the industrial heart of Japan. (There is a striking parallel here. Gen. Dwight D. Eisenhower had stated with regard to Germany that it was necessary to conquer the Ruhr, the industrial heart of Germany. Neither Eisenhower nor MacArthur seemed to understand that the heart of a great nation can be stilled by strategic air operations, as well as by occupation by troops.) General MacArthur believed Russia would demand and get Manchuria, but thought she should pay for it by joining in the fight against Japan. He was quoted as saying that he understood the Navy still favored a plan whereby Japan would be surrounded with air and naval bases, and eventually blockaded and bombed into submission. MacArthur contended that this would never succeed.

On April 20, 1945, General MacArthur analyzed the strategic problem under three possibilities:

> Course 1. Encircle Japan by further expansion to the westward, deploying maximum air forces preparatory to attacks on Kyushu and Honshu in succession or directly against Honshu.
> Course 2. Encircle Japan by further expansion to the westward with a view to its complete isolation, and endeavor to bomb Japan into submission without effecting landings in the homeland.
> Course 3. Attack Kyushu and install air forces to cover a decisive assault on Honshu.

He dismissed Course 1 as time-consuming and diversionary away from the decisive area—the plain of Tokyo. Turning down Course 2 as time-consuming and ineffective, he said:

> It assumes success of air power alone to conquer a people in spite of its demonstrated failure in Europe, where Germany was subjected to more intensive bombardment than can be brought to bear against Japan, and where all the available resources in ground troops of the

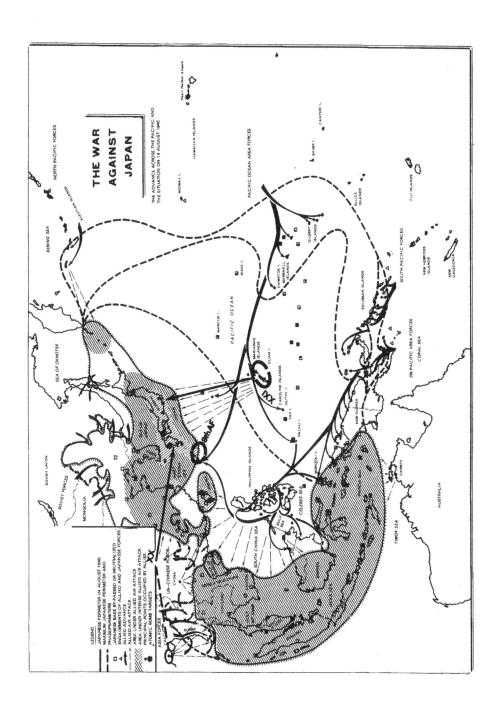

THE WAR AGAINST JAPAN

THE ADVANCE ACROSS THE PACIFIC AND
THE SITUATION ON 14 AUGUST 1945

LEGEND

JAPANESE PERIMETER IN AUGUST 1945
MAXIMUM JAPANESE PERIMETER AND
PHASE PERIMETERS
JAPANESE BASE BY-PASSED OR NEUTRALIZED
ENGAGEMENTS OF ALLIED AND JAPANESE FORCES
ALLIED ADVANCE
ALLIED AIR ATTACK
AREA UNDER ALLIED AIR ATTACK
AREA UNDER INTENSE ALLIED AIR ATTACK
PRINCIPAL POINTS OCCUPIED BY ALLIES
ATOMIC BOMB TARGETS

United States, the United Kingdom and Russia had to be committed in order to force a decision.

He recommended Course 3.

In calling his conference with the Joint Chiefs for June 18, the President stressed the cost of invasion in terms of casualties. He wanted to know the time needed and the losses that would ensue from an effort to defeat Japan by isolation, blockade, and bombardment by sea and air forces. He asked General Marshall for his views. Marshall said he personally believed the operation against Kyushu was the only course to pursue. He felt air power alone was insufficient to put the Japanese out of the war, adding that it was unable alone to put the Germans out. General Eaker was present, representing General Arnold who was in Guam at XXI Bomber Command Headquarters. Arnold had been reached, and he asserted that bombing could end the war. Still, he instructed Eaker to support General Marshall's position.

General Arnold later divulged his reasons for favoring the invasion of Kyushu. He held, with General LeMay, that Japan was already tottering and air power would complete the collapse. But capture of Kyushu would afford certain benefits—areas for basing forty groups in an additional air force. These groups, chiefly equipped with B–17s, would be close to targets in Honshu. The air units were actually available for transfer to the Pacific. And the capture of Kyushu would make it unnecessary to invade Honshu. Besides, this policy position would be an expression of loyalty to General Marshall. The latter had stood "in loco parentis" behind the birth and growth of the Army Air Forces, and had given evidence of supporting a separate Air Force, coequal with the Army and Navy after the war. General Arnold knew, as did the other Chiefs, that Japan had already started peace negotiations through the Russians in Moscow, who deliberately failed to forward the peace feelers. Admiral King concurred with General Marshall.

Admiral Leahy, however, voiced considerable concern over casualties and seemed to favor blockade and bombardment. He asked General Marshall what the casualty rates had been in the other Pacific invasions and how many troops would it take to invade Kyushu.

Marshall said the plan for invading Kyushu called for 766,700 men. Admiral Leahy said the Okinawa casualties (34,000 Army, 7,000 Navy) constituted about 35 percent of the the force. If this yardstick was applied to Kyushu, the casualties would be numerous indeed (268,000). Admiral King thought the casualty rate would be somewhere between that on Luzon and that on Okinawa. Admiral Leahy went on to question the insistence on unconditional surrender, asserting that lesser terms would still allow our absolute control of Japan. The President finally accepted General Marshall's views, and the target date for invading Kyushu was set at November 1.

On his trip to the Pacific, General Arnold had viewed the scene firsthand from the Command Headquarters in Guam. He was impressed with the devastation already visited upon Japan and with the immense air power that was in place. He also saw the mounting strength of the Eighth Air Force, one wing of which was established in Okinawa and the rest in transit from Europe and the United States. Then, too, Arnold received a preliminary report of the Bombing Survey's findings on the effect of the strategic war against Germany. It was a staggering testimonial of the impact of strategic air warfare on a modern state at war. General Arnold was quoted at the time: "If we could win the war by bombing, it would be unnecessary for the ground troops to make a landing on the shores of Japan. Personally I was convinced it would be done. I did not believe Japan could stand the punishment from the air that Germany had taken." Arnold sent General LeMay back to Washington to brief the Joint Chiefs and, if they concurred, the Secretary of War and the President. LeMay had arrived too late. The President had already agreed to the policy of invasion and the machinery had been set in motion, not only for the invasion of Kyushu but for the subsequent invasions of Honshu.

At the Potsdam Conference, President Truman learned of the successful test of the "atomic device." He queried his advisors and top commanders about using it. They agreed to its use, with one exception—General Arnold, the man whose aircraft would deliver it. Arnold, just back from the Pacific, questioned the need to drop the atomic bomb to assure Japan's defeat without an invasion. Japan had already been weakened by blockade and beaten to her knees by air

252

bombardment. In August, September, and October the Twentieth and Eighth Air Forces could double the total tonnage dropped on Japan to date. That should be sufficient to force surrender, since Japan was on the verge of collapse. However, if it became a question of dropping the atomic bomb or launching an invasion, he favored the bomb. Other considerations clinched his conviction that the bomb should be dropped. He later strongly supported the decision to use atomic weapons.

In anticipation of the President's decision to use the atomic bomb, potential targets had been selected. On orders from General Arnold, Col. Cecil E. Combs, Twentieth Air Force Deputy for Operations, had set aside four cities not yet bombed and passed the word to LeMay that they were not to be attacked. These were Hiroshima, Nagasaki, Kokura, and Niigata.

Second Change of Command

With Victory in Europe in May 1945, the second phase of global grand strategy was put in motion. Forces released from combat in Europe were transferred to the Pacific and preparations were made for the final offensive against Japan. On July 16, 1945, a major reorganization of the air forces in the Pacific took place. General Arnold turned to the strategic air team that had been so successful in the air war against the Third Reich. Gen. Carl Spaatz, Commander in Chief, U.S. Strategic Air Forces in Europe, was chosen to command the strategic air assault against Japan. His new designation was Commander in Chief, U.S. Army Strategic Air Forces in the Pacific, headquartered on Guam. He reported directly to General Arnold, who would continue to command the strategic air forces from Washington, as executive agent of the Joint Chiefs of Staff.

The Fifteenth Air Force in the Mediterranean was demobilized, but its Commanding General, Lt. Gen. Nathan F. Twining, was sent to the Pacific as a member of Spaatz's winning team. He would take command of the Twentieth Air Force with headquarters in Guam. The veteran Eighth Air Force, under the other member of the command team, Lt. Gen. James H. Doolittle, would be returned to the

United States, reequipped and trained with B–29s, and moved to Okinawa. The old XX Bomber Command Headquarters would be absorbed in the new Eighth Air Force Headquarters. The XXI Bomber Command would be reconstituted as the Twentieth Air Force. Again there was an awkward problem. General Arnold sent for General Twining and told him there was going to be a reorganization of the entire command structure in the Pacific: "I want Spaatz and Doolittle and you to take over right away. Now get on with it."

General LeMay was relieved as Commanding General, XXI Bomber Command, and General Twining assumed command of Twentieth Air Force. (Through oversight or neglect, General Arnold failed to acquaint LeMay with the decision he had reached, so it remained for Twining to answer LeMay's query on his arrival, "What are you doing here?" Perhaps Arnold had expected Spaatz to notify LeMay.)

General Twining's comment upon heading what had been the XXI Bomber Command and was now to be the Twentieth Air Force was typical—and appropriate. He said, "Taking over this outfit from Curt LeMay is about like taking over the Notre Dame football team from Knute Rockne." Fortunately, General LeMay's broad experience and proven talents were saved for continued application in the strategic air war. General Spaatz made him his Chief of Staff—a role that would keep him active in the final phase of the strategic air war against Japan. Lt. Gen. Barney M. Giles became General Spaatz's deputy.

General Twining had barely settled into his new command when he received orders to deliver the atomic bombs. Twining literally possessed no knowledge of the atomic bomb, for as Fifteenth Air Force Commander he had been deeply engrossed in mounting maximum-effort combat missions in Europe. After a supersecret briefing, he saw no need to waste time in questioning the judgment of his superiors.

The Finale

During the course of the war, the Twentieth Air Force flew

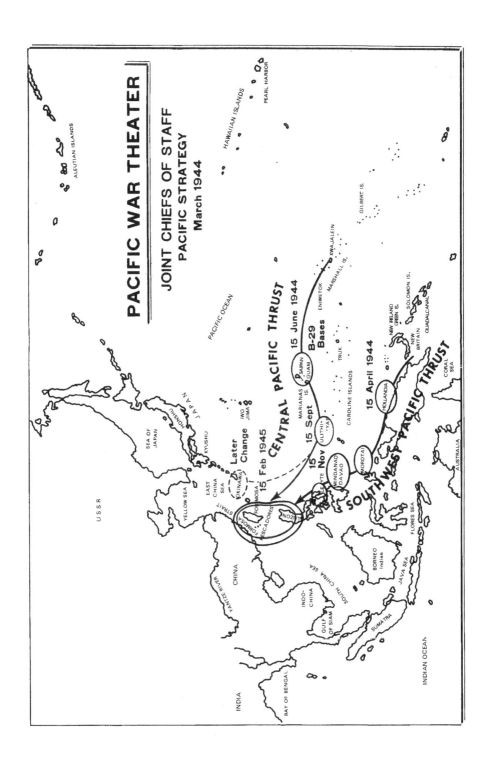

US ARMY AIR FORCES IN THE PACIFIC
US ARMY STRATEGIC AIR FORCES IN THE PACIFIC
AS OF 15 August 1945

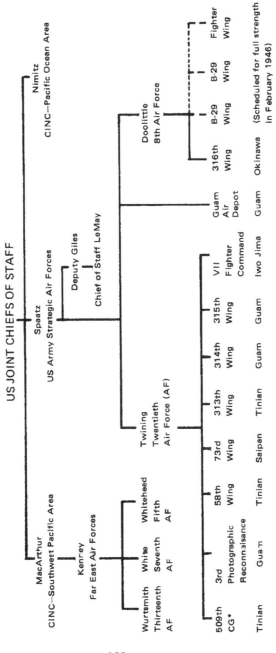

*509th Composite (Atomic) Group

31,387 bomber sorties; 3,058 of which were flown by the XX Bomber Command, 28,329 by the XXI. The war had taken 414 B–29s, 80 from the XX Bomber Command and 334 from the XXI. Losses on combat missions averaged 1.3 percent of sorties airborne, with a total of 147 bombers lost. Of these combat losses:

> 50 percent were caused by enemy fighters.
> 36 percent were caused by enemy antiaircraft.
> 13 percent were caused by a combination of both.
> 1 percent were self-inflicted by accident.

Fighter losses were 80. By the end of the war the Twentieth Air Force comprised:

Bombers	B–29	1,042
Fighters	P–47	733
	P–51	349
	Night	18
Reconnaissance	F–7	26
	F–13	52
Staff and Transports		93
		2,313

The total inventory of B–29s on hand in the Army Air Forces was about 3,700.

On the basis of photo coverage, intelligence estimated that 175 square miles of urban area in 66 cities were wiped out. Total civilian casualties stemming directly from the urban attacks were estimated at 330,000 killed, 476,000 injured, and 9,200,000 rendered homeless. There were 2,210,000 houses demolished or burned down and another 90,000 were partially damaged. This bombing "dehoused" 50.3 percent of the 1940 population of these cities. A total of 159,862 tons of bombs was dropped. Japanese casualties resulting from the strategic air attack, from all causes, was estimated at 900,000 deaths and 1,300,000 injured. Following are a few quotes from Japanese sources on the effectiveness of American air power:

"If I were to give you one factor as the leading one that led to your victory, I would give you the Air Force."

> Admiral Asami Nayano
> Imperial Japanese Navy
> Chief of Naval Staff and Supreme
> Naval Advisory to the Emperor

"If I were to give you the decisive factors in the war in the order of their importance, I would place first the Air Force."

> Vice Admiral Shigeru Fukudome
> Imperial Japanese Navy
> Chief of Staff, Combined Fleet

"The determination to make peace was the prolonged bombing by the B–29s."

> Prince Fumimaro Konoye
> Premier of Japan

Japan accepted defeat while still possessing over 2.5 million combat-equipped troops and 9,000 airplanes capable of being equipped and flown as kamikazes. No Allied troops were present on the soil of the Japanese home islands when Japan surrendered.

A FLIGHT OF B-29s, by John McCoy. (Courtesy USAF Art Collection)

Chapter VII

Summing Up

There are many dangers associated with passing judgment on the strategic offensive against the Axis in World War II. In the first place, those of us who participated in the plans and operations are undoubtedly biased in our views, because we are appraising our own efforts.

Secondly, even after forty years and a vast amount of research and writing by many people, there are still gaps in available knowledge. Critical judgments on the diversion of forces and effort away from the agreed-upon grand strategy and objectives may fail to give proper weight to the imperative of tactical urgency, as well as to the pressures for changes in strategy from the highest political levels. Nor is it possible to reconstruct the confusion, obscurity, and ignorance which attend all military operations in war.

Finally, it is easy to be misled into underestimating the most implacable of all our enemies—the ever-present bad weather. Many tons of bombs that were dumped on "other" targets may represent the bombing of secondary targets when the cloud cover at primary ones was heavier than predicted. The degree to which this diminished the efficiency of the various strategic air offensives will, of necessity, remain a matter of speculation. Judgment of operational capability affected selection of vital target systems, particularly since this was a new art in warfare. Moreover, selections were sometimes made by civilian industrialists whose judgment of industrial effect was highly respected, but who should not have been expected to judge military capability to destroy or paralyze. To cite one example, the Committee of Operations Analysts dropped German electric power from first to thirteenth priority, not because it was not vital, but because they considered its paralysis to be beyond military capability. The relatively small amount of bomb tonnage needed to destroy the German electric power system was actually available and could have been applied.

The Strategic Air War against Germany

A distinguished body of modern historians has reached critical and adverse conclusions about the bomber offensive in Europe. In public places it has been openly proclaimed that the offensive was ineffective, inefficient, and wasteful. No doubt it was more ineffective, inefficient, and wasteful than it need have been. The U.S. Strategic Bombing Survey noted that the strategic air offensive could, in some instances, have been better applied. But as both a careful student and a participant, it seems patently clear to me that the Combined Bomber Offensive was a stunning success.

It provided the sine qua non for the invasion of Western Europe. It achieved its intermediate objective of overriding importance, "elimination of effective air opposition." It paved the way for the landings over the beaches and for the breakout from the beachhead. It destroyed the sources of fuel production on which all elements of the Wehrmacht depended. And it succeeded in delaying the arrival of enemy forces in the crucial few days after D–day.

After the invasion and breakout from Normandy, strategic air warfare provided a major contribution to victory in the subsequent combined operations on the Continent. It was a full partner with air-supported ground operations in bringing Germany to defeat. One of the most powerful nations in modern history was rendered impotent by air power. The viability of the economic system of Germany was destroyed. In the words of the U.S. Strategic Bombing Survey: "It was decisive."

Given the actual development of escort fighters, it also seems certain that any of the three strategic air plans (AWPD–1, AWPD–42, and the CBO) could have been carried out as planned. And the Combined Bomber Offensive could have included the destruction of most of the German powerplants and the disruption of the power distribution system by demolishing the switching stations. Further, it appears to me that the U.S. strategic air forces should not have been dismembered by sending forty percent of the aircraft to the Mediterranean to be used chiefly for theater objectives. The air power could have been better used to destroy and disrupt the electric power system. Coupled to this would be the collapse of the synthetic petroleum system, the loss of nitrogen for explosives, and disruption of the German transportation system. Altogether, they would have produced in May or June of 1944 the chaos which characterized the German war industry and the German state in January, February, and March of 1945.

I also feel it would have been possible to achieve this fatal chaos before the Normandy Invasion. The greatest single deterrent to this achievement was probably the decision to invade North Africa, and later to extend military operations the length of the Mediterranean, including Italy. This was, of course, a political decision. Even during a war, one can not quarrel with the right of political leaders to base major decisions on political rather than military factors. The action was quite within the bounds of American political philosophy. The U.S. Joint Chiefs of Staff had their day in court, expressing with candor and vigor their opposition to this Mediterranean strategy. They contended it was a dangerous diversion from the main military objective—the defeat of Germany. President Roosevelt made it clear he understood the military reasoning of his professional military advisors. But he had other elements to deal with as well. Thus, the right of the President and Prime Minister Churchill to override the advice of the U.S. Joint Chiefs and reach a political decision, and the propriety of their action in this case, are beyond question. The decision's outcome must be evaluated in terms of political accomplishments. Its effect on military achievements and other political goals should likewise be weighed.

From the military point of view, the decision confirmed the dire predictions of the U.S. military advisers. The Mediterranean Theater absorbed enormous resources and energies and drew the Allies into an area of conflict unlikely to make a timely and maximum contribution toward military victory over the principal enemy. This diversion of effort and the attendant critical delay of the main offensive were felt most acutely in the prosecution of the air offensive against Germany. In particular, the decision to invade Italy following the conquest of Sicily entailed a massive, time-consuming, and costly campaign that sapped the energies of the available heavy bombers in support. Ultimately, the strategic air bases in the vicinity of Foggia, Italy, were significant assets in the strategic air offensive. Even so, they were not appreciably better situated than those in Sicily, Sardinia, and Corsica would have been. There was sufficient base capacity there and in England to accommodate the entire strategic air forces. This delay and diversion were most unfortunate in terms of their preventing the "fatal weakening" of Germany before the Normandy Invasion and adding to the invasion's subsequent cost.

Had the Allied heads of government stood steadfast in support of the plans (chiefly the air plans) they had initially accepted, the strategic air offensive against the vitals of Germany could have been mounted earlier and in greater force. Major air strikes on the Luftwaffe fighter component began in February 1944 after at least a four-month delay. Equal air forces had been on hand in October 1943 but forty percent of them were in the Mediterranean, not under a common strategic air force commander. Had Big Week begun in October, with all available bombers operating under unified command, there could have been six months of air assault and the fatal weakening of Germany prior to the invasion. The collapse of Nazi Germany's industrial and economic heart and the loss of munitions support for its armed forces, which occurred in January 1945, could have been brought about before the invasion.

Despite the delays and the dilution of the strategic air offensive against Germany itself, there is good reason to believe that the "fatal weakening" could still have been produced previous to the invasion, if General Eisenhower and his staff had been willing to accept the urgent recommendations of the strategic air force commanders. The Combined Chiefs of Staff should not have yielded complete control of the strategic air forces for six months, even in the face of Eisenhower's open threat to resign his command.

In short, the heads of State and the Combined Chiefs of Staff could have supported their decision at Casablanca with the same determination and unwavering persistence of bomber and fighter crews flying to their objectives. The Committee of Operations Analysts could have confined themselves to listing industrial targets in Germany in order of their effect on the state and its war-making capacity, without speculating on operation feasibility. The Supreme Commander, Allied Expeditionary Forces, could have understood the advantages the strategic air offensive could have brought to him. Had they done these things, the final invasion and land operations would certainly have been far less bloody and less costly. The invasion might have been a major mopping-up and occupation operation.

In summary, the greatest U.S. contribution to the strategic concept of air warfare and its practical application was made by Col. Harold L. George. The idea was first developed by George and his associates at the Air Corps Tactical School. Under his guidance as Chief of the Air War Plans Division, the concept was translated into sound strategic plans for employment of U.S. air power. This was done in the face of strong opposition from proponents of surface warfare. The concept envisioned undermining of the enemy's will and his capacity to wage war, by bombing selected industrial, economic, and military systems. The most persuasive testimony of the soundness of Colonel George's precepts was their passing the crucial test of the world's first great air war. The result was a Germany in chaos, bereft at last of the power to subjugate the free people of Europe.

The Strategic Air War against Japan

Further proof of the precepts of strategic air power lay in the assault on Japan. The defeat of that nation and its surrender were without invasion and with military forces still intact. Devastated and its will broken, Japan could not wage war nor protect its people. Unquestionably the Japanese could have continued to resist, killing thousands of invading Americans and losing thousands of their own. But the potency of the air offensive convinced the Japanese that defense against it was impossible and resistance futile. Even more important, I believe Japan could have been defeated without widespread urban destruction.

The decision to switch to urban incendiary attacks was not necessarily faulty. Persistent cloud cover frustrated efforts to destroy selected targets by optical bombsighting. And the delay in acquiring AN/APQ–7 radar sights would simply have fortified the claims of those who saw invasion as the only reliable option for the defeat of Japan. Moreover, Japanese structures and cities were uniquely vulnerable to incendiary attack. There may have been factors bearing on the decision of which I am unaware. But given the circumstances as they existed, including a dedication to grand strategy based on invasion, I consider the decision to launch incendiary attacks on Japanese cities quite sound. The effects were decisive.

The fault was with the grand strategy. Invasion should not have been regarded as the sine qua non of victory. There was an intense concern with "time," caused by the arbitrary selection of a November 1945 invasion date. Still, there should have been no limitation on strategic operations dictated by the shortage of time. Time was on our side. With every day that passed, the combination of sea blockade, aerial mining, and strategic bombing was bringing Japan nearer to inevitable disaster.

The question of whether grand strategy should have been changed is to a degree academic and pointless. Certainly the Army Air Forces could not have changed it alone. There is, however, another very significant point. The turn to incendiary area attacks and the devastating atomic bombs did not in themselves prove that selective strategic bombing should be abandoned elsewhere or under other circumstances. Selective bombing was decisive against Germany and could have been decisive against Japan. Improvements in weapons and sighting techniques have multiplied the effectiveness of conventional weapons attack perhaps a hundredfold, surmounting the limitations imposed by "our most implacable enemy," the weather. Technology is opening a path toward defense against nuclear missiles. Such a defense of our military capabilities and most particularly of our urban centers—the focus of our "national will"—offers promise of inhibiting nuclear war. If such a condition transpires—and it is crucially important to the American nation that it should transpire—then wars of the future may again be determined by accurate delivery of non-nuclear weapons against properly selected targets. Then selective destruction by strategic air forces with conventional weapons may once more be the instrument for "fatal weakening" of a great industrial power and the arbiter that hastens the peace agreement. It is an option we should furnish ourselves.

Ten years before this climactic assault on Japan, I proposed at the Air Corps Tactical School three basic functions for employing armed forces in support of national purpose and national policy. These were (1) the forceful acquisition of enemy territory, either for permanent acquisition or in order to control the enemy nation and its capability to resist; (2) the application of compelling force, without acquisition of enemy territory or the intent permanently to acquire, in order to destroy or paralyze his capability to wage effective warfare and to sustain the "will to resist" of the enemy people; and (3) the provision of defenses which will sustain our own capability to fight and to bolster the will of our people to endure and persist. This framework still has merit for evaluating military requirements and alternatives in support of national purpose.

Invasion of the Japanese home islands was not an imperative requirement. Reviewing the principles and precepts on which AWPD–1 and AWPD–42 rested, it is quite apparent that, in the case of Japan, invasion was merely a form of compelling and not an end in itself. We did not want to hold Japanese territory permanently. If this had been our aim, invasion would have been a must. The Japanese would not have surrendered even after the atomic bombings, had our purpose been to dismember their nation. What we wanted was to prevent the Japanese expansion, strip Japan of its conquests, and remove the menace of Japanese aggression from the Pacific basin. We needed to exert a compelling force to this end, and it could be imposed by sea blockade and air bombardment as well as by invasion. To be sure, temporary *occupation* by ground forces would be needed while civil order was reestablished under favorable terms. But forceful invasion was just one of several alternatives. Nor was "unconditional surrender" vital to our war aims.

The destruction of the cities and the enormous loss of Japanese civilian lives were in no sense an objective of the United States Government or of the strategic air offensive. They were means toward achieving the ultimate goal—capitulation of the Japanese Government. The wholesale destruction of the Japanese cities entailed an unwelcome reconstruction burden after the war, and the excessive loss of life could not be compensated for at all. An alternative would have clearly been preferable, but it would have required the capability to destroy targets in any type of weather. We achieved this capability at the close of the conventional-weapons air war against Japan.

Whether to drop the atomic bomb caused much soul searching. Preparing for the Allied meeting at Potsdam, President Truman asked his chief advisors (military, political, and scientific) if they favored dropping the bomb.

But the problem was more subtle than first appeared. It was not confined to the morality of killing Japanese civilians with a single weapon; it also embraced the potential loss of half a million or more American lives and perhaps ten times that many Japanese lives (civilian and military) through invasion and subsequent battles in Japan. The atomic bomb was needed both to convince the Japanese that further resistance was futile, and to convince the American army that invasion was unnecessary. The result would be a tremendous saving in Japanese and American lives. The "bomb" may not have been needed to bring defeat to Japan, but it was needed to save the Army from its obsession with a costly invasion. And the bomb's demonstrated power would be required after the war to deter Russian domination of Europe.

As for Japan, the U.S. Strategic Bombing Survey stated:

> The Bombing offensive was the major factor which secured agreement to unconditional surrender without an invasion of the home islands—an invasion that would have cost hundreds of thousands of American lives. The demonstrated strength of the

United States in the B–29 attacks contrasted with Japan's lack of adequate defense made clear to the Japanese people and to the government the futility of further resistance. This was reinforced by the evident deterioration of the Japanese economy and the impact it was having on a large segment of the population. The atomic bombs and Russian entry into the war speeded the process of surrender already realized as the only possible outcome.

It seems clear that, even without the atomic bombing attacks, air supremacy over Japan could have exerted sufficient pressure to bring about unconditional surrender and obviate the need for invasion. Based on a detailed investigation of all the facts, and supported by the testimony of surviving Japanese leaders involved, it is this Survey's opinion that certainly prior to 1 December 1945, and in all probability prior to 1 November 1945, Japan would have surrendered even if the atomic bomb had not been dropped, even if Russia had not entered the war, and even if no invasion had been planned or contemplated.

An Alternative Grand Strategy for World War II

The strategic air offensives against Germany and Japan, carried out in the context of the Allied grand strategy, were magnificent and decisive accomplishments. But, as is always true in history, other courses of action could have been pursued. A different grand strategy might have been equally decisive and perhaps more efficient. One such alternate overall grand strategy for conducting World War II might have had these broad dimensions:

First Phase

I. Strategic offensive against Hitler's Germany, with:

(1) A sustained and unremitting air offensive against the sources of German military, economic, and social strength through selective bombing of:

    (a) The German aircraft engine industry.

    (b) The German electric power system.

    (c) The German transportation systems.

    (d) The German oil and chemical industries.

    (e) The German antifriction bearing industries—coupled with air combat to defeat the German fighter forces.

267

(2) Provision for (a) invasion of the Continent after completion of the strategic air offensive (if invasion should then be necessary), and subsequent defeat of German ground forces, or (b) occupation of Germany if the air offensive caused collapse of military power or produced surrender.

II. Initial defensive operations in the Pacific with minimum diversion of resources from the air war against Germany, and to curb the expansion of the Japanese aggression and provide adequate surveillance measures to prevent surprise attack.

Priority allocation of resources to forces engaged in the European war.

Second Phase

As soon as victory in Europe could be assured, development of forces for the war against Japan and initiation of such military operations for regaining or securing essential base areas as could be undertaken without impairing the success in Europe, coupled with intensive sea operations against Japanese shipping and the Japanese navy.

Third Phase

On defeat of Hitler, reallocation of priorities and transfer of resources to the Pacific for the defeat of Japan, primarily by sea blockade and selective air bombardment, more specifically to complete such of the following as had not been accomplished in phase two:

(1) Principal thrust across the Central Pacific to defeat sea forces and to capture the Marianas, Guam, Okinawa, and Iwo Jima as air bases for the strategic air offensive; the capture of sea bases essential to effective prosecution of a sea blockade and control of essential sea areas. Japanese forces overseas to be cut off from the home islands and left to die or surrender for lack of sustenance.

(2) Conduct of an effective sea blockade of the Japanese home islands, including sinking or capture of Japanese ships.

(3) Conduct of an effective strategic air war to bring about the collapse of Japanese resistance and to undermine the civil and social

structure through selective air attack, using both visual and APQ–7 radar techniques against:

(a) The Japanese Air Force, through destruction of the Japanese aircraft engine and airframe industry.

(b) The Japanese electric power system, primarily through destruction of thermal power plants and switching and transformer stations in the power transmission system serving the principal industrial areas.

(c) The Japanese transportation systems, including Japanese sea transportation (accomplished through aerial mining of home waters, and air attack of shipbuilding and repair facilities and ports), and the principal railroads, which were meager in capacity and very vital and vulnerable.

(d) Japanese steel industry, through destruction of coke ovens.

(e) Petroleum storage and refineries.

(f) The Japanese food resources by destruction of fertilizer chemicals.

(4) Preparation for:

(a) Incendiary attack of Japanese urban areas, if this became necessary to bring about capitulation of the crippled nation.

(b) Atomic attack of Japanese urban areas, if necessary.

(c) Occupation, if Japan surrendered.

(d) Invasion if all else failed.

Secondary effort: operations in the Southwest Pacific to recapture the Philippines, isolate large bodies of Japanese troops, and impose heavy casualties.

This proposed air strategy for Japan bears an interesting resemblance to that of AWPD–1 for Europe. Both proposals stemmed from the basic concepts developed at the Air Corps Tactical School.

Any serious consideration of this speculation, and any derivation of lessons must take into account these circumstances in which the war was fought:

(1) Security of the American homeland. The United States was in

no danger at any time. There was no threat to the American people and no external leverage directed against the civil will to resist. The primary limiting factor at home was domestic impatience. The industrial machine was intact and unhampered.

(2) We had time to build and react. Our Allies in Europe held the enemy at bay while we armed.

(3) There were major drains on the German economy. The Germans were fighting a major war on the Eastern Front. The efficiency of the U.S. strategic air offensive was conditioned by the strain inflicted upon German industry by the war with Russia, and later by large-scale operations in Western Europe and the Mediterranean. But presumably this pressure on Germany would have continued, even without the American and British invasion of Normandy. And the decisive effectiveness of the air offensive did not depend on the Normandy Invasion.

(4) Japan was an island nation with insufficient resources at home to support the war and to maintain its population. This significantly enhanced the efficacy of the strategic air offensive. Furthermore, Japan's highly flammable cities were very vulnerable to incendiary attack.

Finally, in considering the results of our incendiary attacks versus selective bombing, we must recognize a most unwelcome but nonetheless real concurrent effect. Incendiary destruction of great cities has had a powerful and redundant impact upon the United States Air Force. Forgetting the compelling effectiveness of selective bombing against Germany, Americans remember only the slaughter of a million civilians in Japanese cities. A most grievous outcome of our abandoning traditional "selective target" bombing for incendiary destruction of sixty-six Japanese cities was a deep and pervasive revulsion among the American people against strategic bombing of all sorts. This reaction was more powerful and debilitating to the Air Force than the cumulative efforts of the German and Japanese air forces.

Should civilian reaction be permitted to cripple the United States Air Force by shackling the strategic air offensive completely—whether or not it is dedicated to selective bombing? If so, it may deny to the

United States its most effective means of compelling by force in just causes. Actually, if we are denied the efficient application of strategic selective bombing, we will have no means of exerting strategic power whatever, short of massive nuclear exchange. To avoid this crippling, the American public must be better informed on the power and efficiency of conventional weapons, and on selective bombing as a decisive factor in winning wars. Selective target bombing in World War II proved to be the best way to destroy the war-making capabilities of a modern industrialized nation. And it is likely to be far less inhumane than the mass killings on the battlefields, or the vengeful actions of an invading army against helpless civilians in cities. Selective bombing with conventional bombs and other weapons is now many times more effective than it was in the Second World War.

Postscript: Forty Years Later

As I reflect back, later, on the only two great strategic air wars the United States has ever fought, many lessons emerge that can be applied to our ever-present need for security. The principles and concepts underlying the American doctrine of selective strategic air warfare bore up remarkably well in the cauldron of World War II. The devastation of Germany and Japan in 1945 testified eloquently to the power of the strategic air strike force, even before the dropping of the atomic bombs. Germany reached economic and industrial collapse while her borders were still intact. Japan surrendered without a single American soldier on her home soil. Among the strategic precepts confirmed by experience are:

(1) Modern great nations *are* dependent upon industrialized systems for the prosecution of war and for the sustenance of the civil structure. Destruction or crippling of those vital systems through correct strategic targeting can lead to national collapse.

(2) Conventional bombs and warheads *can* destroy any manmade structure or system. New weapon-delivery systems have improved accuracy so markedly as to multiply the destructiveness of conventional weapons manyfold.

271

(3) The air strike force *did* deliver such weapons with adequate accuracy, without incurring intolerable aircraft losses or causing excessive civilian casualties.

(4) Area attack of urban areas is an effective last-resort measure.

(5) Defense of the source of power—our people—is essential before an efficient air offensive can be launched or sustained.

(6) Bolstering the national will through defenses is also necessary to prevent collapse of national resolution in crisis. Wars can be lost without fighting at all.

Few will question the first two precepts in terms of World War II, or in regard to present and future applications. As to the third, new conditions must be examined. Air power has basically two limiting factors: the "will of the people" and of their civilian political leaders to apply air power, and the capability to penetrate enemy defenses without intolerable losses.

Limitation stemming from a lack of will on the part of the people and their civilian political leaders is something new to us. That civilian "will" has never before been subjected to danger and threat from a foreign foe. Since the Civil War in the 1860s, our citizens have been safe and secure at home. Civilians suffered because of the loss of friends and relatives, but they were themselves quite safe and secure. A new element confronts Americans now—national fear.

Fear can bring military defeat by causing our civilian leaders to curb the power of military forces to deal vigorously with an enemy. This is not new. Britain had to swallow the humiliation of Munich because her cities were vulnerable to air attack and her air defenses were not yet ready. Political fear inhibited all effective action by the French military forces in 1939, when the opportunity to act vigorously was ripe. The delay bred of fear led to the defeat and humiliation of France. Whether this outcome was preferable to the casualties that might have ensued from prompt military victory, only Frenchmen can judge.

The same fears restrained British military action early in the war, and much of that inhibition came across the channel from France. It took that vigorous and courageous political leader, Winston Churchill, to guide the British people in facing up to danger. But even here the great British politician could not have prevailed, had not he and a handful of others provided for a belated but effective air defense system for British cities.

After the war, there was a period of panic in Europe as our Allies realized they were powerless to oppose the massive Russian armies camped in East Germany and poised for a thrust through Western Europe. The new North Atlantic Treaty organization (NATO) set goals of 200 divisions, then 150, then 100, and finally 80, as each country defaulted its required contribution. Finally in desperation and with reluctance, NATO turned to American air power to save it from domination by Russian armies or the fear of Russian aggression. The solution, based on enormous U.S. nuclear superiority and relative safety of American cities, worked admirably for 2 decades until the Russians developed a powerful atomic threat of their own. During these 20 years, the threat of U.S. atomic air power repeatedly frustrated Russian threats on Berlin. But the growth of Russian strategic atomic power has eroded our initial great advantage.

Since then we, too, have felt the debilitating hand of political fear. In Vietnam we would not let our military leaders operate efficiently against North Vietnam until very late in the struggle. We feared escalation would bring in Soviet or Chinese forces. Bombing of selected targets in Hanoi and Haiphong ultimately produced prompt results at the peace table. By then we were weary of the struggle and were settling for withdrawal of our troops and recovery of our prisoners of war. We were not directly afraid of the North Vietnamese. We feared that their sponsor, the Soviet Union, would openly enter the war and perhaps escalate it to an international nuclear exchange.

Our fear may or may not have been well founded. Military strategists discounted the likelihood of Soviet nuclear escalation, since we had a huge nuclear superiority in the early days of the war in Vietnam. Civilian leaders, however, took quite a different view. Their fear may well have been the telling factor that shaped our destiny then. It may do so in the future. Soviet nuclear power is very real indeed today and our cities are defenseless. Our allies in Europe are confronted with a double fear—Soviet nuclear power and enormous

273

Soviet conventional power. There probably is no sure and certainly no easy solution. But one requirement stands clearly on the horizon: If we intend to support our rights and aspirations abroad and fulfill our pledges and obligations, we must have the offensive power to compel by our military forces, especially our air forces. We must also have a *defense* for our cities which can bolster our will and preserve our industry and heritage. Both are needed to give credibility to deterrence against direct attack of the United States, and against imposition of political and economic hegemony over important allies and trading partners. These conditions constitute a great change from the national security we enjoyed in World War II. The strategic air offensive proved decisive in that war. But before it can be used again, we must find a way to create for ourselves the security at home that was our legacy then.

Fortunately, new technology offers fresh hope for devising a system of antimissile defense for our country, and the President has called for a major effort to develop that technology into an effective system. It is the sine qua non of American military capability and will to support our national goals.

Appendix*

The German Electric Power Complex as a Target System

As stated earlier, initially the German electric power system had been adequate to its demands. There was sufficient capability to permit boilers and turbine-generators to be shut down periodically for maintenance. But, by 1939, the peacetime demands were putting great strain on the capacity of the system, and with the outbreak of war the demands rose rapidly. Power was rationed first with regard to civilian non-war use. But as the demands for munitions rose, the entire reserve capacity was absorbed, and still it was necessary to ration vital industries. By 1944 many vital industries were rationed at thirty percent below their needs.

It became impossible to allow "stand down" for maintenance and this also began to be felt. Power availability fell considerably below normal "plate" capacity.

Little effort had been made to increase the power capacity at the outset of the war, since the war was expected to be of short duration. But in 1941 an attempt was made to build ten large new plants. None of them was completed prior to the end of the war. However, existing plants were expanded on the following scale:

*Haywood S. Hansell, Jr., *The Air Plan that Defeated Hitler* (Atlanta, Ga., 1972), pp 286–297. In some instances, author has revised the figures in this appendix.

1942 900,000 additional KW
1943 850,000 additional KW
1944 875,000 additional KW

Since the total theoretical installed capacity came to 22,000,000 KW in 1944, of which the actual peak extraction was about 16,000,000 KW, this increase in existing plant capacity was small and was hardly felt. Of the theoretical installed capacity of 22,000,000 KW, 13,300,000 KW was incorporated in the national integrated system. The remainder was either in large factory plants, in the national railway system, or in a large number of small installations which were not included in the generally available power pool.

Of the 13,000,000 KW theoretical capacity of the integrated system,

79% was in coal burning plants.
21% was in the hydroelectric power plants.

About twenty percent of the entire generating capacity was established in the industrial area around Leipzig. Another twenty percent was established in the Ruhr. The hydroelectric plants, comprising another twenty percent, were in southwest Germany.

The distribution of the more important electrical power stations came from some ninety-five power generating stations:

Over 200,000 KW   5
100,000 to 200,000 KW   40
50,000 to 100,000 KW   50
                        95

The total number of large stations was 45. Their capacity was a total of 8,000,000 KW, or nearly two-thirds of the capacity of the installed integrated systems.

This complex, vital, and over-stressed system was operated under the constant control and supervision of the National Load Dispatcher in Berlin, who in turn operated through twelve District Load Dispatchers, each having a major switching system.

Actually the maximum peak capacity that ever flowed through the system rated at 13,000,000 KW was 9,700,000 KW. Thus the 45 plants with a theoretical capacity of 8,000,000 KW constituted the great majority of power which was in such urgent demand by industry.

The integrated "grid" which was the cause of such concern to the Committee of Operations Analysts and the air planners turned out to be far less flexible than they had believed. The report of the USSBS says "A statement by the National Load Dispatcher discloses that the capacity of the transmission system was such as to permit an exchange between adjacent districts, of approximately 10 percent of the larger district's capacity." Thus the system was much less flexible than we had thought.

The report has the following to say about transmission systems:

> The ability to use electric power transmitted over a transmission line depends upon rather severe limits of receiving-end voltage. Any voltage variation beyond the band of 90 percent and 110 percent of normal leads to damage of connected utilization equipment. At some value between 80 and 85 percent of normal voltage, the whole transmission system becomes unstable and will suddenly collapse with coincident wide-spread damage to utilization equipment.
>
> When generating facilities are lost, the transmission system capacity drops at the same time because of the loss of synchronous equipment in the generating stations (turbo-generators), which was the terminal equipment of the transmission system. Destruction of generating facilities, therefore, has a two-fold effect: the direct loss of generating capacity of the area, and the simultaneous reduction of transmission line capacity into the area.

An integrated system contains a complex array of voltage regulators and relays and circuit breakers and switches intended to prevent and arrest damage which may be caused by sudden increases of load and sudden drops in capacity and voltage. These control complexes and safety devices are limited in the degree to which they can accommodate sudden major changes in load and voltage.

The complexes are usually integral with or immediately adjacent to the powerhouses, as are the large transformers.

The Bombing Survey concluded that all evidence indicates that the destruction of power generating and switching installations would have had a catastrophic effect on Germany's war production. The survey might have added that it would have had a catastrophic effect on Germany's civilian economy and social structure as well.

Was the destruction and disruption of the German Electric Power System within the capacity of the available strategic air forces? More specifically:

(a) Could the disruption of the German electric power system have been accomplished in addition to the other operations actually carried out before the invasion, with the forces actually made available?

(b) Could the disruption of the German electric power system have been carried out in addition to the other priority objectives of the CBO, shortly after the invasion?

(c) Would the disruption of the German electric power system in addition to the other primary objectives, have "fatally weakened" the German ability to support the war and thus have brought the German state to collapse at an earlier time?

What size force was required to destroy and disrupt the German electric power system?

Computation of bomber force requirements to assure destruction and collapse of the German electric power system can now be made on the basis of actual war experience, and involves consideration of a number of steps.

1. What is the number of generating plants and switching stations that would have to be put out of operation?

Dr. Carl, a German electric power engineer, submitted a report to the German National Load Dispatcher describing the targets whose destruction would bring about collapse of the system. His report was dated February 23, 1944.

He considered that the U.S. and British strategic air forces would be apt to attack a few transformer points between districts, such as Braieweiler and Kelsterbach sub stations. "After putting this inter-district grid out of operation, the intra-district power supply could be paralyzed by individual attacks on 56 of the most important generating stations whereby two-thirds of the entire German power production could be eliminated."

Another German study lists nine transformer stations and forty-one generating stations.*

For the purpose of this analysis, the target systems will be taken at fifty-six generating stations and nine transformer and switching sub stations.

2. What number of hits and size bombs would be required to knock out an electric power generating station?

The typical thermal electric power station in Germany had its most vulnerable and vital elements housed in a power house about 400 feet by 500 feet in dimensions. The entire complex, including transformers, switchgear, condensers, pumps, and other equipment occupied an area of about 25 acres, or an area about 1000 feet by 1000 feet.

All the facilities were vulnerable to heavy high explosive bombs, which should have delay fuses. Five hundred-pound bombs or larger were found to be adequate to cause irreparable damage. Since no spares for heavy equipment were available, the restoration of operation would have to await manufacture of replacement equipment.

After examining twenty-five generating stations which had been damaged by air attack, the Electric Utilities Report of the U.S. Strategic Bombing Survey had this to say:

> . . .from the foregoing it can readily be seen that an electric generating station or a switching and transformer station is a highly integrated mechanism, each unit playing a vital part in the functioning of the plant as a whole.
>
> The layout in all cases covers a large area, is easily traced by transmission lines, and is easily recognized from the air. It has been demonstrated to be exceedingly vulnerable to air attack, and even a chance hit may be so damaging as to close down a plant completely From the standpoint of generating station engineers and operating

---

*USSBS German Electric Utilities subcommittee report.

men, the vulnerability of a generating plant to air attack in wartime is a continued nightmare.

The recuperability of a generating station to a major failure even in normal times is slow. No two plants are alike, and often the individual pieces of equipment are specially designed to meet a given set of conditions. The possibility of maintaining adequate spares to cover contingencies in such 'custom-made' plants does not exist.

As indicated earlier, examination of these plants which had received damage incidental to attack on adjacent targets led the USSBS to conclude that .2 tons of bombs per acre would put a plant out of commission for several months, and .4 tons of bombs per acre would put a plant out of commission for a period lasting from 6 to 18 months.

Since a powerhouse proper averaged about four acres in extent, this would require two hits with 1100–pound bombs to put the station out of commission for several months, and 3 hits with 1100–pound bombs to knock it out for 6 to 18 months.

The entire area of the generating complex, covering 25 acres, or an area of 1000 feet by 1000 feet, should receive 10 tons of bombs or 20 hits with 1100–pound bombs to knock it out for 6 to 18 months.

3. What size force is required to knock out a generating station, as determined by actual bombing accuracy and prevailing tactics?

In computing requirements to knock out a generating plant, the current bombing tactics employed by the Eighth Air Force, that is to say, formation pattern bombing by combat boxes of 18 aircraft at 20,000 feet and the actual bombing accuracy and distribution recorded for the Eighth Air Force in 1943 and 44 will be used:

Average radial error of the center of the bombing pattern from the aiming point: 875 feet.

Circular probable error of the center of the bombing pattern about the aiming point: 820 feet.

Average dimensions of bomb pattern: 2400 feet by 2400 feet.

One combat box of 18 bombers carrying 1100–pound bombs could deliver 108 bombs.

Considering first the powerhouse only (400 feet by 500 feet), a combat box would provide a 75 percent probability of making at least 1 hit with 108 bombs.

If one combat wing (3 combat boxes or 54 bombers) is used against one powerhouse target, the probability of at least one hit is 98.5 percent, and the probability of at least 2 hits is 84.5 percent.

If two combat wings (6 combat boxes or a total of 108 bombers) are used against 1 target, then:

The probability of at least 1 hit is 99.99%.
The probability of at least 2 hits is 96.5%.
The probability of at least 3 hits is 89%.
The probability of at least 4 hits is 77%.
The probability of at least 5 hits is 54%.
The probability of at least 6 hits is 18%.

This is a conservative method of estimating probable hits.

The probability of making at least three hits with two combat wings is thus about ninety percent.

The normal expectancy (fifty percent probability) of hits within the powerhouse itself from one combat wing is eight.

Thus, if 2 combat wings (6 combat boxes or 108 bombers) attacked each power generating station, they would have virtual assurance of at least 1 hit in the powerhouse, a 96.5 percent probability of knocking it out with 2 hits for several months and 89 percent probability of 3 hits, knocking it out for 6 to 18 months.

As for the total target area: (1000 feet by 1000 feet)

The normal expectancy (fifty percent probability) of bombs within the target if two combat wings are used is fifteen percent. This would provide a normal expectancy of ninety-seven hits within the target area. Actual experience showed that fifteen percent of all bombs dropped by all methods (visual bombing and instrument bombing) by the Eighth Air Force against the oil targets fell within the target area.

4. What is the number of successful attacks and what is the weight

of bombs required to knock out two-thirds of all German electric power?

If 65 targets were attacked (56 generating stations and 9 transformers and switching stations), it would require 65 successful missions by 2 combat wings each if it were considered desirable to seek such a high probability of destruction at each target (90 percent). Since each combat wing would utilize 54 sorties and deliver 178 tons of bombs, this would involve a total of 23,140 tons of bombs delivered in daylight precision bombing by 7,020 sorties.

But even such high probabilities of success as those chosen still leave a chance that some targets will not be completely knocked out of operation on the initial attacks.

To allow for re-attack of generating stations which continue to provide some power and to allow for vicissitudes of weather, an additional provision for attacking half the targets a second time might be called for.

Under these circumstances, the weight of attack required to provide ninety percent probability of successful destruction of each target contributing to two-thirds of Germany's electric power capacity, by normally successful daylight precision bombing, may be taken as:

23,140 tons	7,020 sorties
11,570 tons	3,510 sorties
34,710 tons	10,530 sorties

Another method of computing the force required is somewhat more conservative and calls for higher numbers of sorties. Attacking generating stations in missions of 4 task forces of 2 wings each (108 bombers) against groups of 4 targets gives a 95 percent probability of destroying at least 3 targets on each mission, which may be accepted as practical certainty. Sixty-five targets would take 22 missions, totaling 9,504 sorties and 31,363 tons of bombs. Allowance for weather would raise this to 14,250 sorties and 47,844 tons of bombs, to achieve 95 percent probability of success against all of the 65 targets, with a 50 percent cushion for weather.

The task of knocking out the electric power system actually was much less difficult than that of knocking out the synthetic oil production—and keeping it out.

This tonnage (about 35,000 to 48,000 tons) is a small portion of the total effort available in March, April, and May of 1944. During the period March–May 1944, the U.S. Strategic Air Forces flew over 60,000 sorties and dropped 198,000 tons of bombs, of which only 6,080 tons were on oil targets. Thirty-five thousand tons (or 48,000 tons) is a small portion of this effort. Obviously this is not the problem. In comparison with the total sorties (over 50,000) and tonnage of bombs actually dropped (150,000) by these air forces after Big Week in the time period before May 15, these numbers of sorties (21 or 28 percent) and tonnage (23.3 or 32 percent) of bombs for electric power is small. After May 15, the entire effort of the strategic air forces should properly have been directed to close preparation for the invasion itself. The total tonnage dropped by U.S. air forces on all targets in May was 96,464 tons. Half of this would be 48,232 tons, more than enough to have paralyzed German electric power. The RAF dropped 51,000 tons in May. The combined total from both air forces in the last half of May was 74,000 tons, which should have been ample to disrupt the French railroads.

5. Were there enough days of visual bombing opportunity to have accommodated the precision attacks against electric power targets prior to the invasion?

Some guidance can be obtained by consideration of the number of days in the spring of 1943 on which the Eighth Air Force was launched against targets in which visual bombing conditions were predicted.

In the three months, March through May 1943, there were 25 such missions, 19 of them between 1 March and 15 May. In 1944 about 150,000 tons of bombs were dropped in this time period.

It might be expected that in the corresponding two and a half months of 1944 a similar number of daylight missions had been possible.

Oil targets would have absorbed 4 of those days and 6,000 tons of bombs, leaving 15 visual bombing days and 144,000 tons for targets other than oil. However, the winter of 1944 was especially severe, there was an unusual amount of overcast, weather forecasts were unreliable, and weather distribution was seldom in the pattern desired. To take care of the vicissitudes of weather, allowance has been made for diversion of one half of the sorties away from the primary targets to secondary targets. This would require re-attack of half of the targets.

To repeat, it is most unlikely that the weather would have have been so accommodating as to arrange for clear skies at the places desired. But this allowance for inaccurate weather forecasting and for unfavorable weather distribution provides a cushion that is ultra conservative. The bombing effort could have accounted for the destruction of two-thirds of Germany's electric power capacity in two and a half months even in the face of unusually bad weather.

The rate of repeat attacks for German electric power targets is quite a different matter from that for synthetic oil plants. The latter can be repaired by men with cutting torches, reinforcing plates, and welding tools. But the boilers that have been wrecked or the large steam turbines, or the electric generators, or the high voltage transformers and switches do not lend themselves to such treatment—and there were no spares or reserves. A power plant or switching station that is really heavily damaged is out of commission for a long time.

If rail transportation in Germany had been established as a secondary and alternate target system, a very large tonnage could still have been directed that way. The missions which found the electric power targets obscured could have been employed against transportation. Marshaling yards are sufficiently large to warrant attack in poor visibility, or even by electronic bombing techniques. To be sure, the large 1100–pound bombs with delay fuses would not have been of optimum size for marshaling yards, but they would nevertheless have been effective.

To utilize the available tonnage against electric power targets in Germany it might have been necessary to shuttle strategic operations from the Fifteenth Air Force in Italy to bases of the Eighth Air Force in England—an operation similar to that employed earlier by the Eighth in operations in the Mediterranean.

The tonnage actually dropped exclusive of the oil targets between 1 March and 15 May was adequate to have destroyed the German electric power system before the invasion, and still have left 15 days in May for attack of transportation in France to the extent of 48,000 tons of direct attack on the railroads.

This takes no account of the bombing of RAF Bomber Command, which contributed heavily to the "transportation plan" in France.

General Eisenhower was reported to have been exceedingly pleased with the results of the 48,500 tons of bombs delivered by all the Allied air forces against French rail transportation before the invasion. This had risen to 84,000 tons by the end of June.

These analyses are based on the assumption that the grand strategy had proceeded exactly as it actually did evolve. If, however, the offensive operations in Italy had been reduced to probing actions and the capture of Sardinia and Corsica after the surrender of Sicily, there would have been no difficulty in concentrating the efforts of the strategic air forces against their primary targets in Germany.

It appears that, even with the delay in build-up of the U.S. Strategic Air Forces, it still would have been possible to wreck the German electric power system before the invasion, without lessening the air attacks which were actually carried out on the German Air Force and the German oil industry. In this case, electric power would have had to enjoy priority over transportation in France until the middle of May 1944. Even then transportation would have absorbed a very heavy tonnage as a secondary target system of U.S. daylight operations and as a target of Bomber Command. If RAF Bomber Command had also supplemented the attacks on electric power by night attack on cities containing the largest generating capacities or the most critical switching control centers, the total effect on electric power would have been truly devastating.

There were enough fighters available by this time to provide escort for these operations.

These calculations share a common error with AWPD–1 and

AWPD–42: they presume that it is necessary to destroy two thirds of the generating capacity to cause the complete collapse of the entire system. As indicated earlier, the collapse would have been self-induced long before this number of plants had been knocked out.

Whether these operations could have been authorized and carried out before the invasion in the face of Eisenhower's vehement support of the French Rail Transportation Plan, seems highly doubtful. But they could certainly have been carried out shortly after the St. Lo breakout, using less than one-fifth of the tonnage of the U.S. Strategic Air Forces which were diverted from CBO targets, primarily to the support of the ground campaigns.

Glossary

A6M2 Model 21 Zero-Sen (Japanese)
: Single-engine, single-seat, low-wing monoplane, built by Mitsubishi and Nakajima. Used by army and navy. At Pearl Harbor the A6M2 Model 21 proved equal or superior to any Allied fighter. Armament, 2 fuselage-mounted machineguns and two 20–mm wing cannon, plus two 132–lb bombs. Maximum takeoff weight was 5,313 pounds; highest speed, 316 miles per hour at 16,570 feet; service ceiling, 33,790 feet; and greatest combat range, 1,165 miles.

ABC–1
: Short title for a series of British-American joint meetings and final report. Starting January 29 and ending March 29, 1941, representatives of the two military staffs discussed military and naval strategy, joint operations, geographical responsibilities, force structure, command arrangements, and limited operational plans.

Anglo-American Conference
: Held in Washington from May 12 to May 27, 1943. Attending were President Roosevelt, Prime Minister Churchill, and their advisers, including the Combined Chiefs of Staff. Conferees set May 1, 1944, as the date for the Normandy Invasion; authorized seizure of Azores unless Portugal granted use of bases on these islands; and agreed to increase the quantity of gasoline flown over the Hump from India to China.

B–17 (American)
: Four-engine, midwing bomber, developed in 1930s by Boeing. Used widely during World War II in Europe and the Mediterranean theaters. Nine crewmembers. The F–model, used in the Schweinfurt-Regensburg raids of August 1943, had maximum takeoff weight of 72,000 pounds; top speed of 311 miles; and a service ceiling of 35,000 feet. It carried a bombload of 20,800 pounds. Total produced for the AAF, 1940–1945: 12,692.

B–24 (American)
: Four-engine, midwing bomber, developed by Consolidated Vultee and used in World War II. Eight to 10 crewmembers. Flew in all combat theaters but was especially useful in the Pacific Theater on long-range missions. Served as a bomber, tanker, and transport. The first model used operationally by Army Air Forces bomber units was the B–24D

in 1942. The D had a maximum takeoff weight of 60,000 pounds; top speed of 303 miles per hour at 25,000 feet; service ceiling of 32,000 feet; and a combat range of 2,850 miles. Later Ds carried a bombload of 12,800 pounds. Total produced for the AAF, 1940–1945: 18,190.

B–25
(American)

Made by North American, the twin-engine, single-wing B–25 was one of Army Air Forces' best medium bombers of World War II. Three to 6 crewmembers. Bombload was 3,000 pounds. The B–model added a power-operated turret, with a 2–gun retractable ventral turret replacing the prone gunner's position in the tail. The Doolittle raid to Japan in April 1942 from the USS *Hornet* was flown in B–25Bs. The B–25B's maximum takeoff weight was 28,460 pounds; top speed, 300 miles per hour at 15,000 feet; service ceiling, 23,500 feet; and combat range, 1,300 miles. Total produced for the AAF, 1940–1945: 9,816.

B–26
(American)

Built by Martin, the B–26 Marauder was a twin-engine, single-wing, medium bomber. Three crewmembers. Sent to Australia in December 1941, B–26As saw action in the Pacific theaters from 1942–1945. Beginning in 1942, they also operated from bases in Alaska and, in November 1942, from North Africa. The B–model commenced operations in Europe in May 1943 with Eighth Air Force. The Ninth Air Force used B–26Bs very successfully in a tactical role, supporting the invasion of Europe from the United Kingdom. The B–26B's maximum takeoff weight was 34,000 pounds; best speed, 317 miles per hour at 14,500 feet; service ceiling, 23,500 feet; and combat range, 1,150 miles. Total produced for the AAF, 1940–1945: 5,157.

B–29
(American)

Built by Boeing and used predominantly in the Pacific, the B–29 featured a pressurized cabin, highly advanced remote-control firing system, and a bomb capacity of 20,000 pounds. Powered by 4 Wright R–3350 radial engines, the bomber had 10 crewmembers. The A–model had a maximum takeoff weight of 141,100 pounds; top speed of 358 miles per hour at 25,000 feet; a service ceiling of 31,850 feet; and a combat range of 4,100 miles. Total produced for the AAF, 1940–1945: 3,763.

B–29 (Superdumbo)
(American)

Used by the Navy as a rescue plane, the B–29 Superdumbo carried inflatable lifeboats which were dropped from the air into the water.

B–32
(American)

Four engine, single-wing bomber, built by Consolidated. Ten crewmembers. Bombload, 20,000 pounds. Maximum takeoff weight was 111,500 pounds; top speed, 357 miles per hour at 30,000 feet; service ceiling, 30,700 feet; and combat range, 2,500 miles. The B–32 lagged far behind the B–29 in development. Only 15 saw limited combat in the Pacific at the end of World War II.

B–36
(American)

Long-range bomber developed by Consolidated. Thought to have potential value in bombing Japan, a contract for 100 B–36s was let in 1943. However, the war was over before the B–36 first flew on August 8, 1946. Normally carried 15 crewmen, including 4 relief men. The B–36s maximum takeoff weight was 410,000 pounds; top speed, 411 miles per hour at 36,400 feet; service ceiling, 39,900 feet; and combat range, 6,800 miles. The Strategic Air Command flew B–36s from 1947 to 1956.

Cairo Conferences

First Cairo Conference was held November 22–26, 1943. President Roosevelt, Prime Minister Churchill, and Generalissimo Chiang Kai-

shek agreed to prosecute the war until Japan's unconditional surrender. They agreed that Japan should be deprived of all Pacific islands
acquired since 1914 and affirmed that Korea should become a free,
independent nation. Chiang Kai-shek agreed to build B–29 bases at
Chengtu, and Prime Minister Churchill agreed to build B–29 bases
near Calcutta, India. Admiral Nimitz was directed to capture the
Mariana Islands as bases for the B–29s.

At the Second Cairo Conference (December 4–6, 1943), Roosevelt,
Churchill, and President Ismet Inonu of Turkey discussed preliminar-
ies for Turkey's entrance into the war. The U.S. strategic forces in
England and the Mediterrean were united under the command of
General Spaatz.

Casablanca Conference   Held in French Morocco from January 14 to January 24, 1943. President
Roosevelt and Prime Minister Churchill considered Allied plans for
invading Sicily and the cross-channel invasion of Europe. They
reached a compromise on the invasion of Sicily and Italy, without
prejudicing the ultimate invasion of Europe from Great Britain.
President Roosevelt announced that the war would go on until the
unconditional surrender by the enemy.

CBO   Combined Bomber Offensive

CEP   circular error probable

combat box   A box formation used extensively in American strategic bombing tactics
in World War II. The term was especially applied to B–17 formations.

comd   command

comdr   commander

F–7 (American)   Single-seat, twin-engine U.S. Navy fighter used in World War II. It flew
from Navy aircraft carriers. Built by Grumman, the F–7 had four
.50–caliber guns in the nose and four 20–mm cannons in the wings.
Could carry two 1,000–pound bombs, or 6 rockets, or a standard Navy
torpedo. The F–7/F–3 was the photoreconnaissance version with
cameras installed aft in the fuselage. The F–7's maximum takeoff
weight was 25,720 pounds; top speed, 435 miles per hour at 22,200
feet; service ceiling, 40,700 feet; and combat range, 1,200 miles.

F–13A (American)   Photoreconnaissance version of the B–29A.

FW–190 (German)   Single-engine, single-seat, monoplane interceptor. Built by Focke-Wulf,
its basic airframe permitted adaption to a close-support fighter,
fighter-bomber, and fighter-dive-bomber. This versatile and highly
efficient aircraft served from late 1940 to the end of the war in Europe.
Armament of the Fw–190F–3 consisted of two 7.9–mm fuselage-
mounted machineguns, and two 20–mm cannon in the wings. Typical
bombload comprised a single 550–pound bomb under the fuselage and
four 110–pound bombs under the wings. Maximum takeoff weight was
10,850 pounds; top speed, 394 miles per hour at 18,000 feet; service
ceiling, 34,780 feet; and combat range, 500 miles.

G4–Mi (Japanese)   Twin-engine, single-wing bomber, developed by Mitsubishi. Called
"Betty" by the Allies, it served throughout the Pacific during World

289

War II. Maximum takeoff weight, 26,645 pounds. Top speed, 265 miles per hour at 13,780 feet. Combat range, 3,132 miles, was achieved by putting 1,100 gallons of fuel into the wings and furnishing no armor protection. Armament consisted of a 20–mm cannon in tail and single flexible guns in nose, rear, and belly positions. Due to heavy combat losses, later models afforded some protection for crew and fuel.

Gee
A medium-distance radionavigation system or aid. An aircraft's position was determined by an air traffic controller viewing a scope. The system measured the difference between the time of arrival of synchronized pulses broadcast by a master and two slave stations. One of the broadcast stations was fixed on the aircraft. Developed by the British before World War II.

GHQ
General Headquarters

He–111
(German)
All-metal, single-wing, twin-engine, medium bomber, built by Heinkel. Most widely used and versatile version was the He–111H–6. Five or 6 crewmembers. Bombload, 4,410 pounds. Performed a variety of roles besides that of medium bomber. For example, it became a first-rate torpedo bomber, carrying 2 of these weapons. Maximum takeoff weight was 27,400 pounds; top speed, 258 miles per hour at 16,400 feet; service ceiling, 25,500 feet; and combat range, 760 miles.

Hump
An eastern range of the Himalaya Mountains lying between China and India and Burma. Army Air Forces flew thousands of air transport missions "Over the Hump" from India to China in World War II.

Iceberg
Operation *Iceberg* was the Allied combined naval-land amphibious offensive in World War II to capture Okinawa, the largest island of the Ryukyu Islands. The objective was to take Okinawa in order to establish air bases for conducting the air war against Japan.

initial point
A point on the ground, indentified visually or by electronic means, over which an aircraft begins a bomb run or a run over a drop zone.

Ju–88
(German)
Twin-engine, single-wing aircraft, developed by Junkers. Four crewmen. Used in various modifications: horizontal bomber, dive bomber, torpedo bomber, day or night fighter, or reconnaissance aircraft. The Ju–88G–7 night fighter was fitted with 4 forward-firing 20–mm cannons, 1 rear-firing 13–mm machinegun, and a pair of cannons firing obliquely upward. Maximum takeoff weight was 32,250; top speed, 389 miles per hour at 29,800 feet; and combat range, 1,380 miles.

Ki–43–Ia
(Japanese)
Single-seat, one-engine monoplane, developed by Nakajima. Known as "Oscar" to the Allies, this fighter and subsequent models performed widely in the Pacific as interceptors and long-range escorts. The Ki–43–Ia had only a pair of 7.7–mm machineguns mounted in the upper-wing. Heavier guns were installed in later models. Maximum takeoff was 5,695 pounds; top speed, 308 miles per hour at 13,120 feet; service ceiling, 38,500 feet; and combat range, 745 miles.

Ki–45–Kai-C
(Japanese)
Manufactured by Kawasaki, this twin-engine, single-wing, day/night fighter carried a crew of 2. Dubbed "Nick" by the Allies. Armament

comprised a single 37–mm gun forward, twin fixed 20–mm guns amidships (firing forward and upward), and on some aircraft a small searchlight in the nose. Maximum takeoff weight was 12,125 pounds; top speed, 336 miles per hour at 19,685 feet; service ceiling, 32,808 feet; and combat range, 746 miles. Nick was active in the southern battle areas of the Pacific war, proving a perfect aircraft for escort and patrol between the widely dispersed islands. Later, it assumed night defense of Japanese cities against B–29 strikes.

Ki–61–Ia
(Japanese)

Single-wing, one-seat, single-engine, fighter-interceptor built by Kawasaki. Nicknamed "Tony" by the Allies, it served in virtually every theater of the Pacific, and at one time formed a major part of Japan's home fighter force. Armament, 2 fuselage 7.7–mm guns and 2 wing-mounted 12.7–mm guns (later models strengthened this armament). Maximum takeoff weight was 7,650 pounds; top speed, 348 miles per hour at 16,404 feet; service ceiling, 32,808 feet; combat range, 1,118 miles. Tony was one of the best interceptors against the B–29s. Pilots often made "kills" by ramming the target rather than using their guns.

Ki–84–Ia
(Japanese)

Known to the Allies as "Frank," this one-seat, single-engine, Nakajima aircraft served as a day/night fighter, dive bomber, and ground support fighter. Armament, a pair of 20–mm wing cannon and twin 12.7–mm guns in the upper engine cowling. It could carry two 550–pound bombs under its wings. Maximum takeoff weight was 8,267 pounds; highest speed, 388 miles per hour at 19,685 feet; service ceiling, 34,450 feet; and combat range, 1,025 miles.

Ki–102B
(Japanese)

Twin-engine, two-seat, attack fighter, developed by Kawasaki. Known as "Randy" by the Allies. It resembled the Ki–45–Kai-C ('Nick'), but had better performance. In its nose were two 20–mm cannon. The wings had 57–mm cannons (with 150 shells and a firing rate of 80 rounds per minute). A 12.7–mm machinegun in the rear cockpit fired obliquely upward to the rear. Two 550–pound bombs could be carried under the wings. Maximum takeoff weight was 16,094 pounds; top speed, 360 miles per hour at 19,685 feet; service ceiling, 32,808 feet; and combat range was 1,243 miles.

kamikaze

Japanese for "divine wind." A tactic used by certain Japanese pilots during World War II, in which they flew their airplanes as missiles against Allied targets. This tactic was an act of self-destruction by the pilots and desperation by Japanese military leaders.

Lancaster Mk.1
(British)

Built by Avro, the 4–engine, single-wing Lancaster was the backbone of RAF Bomber Command's offensive against Germany from 1943 to 1945. Crew of 7. It was the most famous and most successful heavy strategic night bomber used over Europe. The maximum bombload, 14,000 pounds, consisted of a wide range of high explosive and incendiary weapons. Maximum takeoff weight was 63,000 pounds; top speed, 281 miles per hour at 18,500 feet; service ceiling, 23,500 feet; and combat range, 2,695 miles. Throughout the war, the MK.1 model and later versions of the Lancaster delivered 608,612 tons of bombs in 156,000 sorties against Germany and Italy.

Me–109 (Bf–109)   Single-engine, single-seat, low-wing fighter, developed by Messerschmitt.
(German)   Used in the Battle of Britain and throughout the war. One of the finest models was the Me–109F–3. Its armament consisted of one 15–mm cannon and two 7.9–mm machineguns. Maximum takeoff weight was 6,054 pounds; top speed, 390 miles per hour at 22,000 feet; service ceiling, 37,000 feet; and combat range, 440 miles.

Matterhorn   Strategic air operation approved by President Roosevelt in November 1943 for the bombing of Japan by B–29s flying from China. The bombers were based in India, but were staged through Chengtu, China before striking Japan.

Norden bombsight   A gyroscopically stabilized synchronizing bombsight used mainly for strategic bombing in World War II. Utilizing preset data and manual operation by the bombardier, the Norden bombsight computed the correct dropping angle and, in connection with an automatic pilot or pilot direction indicator, determined the proper course for the aircraft to the target.

Oboe   Radar navigation and blind-bombing system using two ground stations measuring distance to a radar beacon on the aircraft.

Overlord   Overall plan for invasion of Western Europe in 1944.

P–38   Two-engine, single-seat, single-wing fighter with twin booms. Built by
(American)   Lockheed, the P–38 was popularly called "Lightning." One of the best-known World War II fighters, it served in a variety of roles. Extra fuel tanks and twin engines made the Lightning an excellent escort for deep-penetration raids of B–17s and B–24s over Europe and for strike missions in the Southwest Pacific. Armament of the L–model consisted of two .50–inch machineguns and two 1,600–pound bombs. Maximum takeoff weight was 21,600 pounds; highest speed, 414 miles per hour at 25,000 feet; service ceiling, 44,000 feet; and combat range, 450 miles. Total production for the AAF, 1940–1945: 9,536.

P–47   Powered by a single radial engine, the single-seat P–47 was developed by
(American)   Republic and used in World War II as a fighter and fighter-bomber. The D–model's armament comprised eight .50–caliber machineguns and one 500–pound bomb. Affectionately known as the "Jug," the P–47 was reputed to be the toughest fighter of the war, able to absorb tremendous punishment. Maximum takeoff weight was 19,400 pounds; top speed, 428 miles per hour at 30,000 feet; service ceiling, 42,000 feet; and combat range, 475 miles. Total production for the AAF, 1940–1945: 15,585.

P–51   Single-seat, low-wing monoplane, powered by a single liquid-cooled
(American)   engine. Built by North American and widely used in World War II. It escorted B–17s and B–24s on bombing missions over Germany. The D–model's armament consisted of six .50–caliber machineguns and two 1,000–pound bombs. Maximum takeoff weight was 11,600 pounds; top speed, 437 miles per hour at 25,000 feet; service ceiling, 41,900 feet; and combat range, 950 miles. Redesignated the F–51, the

	"Mustang" served in the Korean War. Total production for the AAF, 1940–1945: 14,501.
PB–2 (American)	Developed by Consolidated, the PB–2 was a single-engine, two-seat, monoplane fighter. The A–model carried 2 fixed forward-firing guns and a single .30–inch gun on a flexible mount in the rear cockpit. Maximum takeoff weight was 5,643 pounds; top speed, 274 miles per hour at 25,000 feet; service ceiling, 28,000 feet; and combat range, 508 miles.
pathfinder	An aircraft with a specially trained crew, carrying dropping zone/ landing zone marking teams, target markers, or navigational aids. It preceded the main force to the dropping zone/landing zone, or target.
Potsdam Conference	Held from July 17 to August 2, 1945. Attended by President Truman, Prime Minister Churchill, Premier Joseph Stalin, and other officials. Clement R. Atlee, new British Prime Minister, joined the conference on July 29. Conferees issued "unconditional surrender" ultimatum (July 26) to Japan; considered treatment of Germany during occupation and control period; and provided for the trial of war criminals by an International Military Tribunal which was established soon after the conference.
Quadrant	See Quebec Conference.
Quebec Conference	Convened from August 11 to 24, 1943. President Roosevelt and Prime Minister Churchill reaffirmed target date for Normandy Invasion. Roosevelt and Churchill agreed to accelerate military operations in Far East, especially in Burma; created a Southeast Asia Command with Adm. Lord Louis Mountbatten as Supreme Allied Commander; and acknowledged that the Battle of the Atlantic against the U–boat had turned in favor of the Allies.
RAF	Royal Air Force
Reno IV	An Allied naval-land-air operation to push along the northern coast of New Guinea into Mindanao, Philippine Islands.
rope	Narrow metallic strips of various lengths which, when dropped from aircraft, created false signals on enemy radarscopes.
San Antonio I and II	First planned strategic air strikes against Japan (Nakajima aircraft factory, near Tokyo urban areas).
Sextant	See Cairo Conferences.
SHAEF	Supreme Headquarters Allied Expeditionary Forces
skip bombing	Bombing tactic accomplished by releasing one or more bombs from a plane flying at low altitude, so that the bombs glance off of the surface of the water or ground and strike the target.
SLU	special liaison unit
Stirling Mk-I (British)	Four-engine monoplane developed by Short. The bomb bay of this heavy strategic bomber held a maximum load of 14,000 pounds that could be carried 590 miles. With the load reduced to 3,500 pounds, the bomber's range was 2,010 miles. Since the bomb bay was split into sections, the heaviest bomb that could be accommodated was a 4,000 pounder. This limited the Stirling's effectiveness. Maximum takeoff

293

weight was 59,400 pounds; top speed, 260 miles per hour; and combat range, 2,330 miles. Carrying a crew of 7 or 8, the Stirling Mk-III featured more powerful engines and an improved dorsal gun turret.

Torch	Operation code name for the Allied invasion of North Africa, beginning on November 8, 1942. It was the first major amphibious operation of World War II in the European Theater.
Trident	See Anglo-American Conference.
Tripartite Pact	German-Italian-Japanese ten-year military-economic alliance signed at Berlin on September 27, 1940. It created the Axis powers of World War II.
Ultra	During World War II the Germans used an encryption machine called Enigma. The British, assisted by the Polish and French, broke the code for Enigma and extracted intelligence data which they labeled Top Secret Ultra. This Ultra intelligence data went to only a very few political leaders and military commanders. For the greater part of the war, German Enigma messages were systematically, regularly, and extensively deciphered.
USSBS	United States Strategic Bombing Survey. A survey of bomb damage done by Allied strategic bombing forces during World War II, covering both primary and secondary damage in the European and Pacific Theaters of Operation. Term also refers to the board that made this survey.
V–1	German robot flying bomb with a pulse jet engine that allowed it to be launched form the Continent at targets in England. Called the "FZG–76" by the Germans and the "buzz bomb" by the British. Used in World War II.

Bibliography

For more than fifty years I have studied the theories, applications, and debates on strategic air warfare. These studies, rooted in personal commitments and experiences, are the basis of this memoir. Certain books and official histories, however, were of great assistance in recalling the context, circumstances, and specific dates in a war fought four decades ago. Two sets of official analytical works were invaluable: Wesley F. Craven and James L. Cate, editors, *The Army Air Forces in World War II*, 7 volumes (Chicago, 1948–1958), Reprint Edition, (Washington: 1984); and *United States Strategic Bombing Survey: European Survey*, 208 Reports (Washington: September–October 1945), and *Pacific Survey*, 108 Reports (Washington: June–July 1946). In addition, for this memoir I drew upon my two earlier published works: *The Air Plan That Defeated Hitler* (Atlanta, Ga: 1972) and *Strategic Air War Against Japan* (Maxwell Air Force Base: 1980). Other books and periodicals which were of assistance are cited below.

Additional Works

Coffey, Thomas M. *Decision Over Schweinfurt: The U.S. Eighth Air Force Battle for Daylight Bombing.* New York: David McKay Co, Inc, 1977.

Douhet, Giulio. *The Command of the Air.* New Imprint. Washington: Office of Air Force History, 1983.

Futrell, Robert F. *Ideas, Concepts, Doctrine: A History of Basic*

Thinking in the United States Air Force, 1907–1964. Maxwell Air Force Base, Ala: Air University, 1974.

Hurley, Alfred F. *Billy Mitchell: Crusader for Air Power.* 2d ed. Bloomington, Ind: Indiana University Press, 1975.

IMPACT: The Army Air Forces' "Confidential" Picture History of World War II. 8 vols. New York: James Parton & Co, Inc, 1980.

Liddell Hart, Basil H. *Paris, or the Future of War.* New York: E. P. Dutton and Company, 1925.

Sallagar, Frederick M. *Lessons from an Aerial Mining Campaign (Operation Starvation).* R–1322–PR. Santa Monica: The RAND Corporation, April 1974.

Slessor, Sir John C. *The Central Blue: Autobiography of Sir John Slessor, Marshal of the RAF.* New York: Frederick A. Praeger, 1957.

Speer, Albert. *Inside the Third Reich: Memoirs.* New York: The Macmillian Co, 1970.

Winterbotham, Frederick W. *The Ultra Secret.* New York: Harper & Row, 1974.

Index

Made in United States
North Haven, CT
12 February 2023

32485803R00183